# Chaucer and the Mystics

# Chaucer and the Mystics

## *The Canterbury Tales* and the Genre of Devotional Prose

## Robert Boenig

Lewisburg
Bucknell University Press
London: Associated University Presses

Associated University Presses
440 Forsgate Drive
Cranbury, NJ 08512

Associated University Presses
25 Sicilian Avenue
London WC1A 2QH, England

Associated University Presses
P.O. Box 338, Port Credit
Mississauga, Ontario
Canada L5G 4L8

The paper used in this publication meets the requirements of the American National Standard for Permanence of Paper for Printed Library Materials Z39.48-1984.

**Library of Congress Cataloging-in-Publication Data**

Boenig, Robert, 1948–
    Chaucer and the mystics : the Canterbury tales and the genre of devotional prose / Robert Boenig.
        p.    cm.
    Includes bibliographical references and index.
    ISBN 0-8387-5288-8 (alk. paper)
    1. Chaucer, Geoffrey, d. 1400.  Canterbury tales.  2. English prose literature—Middle English, 1100–1500—History and criticism.
    3. Devotional literature, English (Middle)—History and criticism.
    4. Christian literature, English (Middle)—History and criticism.
    5. Mysticism—England—History—Middle Ages, 500–1500.  6. Christian pilgrims and pilgrimages in literature.  7. Chaucer, Geoffrey, d. 1400—Religion.  8. Mysticism in literature.  9. Literary form.
    I. Title.
PR1875.R45B64   1995
821'.1—dc20                                                    94-33130
                                                                     CIP

PRINTED IN THE UNITED STATES OF AMERICA

# Contents

# Acknowledgments

I wish to acknowledge with gratitude Houghton Mifflin Company for permission to quote at length from *The Riverside Chaucer*, the Metropolitan Museum of Art for permission to print the three illustrations from its *Cloisters Apocalypse*; the journal *Studia Mystica* for its permission to incorporate part of a previously published article, and Scholars' Facsimiles and Reprints for permission to incorporate part of my introduction of *Contemplations of the Dread and Love of God* into this study.

# Chaucer and the Mystics

# 1

## Introduction

Authorial intentionality has of late been much debated.[1] Particularly among the New Critics, who find in old authors a common humanity shared in the text and thus inscribe their own concerns on those of the author, the act of self-expression has often passed for explication. Explicated meanings were often presented as exclusive of others, that is, "true" in an absolute sense, a map to the intentions of Chaucer, Shakespeare, Milton. Even the exegetical critics of the 1960s,[2] endeavoring to free us from this bind for the recovery of the allegorical workings of the medieval mind, replicated an ideology of the past that was totalizing and partially their own. Reader response critics, however, remind us that we create old texts anew when we explicate them.[3] What New Historicists[4] have to add to this debate is the astute insight that the cultural and social circumstances that circumscribe old authors also intersect with the author's intentions in creating a text.

In this book my intention (rather a vector, I suppose, of my own intentionality and the current trends in academic writing) is to explicate Chaucer in terms of a cultural and social intertext—one of which he was well aware. The similarities I will point out among Chaucer and the Middle English mystics do not imply a conscious intentionality on his part either to imitate them or parody them through irony. Instead they demonstrate, I hope, ways in which a dominant mode of literary expression inscribe on him some ways of looking at things, leaving somewhere in his mind a series of images, topoi, clichés, and attitudes that together with his conscious intentions (whatever they were) helped create *The Canterbury Tales*.[5] He may not have had, in other words, a copy, say, of *The Cloud of Unknowing* on his writing stand when working on the Miller's Tale, but his treatment of the pseudomystic Nicholas in that tale has, as I argue below, some interesting connections with that specific text and the larger intertext of Middle English mystical writings independent of his intentions.[6] A large-scale study of what Chaucer shares with the mystical intertext, particularly that dominated by Pseudo-Dionysian ideas, has not been done. I offer these studies as my own reading—not exclusive of those of others—in an attempt to explain how this one of many cultural, social, and political circumscriptions helped shape Chaucer's text. This is not, in other words, a source study.

## Chaucer and the Genre of Devotional Prose

The two, closely related theses of this book are that Chaucer's *Canterbury Tales* shares specific ideas, topoi, and motifs with the large body of Middle English mystical and devotional treatises and that his persistant fragmentation is at least partially explainable in terms of the mystics' doubts about the valency of language. Taking a cue from Dorothy L. Sayers's comments on Dante, Paul G. Ruggiers in *The Art of "The Canterbury Tales"* calls our attention to what I would argue is a central dichotomy for our understanding of Chaucer:

> Our appreciation of the artistry and the thematic intention of the *Canterbury Tales* as an integral poem depends upon our recognition of affirmation and rejection as informing principles of the . . . structure [of the Canterbury pilgrimage].[7]

The Retraction, with its spiritual erasure of a series of Tales left physically unerased in the manuscripts,[8] Chaunticleer's (mis)translation of his Latin tag *mulier est hominis confusio* as "womman is mannes joye and al his blis" (VII, 3164–66)[9] (p. 192[10]) together chart out the range of the simultaneous affirmation and denial[11] from the general to the specific in *The Canterbury Tales* that Ruggiers so rightly explicates.

The present study is my attempt to place this disturbing tendency toward simultaneous affirmation and denial in a specific historical and intertextual[12] environment—one of doubtless several that could be offered. The Middle English mystical writers, some with names, many anonymous, share this tendency to affirm and deny things—ideas, language, reality itself—with Chaucer. I claim neither that Chaucer was himself a mystic nor that his work has any specific mystical or theological meaning of an allegorical nature,[13] only that Chaucer knew of this type of writing and shared some attitudes with the devotional and mystical authors. The thesis of my book is that an understanding of this intertextual sharing of the tendency to affirm and simultaneously deny helps explicate individual passages of *The Canterbury Tales* and, perhaps more importantly, gives us some access to Chaucer's persistent fragmentation. Like the mystics, in other words, Chaucer depicts a universe in which attempts to control things lead to silence and finally fragmentation.[14]

This book is also an attempt to explore those three themes in *The Canterbury Tales* useful in explaining Chaucer's inability to finish things—control, silence, and fragmentation itself. Control—the efforts of characters to manipulate others, themselves, and their tales—is analogous to ways in which an author manipulates his text and audience.[15] Silence—the secrecy and privacy and trace of meaning left unsaid that characters continually impose on themselves and others[16]—becomes, through the medium of medieval mystical theology and its language theory,[17] a metaphor for Chaucer's blank spaces between the "fragments" of *The Canterbury Tales* and at its end. Fragmentation—the way not only poems break off but meanings split in two and actions end uncompleted—is a concept so broad that its implications are ultimately metaphysical as well as literary. I have in this study sought to valorize these terms as the ground of Chaucer's hermeneutics and aesthetics. Other valorizations could have—and should be—made; these, essential in different ways to the act of making and understanding texts, have not yet been fully made about Chaucer and his greatest poem.

The context I have chosen is the vast body of prose treatises of devotion written by the medieval mystics, especially the Middle English spiritual writers like Richard Rolle, Julian of Norwich, the author of *The Cloud of Unknowing,* and, even more important, the numerous anonymous women and men who contributed to the genre works like *Contemplations of the Dread and Love of God, The Twelve Profits of Tribulation, A Revelation of Purgatory, A Treatise of Ghostly Battle,* and *The Abbey of the Holy Ghost.* Texts like these, I argue, share not only attitudes about language with Chaucer but also specific topoi, themes, imagery, and occasionally characters. If the *via negativa* helped to create a persistently fragmentary Chaucer, the very stuff of the mystical and devotional treatises helped create the very stuff of *The Canterbury Tales.* In other words, it is my contention, to borrow a phrase from Stephen Greenblatt,[18] that there is a circulation of social energy at work in the production of Chaucer's—or for that matter any—text. Among all texts available to me for explication, I have chosen Chaucer's *Canterbury Tales,* and among several different types of social en-

ergy, I have chosen that of mystical and devotional writing, a genre
that Chaucer himself valorizes.

During an instructive comparison between Boccaccio's *Decameron* and Chaucer's *Canterbury Tales,* Derek Pearsall writes:

> Chaucer, in England, had no rich and numerous upper middle-class
> audience such as Boccaccio could rely on, but he was used to creating
> his own audience and the taste by which he would be appreciated.
> He wrote in verse [unlike Boccaccio]: in England literary prose was
> primarily used for devotional writing.[19]

Chaucer himself was well aware of this religious use of English
prose. After all, his friend John Clanvowe wrote the devotional
treatise *The Two Ways,* while his other friend Lewis Clifford mentions *The Book of Tribulation* in his will.[20] With the exception of
*The Treatise on the Astrolabe* and *An Equatorie of the Planetis,*
if it indeed is his,[21] all of Chaucer's prose pieces may be classified
as in some sense devotional. His *Boece,* of course a translation
of Boethius's *Consolation of Philosophy,* is properly a work of
philosophy rather than religious devotion, yet it is entirely congruent with Christian doctrine and was so read throughout the Middle
Ages. His own *Tale of Melibee,* a translation of a French rendering
of a work originally in Latin, is a semi-allegorical lesson in resisting
revenge—a cardinal element in Christian moral and devotional
teaching. And the Parson's Tale is, of course, specifically and
overtly Christian, replete with quotations from the Bible and the
anonymous *Summa Virtutum de Remediis Anime.*[22] There is even
evidence that the Parson's Tale was sometimes divorced from its
context and author and entered the great corpus of anonymous
prose devotional literature current in the late-fourteenth and fifteenth centuries; it is, for instance, included anonymously in the
famous Longleat Manuscript 29—a devotional miscellany containing works by Richard Rolle and Walter Hilton and the anonymous *Revelation of Purgatory.*[23] I will return later to a discussion
of the implications of the Parson's Tale as an independent work of
devotional prose.

Chaucer even claims, it seems, to have translated into prose
the famous treatise of Pope Innocent III, *De Miseria Condicionis
Humane.*[24] Alcestis in the Prologue to *The Legend of Good Women*
defends him in part by claiming,

> He hath in prose translated Boece,
> And Of the Wreched Engendrynge of Mankynde,
> As man may in Pope Innocent yfynde.[25]

(LGW, G 414315)

Interestingly, the last two lines are found only in the G-text of the Prologue, leaving not only the text unextant but the ascription to Chaucer perhaps doubtful.[26]

In his Retraction, which of course immediately follows the Parson's Tale in *The Canterbury Tales,* Chaucer makes it clear that devotional prose is the genre of literature by which he wishes to be remembered. After retracting such works as *Troilus and Criseyde, The House of Fame, The Book of the Duchess, The Parliament of Fowls,* and those *Canterbury Tales* which lead to sin, he reverses the evaluation of six-hundred years of subsequent literary criticism by calmly, audaciously, annoyingly stating:

> But of the translacion of Boece de Consolacione, and othere bookes of legendes of seintes, and omelies, and moralitee, and devocioun, that thanke I oure Lord Jhesu Crist and his blisful Mooder, and alle the seintes of hevene. (X, 1087–88)

The interpretation of the Retraction is much under debate, and it is an issue to which I will later return, but the preliminary point here is simple: Chaucer was well aware of the body of prose devotional literature popular during his lifetime and after. One of the suggestions I wish to make in this book is that such works influenced Chaucer—even in writing "the tales of Caunterbury, thilke that sownen into synne" (X, 1086).

To understand the concerns of the late-fourteenth-century English mystics, we must look first at some earlier texts from countries and in languages alien to Chaucer. In what follows I claim neither knowledge of nor direct influence on Chaucer of specifically these—and, in fact, of the Middle English texts—but I do maintain that of the ideas in general. And what follows must of necessity not be a complete history of medieval mysticism, for that of course is a subject demanding of its own right a book much longer than this one. But what follows will serve as an introduction to the important and relevant ideas, particularly those pertaining to the second part of this book's thesis—that the mystics, following the shadowy yet vastly influential lead of the early mystical writer known as Pseudo-Dionysius, taught Chaucer skepticism over the valency of language.

Historians of medieval mysticism conveniently dichotomize its varieties into two—the *via negativa* and the *via positiva,* the ways that negate and affirm human experience and ideas as an adequate basis upon which to experience and know God. There are more properly—at least according to St. Thomas Aquinas[27]—five ways, and a summary of them at this point is useful. Bernard McGinn writes:

> They are: (1) the way of univocation or equivocation, that is, that the terms we use of things can be applied to God either in exactly the same sense or in a completely different sense . . .; (2) the way of negation (*via negationis*), that is, the terms we use of things must be denied of God; (3) the way of causality (*via causalitatis*), which says that the terms we use of things apply to God insofar as he is the cause of all; (4) the way of eminence (*via eminentiae*), namely, that the terms we use of things apply in some higher way to God; and finally (5) the way of analogy (closely allied to the way of eminence), which states that terms used of both creatures and God are partly the same and partly different.[28]

In other words, the way of affirmation maintains that we may apply a word—say, *good*—to God, while the way of negation reminds us, to put it in the language of linguists and literary theorists, that there is a gap between the signifier and signified: "good" is a human construct that cannot describe God. The remaining three "ways," which have been relatively ignored by historians of mysticism, are in effect ways of saving the appearances: the way of causality allows us to call God "good" by extension, since he is the origin of goodness; the way of eminence is actually what medieval logicians called a *quanto magis* argument, for if a person might be said to be "good," how much more (*quanto magis*) ought we to call God "good"; and the way of analogy claims that what we know of a person's goodness may be extended by way of metaphor to apply to God. The latter three thus accept the basic premise of the way of negation yet seek methods to save language as a tool the mystic may use; they may most profitably be thought of as subclassifications of the negative way.

### Pseudo-Dionysius and his Followers

In an anonymous Middle English devotional poem entitled by its editor *Meditations on the Life and Passion of Christ*,[29] the poet describes the vision of Christ glorified in heaven and lists all the important saints who have in their writings or lives given witness to this mystical vision:

Lo, now he goþ, þe duk so fre,
fful of grace and of beaute.
His presence pleseþ man so,
It ouercomeþ alle serwe and wo.
Þat witnesseþ wel seynt Steuene
Whan he sy Ihesu on hy in heuene . . .

(1935–40)

After Steven, the first martyr, comes a list of the others: Peter, Clement, John the Evangelist, Paul, Lawrence, Vincent, Jerome, John Chrysostom,

Bernard, Gregor, Ambros, Dionys,
Alle þey weron clerkes of pris
And of holinesse þei beren gret name,
And alle þei witnessen þe same.
Þe archebishop, seynt Thomas,
Þer-fore suffred a ruly ras;
Vp-on his hed rede men may
Þat he ne dradde any afray.

(1966–74)

This juxtaposition of Pseudo-Dionysius with the holy blissful martyr who occasioned the Canterbury pilgrimage is of course coincidental, but Becket did, as we shall see, have a special devotion to St. Denis, and Pseudo-Dionysian language theory, I argue, had a formative influence on Chaucer's work.

The great transmitter of the mystical negative way to the Western Middle Ages was an anonymous fifth- or sixth-century Syrian monk[30] who appended the name Dionysius to his[31] treatises,[32] thus simultaneously guaranteeing some level of authority for his texts, since the historical Dionysius, surnamed "the Areopagite," was an Athenian follower of the apostle Paul (see Acts 17:34) and—I would argue—ironically divorcing his identity from his "name,"[33] for Pseudo-Dionysius's preoccupation was with the simultaneous naming and failing to name things. Perhaps his most famous treatise is *The Divine Names,* which is largely a catalog of the various names applied to God in the Bible. In the first chapter he writes:

we must not dare to resort to words or conceptions concerning that hidden divinity which transcends being, apart from what the sacred scriptures have divinely revealed. Since the unknowing of what is beyond is something above and beyond speech, mind, or being itself, one should ascribe to it an understanding beyond being.[34]

Here Pseudo-Dionysius coins the paradoxical term so influential among later mystics, "unknowing,"[35] and he does so in a paradoxical, almost playful way—in words denying the validity of words. He in fact is developing ideas that are as central to modern critical theory as they are to medieval mysticism—the gap between signifier and signified and the consequent erasure of meaning. As we shall see, he is well aware of what he is doing.

For him language is almost a measure of desperation, especially when it is applied to God. He writes,

> We use whatever appropriate symbols we can for the things of God. . . . We call a halt to the activities of our minds and, to the extent that is proper, we approach the ray which transcends being. Here, in a manner no words can describe, preexisted all the goals of all knowledge and it is of a kind that neither intelligence nor speech can lay hold of it nor can it at all be contemplated since it surpasses everything and is wholly beyond our capacity to know it. . . . How then can we speak of the divine names?[36]

Despite his skepticism about language, Pseudo-Dionysius goes on in *The Divine Names* to catalog the various modes of expression used in the Bible to describe God—not only nouns, but also phrases and adjectives:

> [The biblical writers] gave it [the Godhead] many names, such as "I am being," "life," "light," "God," "the truth." These same wise writers, when praising the Cause of everything that is, use names drawn from all the things caused: good, beautiful, wise, beloved, God of gods, Lord of Lords, Holy of Holies, eternal, existent, Cause of the ages. . . . he is sun, star, and fire, water, wind, and dew, cloud, archetypal stone, and rock. . . . he is all, . . . he is no thing. And so it is that as Cause of all and as transcending all, he is rightly nameless and yet has the names of everything that is.[37]

Significant here is not only the persistent paradox, but also the reminder that "God" itself is a mere name, thus only loosely connected with its signified. That God is "no thing" is perhaps startling, given the first name listed here, "I am being" (that is, the Hebrew name YHWH—see Exod. 3:19)—an idea with real connections to Eastern, particularly Buddhist thought,[38] one that the early fourteenth-century German mystic Meister Eckhart takes up with enthusiasm.

That Pseudo-Dionysius was aware of the linguistic and philosophical bind he had created for himself is evident throughout his treatises. For instance, speaking to "Timothy," the contemporary of the biblical Dionysius, he says:

> As for me, I pray that God should allow me to praise in a divine way the beneficent and divine names of the unutterable and unnameable Deity, and that he "take not the word of truth from out of my mouth."[39]

The quotation is from Psalm 119 (verse 43)—the long, seemingly interminable alphabetic psalm of 176 verses. A quotation from an overly prolix psalm supporting the unreliability of words is, of course, humorous, but it is a desperate humor: the verse may be taken in more than one way—as both a prayer for help in fitting the signifier and signified to each other, and as a prayer for the opposite—silence. In either case, he needs God's help. Likewise, at the very end of *The Divine Names,* he writes:

> These, then, are the divine names. They are conceptual names, and I have explained them as well as I can. But of course I have fallen well short of what they actually mean. Even the angels would have to admit such a failure and I could scarcely speak praises as they do.[40]

Similarly, at the end of *The Celestial Hierarchy,* his treatise defining for the subsequent Middle Ages the nature of those angels, he writes,

> This, then, is what I have to say regarding the sacred representations. Perhaps it falls a good deal short of making everything clear. Nevertheless I believe it will keep us from the wretchedness of being stuck in . . . fictional appearances.[41]

He is a person stuck in a conundrum, and his attempt to prove by words that words are unreliable is a kind of negative performatory utterance.

What such problematical symbols as words tend towards for Pseudo-Dionysius is silence. In the Invocation to his short treatise, *The Mystical Theology,* he addresses the Trinity in a much-quoted passage among the later mystics:

> Lead us up beyond unknowing and light, up to the farthest, highest peak of mystic scripture, where the mysteries of God's Word lie simple, absolute and unchangeable in the brilliant darkness of a hidden silence.[42]

Or as the anonymous Rhenish co..piler of the early fourteenth-century mystical treatise now known as *The Rothschild Canticles,* a writer heavily influenced by Pseudo-Dionysius, puts it, "He speaks best and most beautifully who keeps silence concerning God."[43] This silence is the medium of the angels, and it has for Pseudo-Dionysius as its attribute the same name used for God, "good":

> The angel is an image of God. He is a a manifestation of the hidden light. He is a mirror, pure, bright, untarnished, unspotted, receiving, if one may say so, the full loveliness of the divine goodness and purely enlightening within itself as far as possible the goodness of the silence in the inner sanctuaries.[44]

Silence is also a name in Pseudo-Dionysian terminology for God's work of creation:

> the Good is the Cause ever for the sources and the frontiers of the heavens, which neither shrink nor expand, and it brought into being the silent (if one must put it this way) and circular movements of the vast heavens.[45]

The disclaimer, of course, is another admission of Pseudo-Dionysius's linguistic dilemma.

One experiences this dilemma not only with the silence of angels but, more importantly, with fragmentation:

> The intelligent and intelligible powers of the angelic minds draw from Wisdom their simple and blessed conceptions. They do not draw together their knowledge of God from fragments nor from bouts of perception or of discursive reasoning. . . . Human souls also possess reason and with it they circle in discourse around the truth of things. Because of the fragmentary and varied nature of their many activities they are on a lower level than the unified intelligence [i. e., angels]. Nevertheless, on account of the manner in which they are capable of concentrating the many into the one, they too, in their own fashion and as far as they can, are worthy of conceptions like those of the angels.[46]

The fragmentation is, in fact, a result of one's point of view. As mortals, we cannot perceive God and his creation as he and it is, so we circle about, inventing imperfect names that must be denied yet accepted as useful—a simultaneous affirmation and denial. In other words, they are signs, symbols, as Charles Peirce and later Paul de Man remind us, an infinite regress from reality.[47] As Pseudo-Dionysius puts it,

By resorting to the perceptible, to imagery, he [God] makes clear that which gives life to our minds. . . . He shows how he came down to us from his own natural unity to our own fragmented level, yet without change.[48]

Such fragmentation, in accord with Pseudo-Dionysius' persistent paradox, simultaneously explains as well as obscures things:

I doubt that anyone would refuse to acknowledge that incongruities are more suitable for lifting our minds up into the domain of the spiritual than similarities are.[49]

Names (as well as sacraments, the subject of his treatise, *The Ecclesiastical Hierarchy*) function for Pseudo-Dionysius as fragmentary codes by which we interpret God and his creation.

This encoding is done by the believer through what amounts to a divinely inspired oscillation. Influenced by the Neoplatonists like Iamblichus and Plotinus as much as by Scripture and Christian tradition, Pseudo-Dionysius adopted the Neoplatonic concept "procession and return" as the structure for his ideas.[50] It is in this structure that it is possible to see exactly how Pseudo-Dionysius can simultaneously affirm and deny meaning to words. In other words, God allows a procession of signifiers, starting from simple ones like "good" and "one" and proceeding to the more egregious anthropomorphisms found in the Bible (God's beard, etc.), to emanate from him. This is the way of affirmation. The believer, starting at the farthest point of variety in this procession, follows the signifiers back to the signified, rejecting each in its turn, ultimately lapsing into silence. This path of return is the way of negation. The various symbols are then both true and untrue[51]—simultaneously. As the Church historian Paul Rorem puts it,

the Areopagite carefully preserved the simultaneity of procession and return, and thus of affirmation and negation. A given expression or symbol about God is denied because of its ultimate dissimilarity, but it is also, and at the same time, affirmed because of its relative similarity. An assertion based upon sense perception might claim, for example, "God is big." The interpretation of that symbolic language would counter with a negation, "Well, God is not really 'big' in that spatial sense" and then continue with an explanatory affirmation on a higher level, "God is 'big' in another way, a way not dependent upon perceptual categories," or, to use Dionyʌian short-hand, "God is super-big. . . ."[52]

The Pseudo-Dionysian universe is, in short, full of words that are unreliable yet useful,[53] signs admittedly fragmentary yet using fragmentation as a means of encoding the silence of God's non- or super-being.

One thinks here of Chaucer's famous passage in the General Prologue about the reliablility of words:

> But first I pray yow, of youre curteisye,
> That ye n'arette it nat my vileynye,
> Thogh that I pleynly speke in this mateere,
> To telle yow hir wordes and hir cheere,
> Ne thogh I speke hir wordes proprely.
> For this ye knowen al so wel as I:
> Whoso shal telle a tale after a man,
> He moot reherce as ny as evere he kan
> Everich a word, if it be in his charge,
> Al speke he never so rudeliche and large,
> Or ellis he moot telle his tale untrewe,
> Or feyne thyng, or fynde wordes newe.
> He may nat spare, althogh he were his brother:
> He moot as wel seye o word as another.
> Crist spak hymself ful brode in hooly writ,
> And wel ye woot no vileynye is it.
> Eek Plato seith, whoso that kan hym rede,
> The wordes moote be cosyn to the dede.
> Also I prey yow to foryeve it me,
> Al have I nat set folk in hir degree
> Heere in this tale, as that they sholde stonde.
> My wit is short, ye may wel understonde.
>
> (I, 725–46)

Christ and Plato certainly, but the Christian Neoplatonist Pseudo-Dionysius is also a referent here:[54] We have an assertion that the signified and signifier be identified together with a disclaimer based, ultimately, on lack of control: "My wit is short," just as the Pseudo-Dionysian person's wit is too short to apprehend the divine nature and name it. Chaucer's contemporary, the *Cloud*-author, has similar doubts about the referentiality of language. As he puts it in his translation/adaptation of Pseudo-Dionysius's *Mystical Theology*, his *Deonise Hid Diunite*:

> It behouiþ us alle þat ben practisers of þis deuinite for to make oure deniinges on þe contrary maner to oure afferminges; for whi we settyng oure affermynges begynnen at þe moost worþi þinges of þees beyng þinges, & so forþe by þe menes we descende to þe leest, bot in oure

deniinges we begynnyn at þe leest, & stien up to þe moste, and eftsones by þe menes, from þe hiest to þe last, & fro þe last to þe hiest aȝein, we foulden alle togeders & done hem awey, þat we mowen cleerliche knowe þat vnknowyng. . . . [55]

This passage is as much Neoplatonic as Christian and is perhaps the most emphatic in all the Pseudo-Dionysian corpus (including the many derivative and related texts) of the central doctrine of medieval language theory drawn from the mystics—the simultaneous affirmation and denial of the referentiality of language.

In the passage from the General Prologue, Chaucer shows this same attitude toward language. Words must be cousin to deeds—a double-edged statement, if ever there was one. Words are similar to yet different from the deeds they purport to describe: we may "know" deeds through words, yet this knowledge folds all together and tends ultimately toward unknowing, loss of control, and silence. The *Cloud*-author, in his treatise *A Pistle of Discrecioun of Stirings,* puts it this way:

For silence is not God, ne speking is not God. . . . He is hid betwix hem, and may not be founden by any werk of þi soule, bot al only bi loue of þin herte. He may not be knowen by reson. He may not be þouȝt, getyn, ne trasid, by vnderstonding. . . . Chese þee him; and þou arte silently spekyng & spekingly silent. . . . [56]

Silence and speech, like words and deeds, are cousins, each arrogating the roles traditionally assigned to the other when the control we exert over our words fails. God falls into the crack between them—an illogical proposition, at least according to the Scholastic philosophers, because there can logically be no middle between them.[57]

As Robinson notes,[58] the allusion to Plato in Chaucer's lines is to the *Timaeus,* filtered through Boethius. But Neoplatonists like Iamblichus and Pseudo-Dionysius were even more concerned with deeds and their cousins words than their master or Boethius were. Chaucer's statement reveals the same simultaneous affirmation and denial that we find in Pseudo-Dionysius. Words proceed from the deed, yet in our return to the deed we perceive that they are not identical, only cousins. Thus Chaucer must apologize for the negation that follows the affirmation: "n'arette it nat my vileynye" (I, 726). It is perhaps significant to note that the pilgrimage Chaucer is talking about here is a literal procession, with the return lost as *The Canterbury Tales* fragments. Perhaps it is even more significant to note that the object of that pilgrimage, St. Thomas Becket, uttered as his very last words as his murder precipitated his own eschatological, literal return to God a prayer to Pseudo-Dionysius:

> I commend myself and the cause of the Church to the blessed Mary, the patron saints of this church and the blessed Dionysius.[59]

I have elsewhere written about the dispersal of Pseudo-Dionysius's ideas to the West and suggested some possible points of entry into fourteenth century England[60]; a summary of the salient points is all, at any rate, needed for this book. The works of Pseudo-Dionysius were first translated into Latin in the ninth century by John Scotus Eriugena, but it is in the twelfth century that Pseudo-Dionysius, conflated with both the biblical Dionysius the Areopagite and St. Denis, patron of France, reached the height of his influence, not only in theological matters but also in political and artistic. His hierarchizing ideas were then used as a theoretical basis for the increasingly hierarchized nature of feudalism,[61] and Abbot Suger appealed to them as the theoretical basis for his ideas about visual art, especially the new Gothic style of architecture emerging at his abbey of St. Denis.[62] Twelfth-century theologians, of course, were most interested in him, beginning with Hugh of St. Victor, who wrote a commentary on *The Celestial Hierarchy,* thus beginning the trend toward dominance that Pseudo-Dionysius's ideas about the *via negativa* have had and continue to have in the discipline of mystical theology—an influence still so great, in fact, that the distinguished historian of medieval theology, monasticism, and mysticism, Dom David Knowles, is reluctant to grant full mystical status to those like Richard Rolle and Margery Kempe who seem most impervious to Pseudo-Dionysian themes.[63]

Pseudo-Dionysius's original influence, however, was on Eastern mystical theology. The seventh-century Maximus Confessor,[64] for instance, attempted a revision of Pseudo-Dionysius's ideas, shifting them away from Neoplatonism and more toward what is known in theological language as *christocentrism,* the doctrine that the Incarnation of Christ is the central divine act.[65] Even if Maximus prefers to save the appearances of language by positing doctrines about Christ as beyond the skepticism of the *via negativa,* he still accepts Pseudo-Dionysius's ideas about the simultaneous affirmation and denial of other language about God; for him we are left "adoring the Logos in silence."[66] Other Greeks, particularly the eleventh-century Symeon the New Theologian, as he is called, reacted against Pseudo-Dionysian themes,[67] yet later Greeks, like the early fourteenth-century Gregory Palamas,[68] whose dates (1296–

1359) make him the exact contemporary of Rolle, overlapping by almost two decades Chaucer's own life, are still driven by Pseudo-Dionysius's ideas.

In the West, the twelfth-century Richard of St. Victor[69] took it upon himself to develop Pseudo-Dionysius's ideas, stressing the role of imagination in the *via positiva* and writing an allegorical treatise on *The Twelve Patriarchs* from the book of Genesis in which he arranged them according to a Pseudo-Dionysian pattern: the final patriarch, Benjamin, who represents Contemplation, is born at the moment his mother, Rachel, who represents Reason, dies. Chaucer's contemporary, the author of *The Cloud of Unknowing,* translated part of this work in his *A Tretyse of þe Stodye of Wysdome þat Men Clepen Beniamyn.*[70]

In the thirteenth century Pseudo-Dionysian ideas eddied into the currents of Scholastic theology. Albertus Magnus[71] wrote a commentary on John Sarracenus's translation of *The Mystical Theology* which had been commissioned by Beckett's friend John of Salisbury,[72] in which he seeks to reconcile Pseudo-Dionysius with Aristotelian philosophy. Albertus was lecturing on Pseudo-Dionysius's *Celestial Hierarchy* when the young Thomas Aquinas[73] arrived in Paris; Thomas became Albertus's scribe for these lectures and followed his master to Cologne and inscribed the next series of lectures, which were on *The Divine Names.* Aquinas adopted the same method of reconciling Pseudo-Dionysius to Aristotle in his own writings,[74] particularly in the *Summa Contra Gentiles* and the *Summa Theologica,* where his Question 13, "On Theological Language," rehashes from an Aristotelian point of view Pseudo-Dionysius's *via negativa.*[75] The Scholastic Franciscan St. Bonaventure[76] was as much interested in Pseudo-Dionysius as the Dominicans Albertus and Thomas, beginning his major work, the *Itinerarium mentis in Deum,*[77] with a reference to *The Mystical Theology* and presenting his own version of the "journey of the soul to God" in Pseudo-Dionysian terms.

At the beginning of the fourteenth century the Dominican Meister Eckhart[78] took up Pseudo-Dionysian themes in a radical way, preferring the rigor of Pseudo-Dionysius's logic to Aristotle's, for he valorized Pseudo-Dionysius's more extreme statements, particularly those about God's *super-* or nonexistence and preferring silence as the ground on which to approach God.[79] The unorthodox tendencies of these ideas landed Eckhart in severe trouble with his order; the proceedings to condemn his writings as heretical were underway at the time of his death in 1327. The next generation of Dominicans, particularly Heinrich Suso[80] and Johannes Tauler,[81] followed Eckhart's lead but avoided his extremes. Tauler influenced Jan Ruusbroec,[82] who likewise stressed silence and the inability of words to signify.[83]

The preceding paragraphs, I hope, show how widespread were Pseudo-Dionysius's ideas among Continental mystics and theologians. But they also suggest several ways in which his ideas arrived in England. The *Cloud*-author, as well as adapting Pseudo-Dionysian ideas in his original writings, translated works of both Pseudo-Dionysius and Richard of St. Victor. This coincidence suggests perhaps the existence of a manuscript compendium containing both *The Mystical Theology* and *The Twelve Patriarchs,* implying some direct or indirect link in late-fourteenth-century England with the library at St. Victor itself. Richard was one of the theologians called in to try to settle the dispute between Becket and Henry II, Becket's friend and retainer John of Salisbury commissioned translations of Pseudo-Dionysius, and Becket died with a prayer to St. Denis on his lips—all indications that an earlier ingress of Pseudo-Dionysian ideas into England during the late-twelfth century was possible. In between, the Dominicans of the late-thirteenth century and early fourteenth—Albertus, Aquinas, Eckhart, Suso, and Tauler—were steeped in Pseudo-Dionysian thought. We can look to the preaching of their English province as another possible disseminator of Pseudo-Dionysian thought.

## The Middle English Mystics

Even though Richard Rolle (1300–1349),[84] the Yorkshire recluse whose dates barely overlap with Chaucer's, is usually described by scholars as resistant to the influence of Pseudo-Dionysius, that is strictly not the case.[85] Admittedly, he prefers a positive mysticism, in which earthly categories (specifically his famous "heat," "sweetness," and "song,") are used rather than discarded on the mystic's approach to God.[86] He nevertheless has read at least some of Pseudo-Dionysius and shows the occasional influence of Pseudo-Dionysian language theory. In his *Ego Dormio,* for instance, he summarizes briefly Pseudo-Dionysius's theories about angels from the *Celestial Hierarchy,*[87] and he often engages in the seemingly favorite activity of the mystics, simultaneously affirming and denying the valency of words.

In his *Form of Living,* for instance, Rolle writes about mystics in general:

Men wenes þat we er in pyne and in penance: bot we haue mare Ioy and verray delyte in a day, þan þei haue in þe worlde all þar lyue.[88]

*Pain* and *penance* are words whose meaning is affirmed in one direction only: recluses often live a harsh life of ascetic practices. But the words are denied in another direction, that of the mystics' approach to God, for then they become *joy* and *delight*. I shall show that St. Cecelia in the Second Nun's Tale uses this same technique of redefining mystic speech in her debate with the evil judge Almachius.

Perhaps a briefer example from Chaucer will help clarify this simultaneous affirmation and denial of the meaning of words that we find in Rolle. In a frequently explicated example from the Knight's Tale,[89] we encounter Arcite's redefinition of the world *prison* after he is released and thus exiled seemingly forever from Emelye's presence:

> "O deere cosyn Palamon," quod he,
> "Thyn is the victorie of this aventure.
> Ful blisfully in prison maistow dure—
> In prison? Certes nay, but in paradys!
> Wel hath Fortune yturned thee the dys. . . ."
>
> (I, 1234–38)

The Pseudo-Dionysian wedge between signifier and signified, easily discerned in the shift from "prison" to "paradise," also splits other words in this short passage—"deere," "victorie," "blisfully," "dure," and "wel." Like the two fictive cousins, the semantic cousins word and deed here have difficulty agreeing. Palamon and Rolle share a common view of language.

The great transmitter of such ideas to Chaucer's England, however, was not Richard Rolle but the anonymous author of *The Cloud of Unknowing,* Chaucer's exact contemporary.[90] He wrote not only that great work but also six other, shorter treatises, *The Book of Privy Counselling, A Pistle of Preier, A Pistle of Discrecioun of Stirings, A Tretis of Discrescyon of Spirites, Deonise Hid Diunite,* and *A Tretyse of þe Studye of Wysdome þat Men Clepen Beniamyn. Deonise Hid Diunite* is, as we have seen, a translation of Pseudo-Dionysius's *Mystical Theology,* while *Beniamyn* is his translation/abridgment of Richard of St. Victor's *Twelve Patriarchs;* the other treatises are original expositions of ideas the *Cloud*-author found in Richard and Pseudo-Dionysius.

How the *Cloud*-author treats his sources is instructive. Ex-

plaining the death of Rachel/Reason and the birth of Benjamin/
Contemplation, he writes,

> Neuerþeles ȝit may a man neuer come to soche a grace by his owne
> sleiȝt, for whi it is þe ȝift of God withoutyn deseert of man. And ȝit
> no man may take soche grace wyþoutyn greet study and brennyng
> desires comyng before. And þat wote Rachel ful wel. And for-þi she
> multyplie hir study, & whette hir desires, iche desire on desire, so þat
> at þe laste, in greet habundaunce of brennyng desires and sorow of þe
> delaiing of hir desire, Beniamyn is borne, and his moder Rachel diȝe.
> For whi in what tyme þat a soule is rauischid abouen hymself by habun-
> daunce of desires & a greet multytude of loue, so þat it is enflawmyd
> with þe liȝt of þe Godheed, sekirly þan dyȝeþ al mans reson.[91]

The language here depicts the soul out of control, ravished above
itself, losing completely its reason in contemplation of God. The
*Cloud*-author's version of the opening prayer of Pseudo-
Dionysius's *Mystical Theology* (quoted above in its original) is
likewise significant:

> I beseche þee for to drawe us up in an acordyng abilnes to þe souereyn-
> vnknowen and þe souereyn-schinyng heiȝt of þi derke inspirid spek-
> ynges, where alle þe pryue þinges of deuinytee been kouerid and hid
> vnder þe souereyn-schinyng derknes of wisest silence, makyng þe
> souereyn-clerest souereynly for to schine priuely in þe derkyst; and þe
> whiche is—in a maner þat is alweys inuisible & vngropable—souere-
> ynli fulfillyng wiþ ful fayere clertees alle þo soules þat ben not hauyng
> iȝen of mynde.[92]

For him Pseudo-Dionysius's word *mystic* is the simple English
word *hid*—as his translation of the title *Mystical Theology* as *Deonise Hid Diunite* would also indicate—and the silence that Pseudo-
Dionysius speaks of is translated both by *silence* and by the word
that is halfway between silence and hiddenness—*privy*—here present as both the adjective and adverb *priue* and *priuely*—and used
in the title of his *Book of Privy Counselling*. As we shall see, this
word is an important one in many of *The Canterbury Tales*, most
notably perhaps in the Miller's.[93]

In the *Book of Privy Counselling*, the *Cloud*-author directly
takes up in an original treatise the Pseudo-Dionysian themes considered here. We must, he maintains, approach God nakedly—that
is, without reason, without categorizing God by our names—to
experience him contemplatively:

Þus schal þi þouȝt & þi feling be onid wiþ hym in grace wiþ-outyn departing, alle corious sechinges in þe queinte qualitees of þi blinde beyng or of his fer put bac; þat þi þouȝt be nakid & þi felyng noþing defoulid, & þou, nakidly as þou arte, wiþ þe touching of grace be priuely fed in þi felyng only wiþ hym as he is; bot blyndly & in partie, as it may be here in þis liif, þat þi longing desire be euermore worching.[94]

Not only do we hear the language of the silent theology that avoids naming God ("priuely fed in þi felyng only wiþ hym as he is"), but we also hear the fragmentation so important to Pseudo-Dionysius ("blyndly & in partie").

The most direct imprint, though, of Pseudo-Dionysius on *The Book of Privy Counselling* is in the passage where the *Cloud*-author lists the divine names:

For wite þou riȝt wel þat in is werk þou schalt no more beholdyng haue to þe qualitees of þe being of God þan to þe qualitees of þe beyng of þi-self. For þer is no name, ne felyng ne beholdyng more, ne so moche, acordyng vnto euer-lastyngnes, þe wiche is God, as is þat þe whiche may be had, seen & felt in þe blinde & þe louely beholding of þis worde IS. For ȝif þou sey "Good" or "Faire Lorde," or "Swete," "Merciful" or "Riȝtwise," "Wise" or "Alwitty," "Miȝti" or "Almiȝti," "Witte" or "Wisdome," "Miȝte" or "Strengþe," "Loue" or "Charite," or what oþer soche þing þat þou sey of God: al it is hid & enstorid in þis litil worde IS. . . . & þerfore be as blynde in þe louely beholdyng of þe beyng of þi God as in þe nakid beholdyng of þe beyng of þi-self wiþ-outyn eny corious seching in þi wittys to loke after eny qualite þat longeþ to his being or to þine.[95]

Pseudo-Dionysius's simultaneous affirmation and denial of language is here, but it is of slightly different character. For the *Cloud*-author all names can be distilled and hidden in the verb *is,* which of course is related to God's name YHWH (see Exod. 3:13–15). Even more interesting is the *Cloud*-author's insistence that names are unreliable not only as applied to God but also to one's self. In this generalizing of the Pseudo-Dionysian gap, he follows his other great mentor, Richard of St. Victor.

His great treatise, of course, is *The Cloud of Unknowing.* In defining his controlling image, he shows how paradoxical words can be in a Pseudo-Dionysian universe, warning his reader of the dangers of language:

& wene not, for I clepe it a derknes or a cloude, þat it be any cloude congelid of þe humours þat fleen in þe ayre. . . . Lat be soche falsheed; I mene not þus. For when I sey derknes, I mene a lackyng of kno-

> wyng. . . . & for þis skil it is not clepid a cloude of þe eire, bot a cloude of vnknowyng, þat is bitwix þee & þi God. & ȝif euer þou schalt come to þis cloude & wone & worche þer-in as I bid þee, þee byhoueþ, as þis cloude of vnknowyng is abouen þee, bitwix þee & þi God, riȝt so put a cloude of forȝetyng bineþ þee, bitwix þee & alle þe cretures þat euer ben maad.[96]

This cloud of unknowing is the Pseudo-Dionysian gap between signifier and signified that we must pierce "with a scharpe darte of longing loue."[97] But more important for my purposes in this book is the second cloud, the cloud of forgetting that we must place between us and earthly things. In the *Cloud*-author, in other words, the Pseudo-Dionysian gap works both ways, surrounding us entirely, fragmenting us both from God and from things in our search for meaning beyond words.

One further Middle English mystical text is well worth considering before I begin my explication of *The Canterbury Tales* proper. Chaucer's contemporary, Julian of Norwich (ca. 1342-ca. 1423),[98] less theoretical and more personal than Meister Eckhart, the *Cloud*-author, and the rest, nevertheless shows how deeply ideas drawn from Pseudo-Dionysius about language, fragmentation, and silence had pierced Chaucer's England. Her *Showings* recount the visions she received of the suffering Christ while she herself was suffering a near fatal illness. Her text is justly celebrated for its influence on T. S. Eliot, Annie Dillard, and others, for its early and important feminist concerns, especially its lengthy explication of the God-as-Mother/Jesus-as-Mother theme,[99] for its emphasis on the all-powerful goodness of God ("all will be well, all manner of things will be well"), and for its unforgettable image of the cosmos as a hazelnut. For my purposes here what is important is a sequence of ideas she expresses in the seventeenth and eighteenth chapters of the long text of her *Showings,* part of her Eighth Showing, that of the desiccation of Christ's face.

Describing it, she notes the dried blood that had streamed down from the wounds caused by the crown of thorns:

> And ferthermore I saw that the swet skynne and the tendyr flessch with the here and with the blode was alle rasyd and losyde aboue with the thornes and brokyn in many pecis, and were hangyng as they wolde hastely haue fallen downe whyle it had kynde moyster.[100]

The philosophical fragmentation here has its literal correspondent in the torn skin hanging from Christ's face, "brokyn in many pecis." This reference to fragmentation might be a result of the physical necessities of her description, not any Pseudo-Dionysian concerns over the nature of language to signify, if it were not for her immediate response to this vision and the literary context in which she places it. The response is silence:

> Theyse were ij paynes that shewde in the blyssed hed. The furst wrought to the dryeng whyle it was moyst, and that other slow with clyngyng and dryeng, with blowyng of wynde from without, that dryed hym more and payned with colde than my hart can thingke, and all other peynes, for which paynes I saw that alle is to lytylle that I can sey, for it may nott be tolde.[101]

The fragments of Christ's skin which lead to silence immediately cause Julian to think of Pseudo-Dionysius:

> And thus tho that were hys fryndes suffered payne for loue, and generally alle; that is to sey, they that knew hym nott sufferde for feylynge of all maner comfort, saue the myghty pryve kepyng of god. I mene of ij maner of people that knew hym nott, as it may be vnderstond by ij persons. That oone was Pylate; that other person was seynt Dyonisi of France, whych was that tyme a paynym. For whan he saw wonders and merveyles, sorowse and dredys that befell in that tyme, he seyde: Eyther the worlde is now at an ende, or elles he that is maker of kyndes sufferyth. Wherfore he dyd wryte on an awter: Thys is an awter of the vnknowyn god.[102]

Not an abstract mystical theologian, but instead a mystic speaking from her own experience, Julian presents a vision of Christ, the controller of the cosmos, out of control on the cross and wounded to fragmentation. Her response is silence and then a reference to the Dionysius she did not label as "pseudo," a philosopher who speculated about the "pryve"[103] doings and the unknowability of God—both before and after his conversion.

If we have dealt at length with Pseudo-Dionysius and his followers, we should not forget the first part of this book's thesis, for before falling into the silence initiated by his Retraction, Chaucer drew much in the way of themes and imagery from the mystics. It is to that aspect of Chaucer and the mystics we turn, following for awhile the way of affirmation.

# 2
## Experience and Authority

Before I explore the tendency toward the simultaneous affirmation and denial that Chaucer shares with the Pseudo-Dionysian mystics, it is appropriate to address two connections that *The Canterbury Tales* has with the Middle English prose genre of devotional and mystical writing that Chaucer valorized in his Retraction—the striking similarities between the Wife of Bath and the early fifteenth-century mystic Margery Kempe[1] and the entry of Chaucer's own Parson's Tale shortly after his death into the vast body of anonymous devotional treatises. The first part of this chapter centers on the Wife of Bath's favorite term, "experience," for Margery Kempe writes of her experiences—some of which her fictional older contemporary, Alice of Bath, shared, others of which, as we shall see, she did not. The second term in the Wife's famous dichotomy of "experience" and "authority" refers, of course, to the power of texts to define and direct experience: the limits of the Parson's Tale as such a defining and directing text will be the subject of the second part of this chapter.

### Margery and Alice

No matter what David Knowles asserted, Kempe is not entirely impervious to the influence of Pseudo-Dionysius, for at one point she has Jesus address her in the words of the Syrian monk and his followers Meister Eckhart and the *Cloud*-author:

> Dowtyr, þu seyst þat it is to me a good name to be called al good, & þu xalt fyndyn þat name is al good to þe. And also, dawtyr, þu seyst it is wel worthy þat I be callyd al lofe, & þu xalt wel fyndyn þat I am al lofe to þe, for I knowe euery thowt of thyn hert.[2]

Those of us accustomed to the discussions of Pseudo-Dionysius and his followers about God's names expect Kempe to turn immediately to the limits of such names, but she here lets the matter drop—a result, perhaps, of the way she assimilated mystical texts.

Herself illiterate, she dictated her autobiographical book in the late 1430s, near the end of her life, to a local priest and occasionally recounts how others had read mystical texts to her:

> He [a young priest she had encountered] red to hir many a good boke of hy contemplacyon & oþer bokys, as þe Bybyl wyth doctowrys þer-up-on, Seynt Brydys boke, Hyltons boke, Bone-ventur, Stimulus Amoris, Incendium Amoris, & swech oþer.[3]

The Bible with doctors thereupon is a Bible with patristic glosses of the type the Wife of Bath finds so repugnant ("Glose whoso wole, and seye bothe up and doun" [III, 119]); St. Bridget's book was translated into Middle English as the *Liber Celestis;*[4] Walter Hilton's book is his *Scale of Perfection;* Pseudo-Bonaventure wrote the *Stimulus Amoris;* and the *Incendium Amoris* was by Richard Rolle. Kempe often reveals how much her life imitates things she found in these and other devotional texts, for she visits St. Bridget's home in Rome and speaks to her still-surviving hand-maid (chap. 39) and often claims to have heard the sweet melody that Rolle makes so much of. We can discern other silent traces of her secondhand reading in, for instance, her attempts to kiss lepers (chap. 74), so similar to those of St. Francis recounted in his *Life,* and her attentions to a poor sick woman while she is in Rome (chap. 34), so reminiscent of the similar ministrations of St. Cathe-rine of Siena.

One particular detail from the experiences of her life that imi-tates the authoritative context of books—and one of special inter-est to readers of Chaucer—is Kempe's efforts to pattern her marriage, however belatedly, after St. Cecelia's.[5] The *Life of St. Cecelia* generally available in early fifteenth-century England was that contained in Jacobus of Voragine's *Legenda Aurea,* but, of course, Chaucer's own adaptation of it for *The Canterbury Tales,* the Second Nun's Tale, was also perhaps available to Kempe. One night, in bed with John Kempe, her husband, she has a mystical experience that owes something both to Rolle and St. Cecelia's *Life:*

> On a nyght, as þis creatur lay in hir bedde wyth hir husbond, sche herd a sownd of melodye so swet & delectable, hir þowt, as sche had ben in Paradyse. And þerwyth sche styrt owt of hir bedde & seyd, "Alas, þat euyr I dede synne, it is ful mery in Hevyn."[6]

Passing over Kempe's seeming quotation of the Wife of Bath, "Allas! allas! That evere love was synne!" (III, 614)—for the sin Kempe continually laments throughout her *Book* is sexual in nature—we are left with a seeming imitation of St. Cecelia, whose *Life* recounts the access she, Valerian, her husband, and Tiberius, his brother, have to the sweet smells of heaven.[7] The difference is that Kempe substitutes Rolle's *song* for the sweet smell.

More to the point, however, is St. Cecelia's negotiation of her marriage. As Chaucer's text puts it,

> The nyght cam, and to bedde moste she gon
> With hire housbonde, as ofte is the manere,
> And pryvely to hym she seyde anon,
> "O sweete and wel biloved spouse deere,
> Ther is a conseil, and ye wolde it heere,
> Which that right fayn I wolde unto yow seye,
> So that ye swere ye shul it nat biwreye."
>
> Valerian gan faste unto hire swere
> That for no cas, ne thyng that myghte be,
> He sholde nevere mo biwreyen here;
> And thanne at erst to hym thus seyde she:
> "I have an aungel which that loveth me,
> That with greet love, wher so I wake or sleepe,
> Is redy ay my body for to kepe.
>
> "And if that he may feelen, out of drede,
> That ye me touche, or love in vileynye,
> He right anon wol sle yow with the dede,
> And in youre yowthe thus ye shullen dye;
> And if that ye in clene love me gye,
> He wol yow loven as me, for youre clennesse,
> And shewen yow his joye and his brightnesse."

(VIII, 141–61)

This murderous angel who would insure St. Cecelia's chaste marriage metamorphoses into a murderous Jesus in Kempe's text, who would do something similar to aid the would-be saint:

Anoþer tyme, as þis creatur prayd to God þat sche myt leuyn chast be leue of hir husbond, Cryst seyd to hir mende, "Þow must fastyn þe Fryday boþen fro mete & drynke, and þow schalt haue þi desyr er Whitsonday, for I schal sodeynly sle þin husbonde."[8]

Christ, mercifully, forgets to do this for Kempe, and she must negotiate her own chaste marriage in ways more difficult than the authority of her text seems to imply. Three years later—and after she bears him a total of fourteen children—John Kempe finally agrees to be Valerian to her Cecelia, and the long conversation (chap. 11) that finally brings him to heel begins with a veiled threat like the one Cecelia levels at Valerian:

> Now, good ser, amend ȝow & aske God mercy, for I teld ȝow ner iij ȝer sythen þat ȝe schuld be slayn sodeynly, & now is þis þe thyrd ȝer, & ȝet I hope I schal han my desyr.[9]

The point is actually twofold. First, Kempe, reader of devotional and mystical texts, seeks to become herself such a text, first by imitating the characters of such texts by appropriating their experiences when possible—hearing Rolle's sweet melodies, for instance—and struggling to appropriate their experiences when not possible—threatening John Kempe with the death Valerian would earn by living unchastely with his wife. Then Kempe turns her own experienced life into a *Life* by seeking out a priest who, reluctantly, agrees to write her words down,[10] thus turning her experience into an authority, which presumably will influence others. Second, her attitude toward both experience and reality here charts the outlines of her similarities to and differences from the Wife of Bath—a woman likewise influenced by texts yet as eager to experience the pleasures of the marriage bed as Kempe is to avoid them.

In general, the experiences of Kempe and her fictional older contemporary are striking. Both are given to autobiographical narrative. Both are middle-class wives who engage, independently of their husbands, in businesses of their own—Alice of Bath in the cloth trade and Kempe as first brewer and then miller. Both are fond of pilgrimages, for the Wife of Bath has left behind her fourth husband to go to Jerusalem, a long and dangerous trip, and Kempe makes that same trip without her husband, stopping off at the second locus of pilgrimage, Rome, on the way back. Both go to Canterbury, and Kempe goes to Compostela, Walsingham, and the Eastern European shrine of Wilsnack as well.

Both give much thought to the pleasures of the flesh. As the Wife of Bath explains:

> . . . I hadde the prente of seinte Venus seel.
> As help me God, I was a lusty oon,
> And faire, and riche, and yong, and wel bigon,
> And trewely, as myne housbondes tolde me,
> I hadde the beste *quoniam* myghte be.
> For certes, I am al Venerien

> In feelynge, and myn herte is Marcien.[11]
> Venus me yaf my `st, my likerousnesse,
> And Mars yaf me my sturdy hardynesse. . . .
>
> . . . . . . . . . . . . . . . . .
> I folwed ay myn inclinacioun
> By vertu of my constellacioun;
> That made me I koude noght withdrawe
> My chambre of Venus from a good felawe.
>
> (III, 604–12, 15–18)

Surprisingly, would-be St. Cecelia Margery Kempe can explain:

> & so þe Deuyl bar hyr on hande, dalying vn-to hir wyth cursyd thowtys
> liche as owr Lord dalyid to hir be-forn-tyme with holy thowtys. And,
> as sche beforen had many gloryows visyonys & hy contemplacyon in
> þe manhod of owr Lord, in owr Lady, & in many oþer holy seyntys,
> ryth euyn so had sche now horybyl syghtes & abhominabyl, for any-
> thyng þat sche cowde do, of beheldyng of mennys membrys & swech
> oþer abhominacyons. Sche sey as hir thowt veryly dyuers men of reli-
> gyon, preystys, & many oþer, bothyn hethyn & Cristen comyn be-for
> hir syght þat sche myth not enchewyn hem ne puttyn hem owt of hir
> syght, schewyng her bar membrys vn-to hir.[12]

But Kempe, of course, withstands these temptations, staying faithful to her only husband—with occasional difficulty (see also chap.
4)—and then to Jesus after she finally negotiates her chaste marriage. Where the Wife of Bath finds sex a delight, Margery Kempe
finds it "abominable." As she explains to one of the frequent male
interrogators who suspect her of Lollardy:

> "Sir," sche seyde, "I take witnesse of my Lord Ihesu Crist, whos body
> is her present in þe Sacrament of þe Awter, þat I neuyr had part of
> mannys body in þis worlde in actual dede be wey of synne, but of myn
> husbondys body, whom I am bowndyn to be þe lawe of martrimony,
> & be whom I haue born xiiij childeryn.[13]

And even that lawful intercourse is a burden to her and cause
of guilt:

> As þis creatur lay in contemplacyon, sor wepyng in hir spiryt, sche
> seyde to owyr Lord Ihesu Cryst, "A, Lord, maydenys dawnsyn now
> meryly in Heuyn. Xal not I don so? For be-cawse I am no mayden,
> lak of maydenhed is to me now gret sorwe; me thynkyth I wolde I had
> ben slayn whan I was takyn fro þe funt-ston þat I xuld neuyr a dysple-
> syd þe, & þan xuldyst þu, blyssed Lorde, an had my maydenhed wyth-
> owtyn ende.[14]

Both Margery Kempe and Alice of Bath, in other words, regret that ever love was sin, but from entirely different points of view. Kempe, in fact, follows closely to the norm of medieval female spirituality, and the Wife of Bath does not—as readers of historians like Bynum and Bell know.[15] For often the woman who felt called to the life of religious devotion had to endure the hardships of intense familial pressure to achieve husbandless chastity—a matter of some importance, as I shall show in my analyses of both the Prioress's and the Franklin's tales.

Perhaps even more important for an understanding of what the experiences of Margery Kempe have to tell us about the Wife of Bath is an understanding of their relationships to that greatest of textual authorities, the Bible. As we know, the Wife of Bath prefers literal to allegorical interpretations of scripture:

> Telle me also, to what conclusion
> Were membres maad of generacion,
> And of so parfit wys a [wright] ywroght?
> Trusteth right wel, they were nat maad for noght.
> Glose whoso wole, and seye bothe up and doun
> That they were maked for purgacioun
> Of uryne, and oure bothe thynges smale
> Were eek to knowe a femele from a male,
> And for noon oother cause—say ye no?
> The experience woot wel it is noght so.
> So that the clerkes be nat with me wrothe,
> I sey this: that they maked ben for bothe:
> This is to seye, for office and for ese
> Of engendrure, ther we nat God displese.
> Why sholde men elles in hir bookes sette
> That man shal yelde to his wyf hire dette?
> Now wherwith sholde he make his paiement,
> If he ne used his sely instrument?
> Thanne were they maad upon a creature
> To purge uryne, and eek for engendrure.

> (III, 115–34)

Kempe, however, can see beyond a literal text having to do with engendering children toward a larger tropological realm:

Anoþer tyme þer cam a gret clerke on-to hir, askyng þes wordys how þei xuld ben vndirstondyn, "Crescite & multiplicamini."[16] Sche, answeryng, seyd, "Ser, þes wordys ben not vndirstondyn only of begetyng of chyldren bodily, but also be purchasyng of vertu, whech is frute gostly, as be heryng of þe wordys of God, be good exampyl ȝeuyng, be mekenes & paciens, charite & chastite, & swech oþer, for pacyens is more worthy þan myraclys werkyng." And sche thorw þe grace of God answeryd so þat clerke þat he was wel plesyd.[17]

Yet Kempe, as orthodox as this answer may be and as dependent as it is on patristic glossing of the sacred text, also has a more direct line of access to the writers of the Bible, one she shares with Alice of Bath. As Jesus explains to her:

Dowtyr, I sent onys Seynt Powyl vn-to þe for to strengthyn þe & comfortyn þe þat þu schuldist boldly spekyn in my name fro þat day forward. And Seynt Powle seyd vn-to þe þat þu haddyst suffyrd mech tribulacyon for cawse of hys wrytyng, & behyte þe þat þu xuldist han as meche grace þer-a-ʒens for hys lofe as euyr þu haddist schame er reprefe for hys lofe. He telde þe also of many joys of Heuyn & of þe gret lofe þat I had to þe.[18]

This context of direct communication with Paul, of course, makes the Wife of Bath's statement of direct access to that great letter writer of the New Testament not quite as implausible as it might seem:

> Right thus the Apostel tolde it unto me,
> And bad oure housbondes for to love us weel.
> Al this sentence me liketh every deel"—
>
> (III, 160–62)

Kempe further remarks,

Sum-tyme Seynt Petyr, er Seynt Powle, sumtyme Seynt Mary Mawdelyn, Seynt Kateryne, Seynt Margaret, er what seynt in Heuyn þat sche cowde thynke on thrw þe wil & sufferauns of God, þei spokyn to þe vndirstondyng of hir sowle.[19]

Direct access to the Bible was, of course, politically and ecclesiastically problematic in the late-fourteenth and early fifteenth centuries. It was a mark of Wycliffe's teachings, and, after John of Gaunt's death, the Lollards that he protected were exposed to danger. Kempe several times was victim of interrogations, spent time in prison, and narrowly escaped being burned. Her orthodoxy, particularly her willingness to interpret Scripture through the accepted patristic glosses—a willingness that the Wife of Bath lacks, exposing her perhaps (if we fancifully extend her life into the fifteenth century) to the flames Kempe with trouble avoided.

Kempe's adversaries were often friars (see chaps. 61 and 62, for
instance), as are, of course the Wife of Bath's (see III, 829–31),
although hers is a more good-natured, far less dangerous opposition. Chaucer's day was more generous to those to whom Paul
spoke directly than that of the next generation.

I suggest that Margery Kempe and the Wife of Bath, with significant differences relating to sex and marriage, are of a piece—
the woman with direct access to God's word, at opposition to the
clergy. It is a type traceable as far back as Christina of Markyate
in England and Hildegard of Bingen in Germany in the twelfth
century—women I will discuss later. When such women, usually
unmarried, banded together in common dwellings yet without religious vows, they were called *beguines,* some of whom, like Margaret Porete (d. 1310), author of *The Mirror of Simple Souls,* were
burned for heresy. The prototype beguine, Mary of Oignes, whose
famous *Life* by Jacques de Vitry occasioned much imitation both
literary and lived (that is, authority and experience), is one of the
mystics whose texts Kempe read at second hand and imitated:

> aftyrward he [a priest who reads to her] red of a woman clepyd Maria
> de Oegines & of hir maner of leuyng, of þe wondirful swetnesse þat
> sche had in þe word of God heryng, of þe wondirful compassyon þat
> sche had in hys Passyon thynkyng, & of þe plentyows teerys þat sche
> wept, þe whech made hir so febyl.[20]

Perhaps the most memorable things about Kempe's life/*Life* are
the great tears and roaring she, out of control, experiences. Experience imitates authority before hiring a reluctant priest to write it
again into authority.

The point about the Wife of Bath, of course, is that she simultaneously is and is not Margery Kempe. She shares in some of the
same attitudes as Kempe and the beguines and others on whom
Kempe modeled her life—pilgrimage, and direct access to the Bible
and religious truth, in particular.[21] Yet the hallmark of the lay-
woman with religious leanings is the attempt at avoiding marriage
and sublimating sexuality into religious devotion. Chaucerian comedy here, in other words, is at least by extension Pseudo-
Dionysian, affirming Alice of Bath's nature of lay-religious with
one hand while denying it with the other.

## The Parson

Margery Kempe has also at least two instructive parallels with
Chaucer's Parson.[22] The first is their Lollard-like tendency to judge

others, particularly for cursing. On trial for Lollardy under the Archbishop of York, she defiantly answers her judge—like, perhaps, St. Cecelia before Almachius:

I xal spekyn of God & undirnemyn [i.e., rebuke] hem þat sweryn gret othys wher-so-euyr I go vn-to.[23]

The Parson, of course, also is accused by the Host of Lollardly because of his tendency to rebuke swearing:

"Sir Parisshe Prest," quod he, "for Goddes bones,
Telle us a tale, as was thi forward yore.
I se wel that ye lerned men in lore
Can moche good, by Goddes dignitee!"
    The Parson hem answerde, "Benedicite!
What eyleth the man, so synfully to swere?"
Oure Host answerde, "O Jankin, be ye there?
I smelle a Lollere in the wynd," quod he.
"Now! goode men," quod oure Hoste, "herkeneth me;
Abydeth, for Goddes digne passioun,
For we schal han a predicacioun;
This Lollere heer wil prechen us somwhat."

(II, 1166–77)

The anonymous Middle English prose devotional text, *The Vision of William of Stranton,* a vision of purgatory, makes clear just how grievous a sin swearing was to people like Kempe and the Parson:

Then Sent John [sayde], "Loo, Wyllyam, thyes wrachys suffers thyes paynes for thay dysmembyrde Gode wyth swerynge of hys body, hys armys, hys eyne, hys sydes, hys wondys, hys nayles, hys sowle, and other of hys membyrs, and þerfore Goddys wyll here endurys þat behovysse them to suffer thys."[24]

Note the direct conversation an apostle has with a believer, reminiscent of those both Kempe and the Wife of Bath claim for themselves. Such a text incidentally does much to explain the Pardoner's comments about swearing (see VI, 629–59).

Perhaps an even more instructive connection between the two is their shared tendency to see earthly pilgrimage in terms of an allegorical heavenly pilgrimage. Near the end of *The Canterbury Tales,* the Parson, of course, redirects the pilgrimage toward religious allegory,[25] even when he paradoxically disclaims interest in allegorical glossing:

> And therfore, if yow list—I wol nat glose—
> I wol yow telle a myrie tale in prose
> To knytte up al this feeste and make an ende.
> And Jhesu, for his grace, wit me sende
> To shewe yow the wey, in this viage,
> Of thilke parfit glorious pilgrymage
> That highte Jerusalem celestial.

(X, 45–51)

Kempe does the same: while on her earthly pilgrimage to Jerusalem, with the very towers of that city in the distance, she too redirects things:

> & so þei went forth in-to þe Holy Lond tyl þei myth se Ierusalem. And, whan þis creatur saw Ierusalem, rydyng on an asse, sche thankyd God wyth al hir hert, preyng hym for hys mercy þat lych as he had browt hir to se þis erdly cyte Ierusalem he wold grawntyn hir grace to se þe blysful cite Ierusalem a-bouyn, þe cyte of Heuyn.[26]

It is, however, not the experience the Parson shares with Margery Kempe that is important for an understanding of his tale, however suggestive their shared tendency to equate literal cities with heavenly. What is important, however, is the Parson's Tale's place among the authoritative texts that make up the genre of Middle English devotional/mystical literature.

The coupled adjectives in the last sentence now demand some attention. In fact, the Parson's Tale is useful in an attempt to join those adjectives, for it demonstrates, by its placement in compendia of Middle English religious treatises when unmoored from the rest of *The Canterbury Tales,* that the dichotomy we have constructed between the words is a modern rather than medieval one. In the early fifteenth-century Longleat Manuscript 29, for instance, the Parson's Tale enters anonymously that genre, joining works like Walter Hilton's *De Vita Activa et Contemplativa* and several others by Richard Rolle—works defining by theory and experience the individual's contemplative union with God—what we would term today specifically mystical treatises. In that manuscript is also the fifteenth-century *Revelation of Purgatory,* a work visionary in nature, in which an anonymous woman has a vision of the torments a nun of her acquaintance suffers in purgatory. The point is that the Parson's Tale is neither "mystical"—that is, concerned with either the believer's methods of achieving or experiences of unity with God—nor visionary. A treatise or "meditation"[27] on penance and the Seven Deadly Sins, it is strictly moral in nature.[28]

The morally devotional and the strictly religious, in other words, mix in this and many other Middle English manuscripts. There is evidence, incidentally, that several others of *The Canterbury Tales* entered this corpus, joining both anonymous and "named" works in religious miscellanies—the Prioress's Tale, the Monk's Tale, and most frequently the *Tale of Melibee*.[29]

There is an organizing principle here, I would suggest, beyond the normal happenstance of book compilation in the late Middle Ages: those interested in moral devotion and mysticism recognized a continuum that ran from the one to the other. In *Contemplations of the Dread and Love of God*,[30] a work in Middle English exactly contemporary with *The Canterbury Tales,* for instance, the anonymous author establishes moral betterment as the ground on which mystical contemplation is built.

He begins his treatise with a nostalgic look back on those of "old time" who were capable of mystical contemplation; specifically as I have elsewhere argued,[31] Richard Rolle:

> I fynde & rede of oure holy faders in olde tyme that for the loue of god they forsoke the worlde and all worldely thynges and lyued in wyldernes by grasse & by rotes / suche men were feruent in the loue of God. But I troue there ben but fewe or elles none that folowen them now. . . . Some of these men as I haue herde and redde were vysyted by the grace of god with a passynge swetenes of the loue of cryste / whiche swetenes for an example they shewed afterwarde by theyr wrytynge to other men folowynge / yf ony wolde trauayle to haue that hyghe desyre or degree of loue.[32]

He laments the inability of his contemporaries to experience God so directly and thus proposes a means by which they can prepare themselves for the three high degrees of love experienced by Rolle and others like him in former generations by starting with four lower degrees. These lower degrees will comprise the access point for the higher, and they are particularly moral in nature:

> For yf thy desyre be sette feruently & louyngly holdynge the unworthy to haue so hyghe a ghoostly gyfte before an other man / & puttest thy desyre to goddes dysposycyon trustyngly he wyll dyspose that is best for the / whether thou haste thy desyre or haue it not. But it is fyrst nedefull to þe that thou haue other [four][33] degrees of loue that the same holy men wrote in theyr treatyse / whiche be not of so hyghe a degree as tho that be reherced before.[34]

The four degrees he proposes are all properly those of moral devotion. He names them "ordained," "clean," "steadfast," and "perfect." The author divides each of his degrees into aspects that he calls "points," and the five points of ordained love govern a person's relationship to the physical world. The first point claims that one should love one's own flesh only insofar as it may be sustained for the service of God. Although he warns his reader to avoid gluttony, the author here cautions as well against overly rigorous asceticism. The second point is that one should not love the world excessively, and again the bivalence is evident. By claiming that excessive love of the world is wrong, the author allows for a moderate love bounded by God's will. The last three points of this degree extend ordained love into the world of interpersonal relationships: one should love one's neighbor for God's sake, one's friend for his good living, and one's enemy for the consequent spiritual reward.

Clean love governs a person's inward moral realm. The first point sounds paradoxical and thus demands some explanation: one should love no vice with virtue. In brief, this point is a warning against hypocrisy, for one should be virtuous not for the praise of others but for the proper inward motive. In the second point the author admonishes his reader to persevere in the fight against habitual sins, and in the third point he reminds us that little sins can be just as deadly to the soul and detrimental to the progress of love as great ones.

The points of the third degree, steadfast love, are practical in that they suggest how to maintain one's progress in love. Briefly, the five caution one to love God with all one's desire, to remember God at the beginning of any good work, to do nothing wrong for the sake of some good that might come of it, to control oneself for the sake of having a fervent will, and to resist giving up because of weariness or temptation. Thus steadfast love deals also primarily with the moral world, but where clean love governs the purging of sins, steadfast love governs the persevering in good.

The last degree, perfect love, combines the contemplative with the moral. In the first point the author shows how the virtues lead to perfection, and in the succeeding five, he shows how individual virtues foster contemplation—good will, prayer, resistance to temptation, patience, and perseverance. The treatise concludes with a meditation on Christ's Passion.[35]

My quotations from and lengthy summary of *Contemplations of the Dread and Love of God* may be justified not only because that work may serve as a fairly typical Middle English devotional treatise contemporaneous with Chaucer and the Parson's Tale, but also because it both inhabits the same ideological universe as that tale and bridges the gap between the devotional and moral. In other words, the compiler of Longleat Manuscript 29 saw fit to include the Parson's Tale in a miscellany containing the mystics Hilton and Rolle because it helps the reader—as do the preliminary four degrees of love proposed by the author of *Contemplations of the Dread and Love of God*—prepare for the mystical contemplation that is Hilton's and Rolle's subject.

Just how closely allied are the intentions of the Parson's Tale to those of *Contemplations of the Dread and Love of God* may be seen by a look at the opening passage of that tale:

> Oure sweete Lord God of hevene, that no man wole perisse but wole that we comen alle to the knoweleche of hym and to the blisful lif that is perdurable, amonesteth us by the prophete Jeremie, that seith in thys wyse: "Stondeth upon the weyes, and seeth and axeth of olde pathes (that is to seyn, of olde sentences) which is the goode wey, and walketh in that wey, and ye shal fynde refresshynge for youre soules, etc." Manye been the weyes espirituels that leden folk to oure Lord Jhesu Crist and to the regne of glorie. Of whiche weyes there is a ful noble wey and a ful convenable, which may nat fayle to man ne to woman that thurgh synne hath mysgoon fro the righte wey of Jerusalem celestial; and this wey is cleped Penitence, of which man sholde gladly herknen and enquere with al his herte to wyten what is Penitence, and whennes it is cleped Penitence, and in how manye maneres been the acciouns or werkynges of Penitence, and how manye speces ther been of Penitence, and whiche thynges apertenen and bihoven to Penitence, and whiche thynges destourben Penitence. (X, 74–82)

Where the author of *Contemplations of the Dread and Love of God* begins by appealing to the sweetness of mystical union achieved by Rolle and his generation, the Parson appeals to "the blisful lif that is perdurable." Where the author of the anonymous text proposes a way of moral betterment, that is, doing positive good, the Parson suggests penitence, that is, turning away from evil. And where the author of *Contemplations of the Dread and Love of God* enumerates and labels the steps along his way, so does the Parson, for shortly he gives his own signpost for the treatise that is to follow:

> The speces of Penitence been three. That oon of hem is solempne, another is commune, and the thridde is privee. (X, 101)

The Parson's penitential treatise, of course, is largely a translation of two works: the *Summa* of Raymond of Pennaforte and the anonymous *Summa Virtutum de Remediis Anime*,[36] the last the source for the material about the Seven Deadly Sins, a treatise loosely related to the similar *Summa vitiorum* of William Peraldus, whose work was once thought to be the direct source of the corresponding section of the Parson's Tale.[37] These works—and Chaucer's compilation—stand, moreover, at the end of a long tradition of explications and systematizations of the virtues and vices. Dante, of course, structures his vast *Divine Comedy* according to the hierarchization of the vices and virtues, but the genre is traceable back to the very early Middle Ages to two roots—the *Psychomachia* of Prudentius,[38] where the personifications of the virtues defeat the vices on the battlefield of the soul,[39] and the penitential handbooks of the eighth through tenth centuries that often instruct the priest to recommend the virtues as metaphorical medicine to heal the vices.[40] The twelfth-century visionary and mystic Hildegard of Bingen shows the centrality of this morally devotional genre to the mystic by writing a morality play set to music and based on the personified virtues' efforts to cleanse and win the soul—the *Ordo Virtutum*,[41] important alike for musicologists, theologians, and literary historians.

As Thomas Bestul has shown,[42] however, the Parson's Tale is more than a compilation of two treatises related to moral development, for to them Chaucer adds some of his own material, notably a meditation on Christ's Passion (X, 255–82). Such meditations were staples of purely mystical literature both in Latin and Middle English, and Bestul suggests analogues from St. Bernard, Bonaventure, Richard Rolle, and the anonymous authors of *The Wohunge of Ure Lauerd*[43] and *A Talking of the Love of God,* among others. This interpolation, in other words, reveals two things—Chaucer's wide reading in mystical literature and his tendency to revise his penitential treatise in the direction of mysticism.

A passage from Chaucer's interpolation will indicate how central the Parson's Tale is to the genre of Middle English mystical literature:

For certes, after the diverse disordinaunces of oure wikkednesses was the passioun of Jhesu Crist ordeyned in diverse thinges, as thus. . . . For this disordinaunce of synful man was Jhesu Crist first bitraysed, and after that was he bounde, that cam for to unbynden us of synne and peyne. Thanne was he byscorned, that oonly sholde han been honoured in all thynges and of all thynges. Thanne was his visage, that oghte be desired to be seyn of al mankynde, in which visage aungels desiren to looke, vileynsly bispet. Thanne was he scourged, that no thyng hadde agilt; and finally, thanne was he crucified and slayn. (X, 274–79)

Note the paradoxical structure of this passage—the one bound who comes to unbind, the despised visage upon which angels long to gaze. The Pseudo-Dionysian simultaneous affirmation and denial of valency to words is, of course, the ground of the paradox.

In *Contemplations of the Dread and Love of God* the linkage of the meditation on the Passion to moral devotion is evident. That text begins with a short and ends with a long meditation on Christ's death on the Cross. Here is the initial, shorter one:

> In what maner he [Christ] bought vs / euery crysten man knoweth or sholde knowe / that no lasse pryce / but suffred his owne precyous body to be all to rente with bytter peynes of scorgynge. He suffred also a garlonde of sharpe thornes pressyd to his heed / whiched [sic] percyd so the veynes that the blood ran doune in to his eyen / nose mouth & eeres. Afterwarde vpon the crosse his bones were drawe out of Joynte / the veynes & the senewes were borsten for strayte dra-wynge / to þe crosse he was nayled honde & foot / and so fayled the blood of kynd with bytter paynes of deth. He betoke his spyryte to the fader of heuen / and than suffred at the last his gloryous herte to be thorugh percyd with a shapre [sic] spere for to gyue his herte blood to bye man body and soule into Joye without ende.[44]

The author of *Contemplations of the Dread and Love of God* is slightly more graphic than Chaucer, but the content and the meaning is roughly the same: meditation has a central role in moral development.

Perhaps the greatest of all medieval meditations on the Passion can clarify this point. The twelfth-century English abbot of the Cistercian foundation of Rievaulx in Yorkshire, Aelred, wrote a Latin rule for his sister, who was entering the life of a solitary anchoress. Aelred's *De Institutione Inclusarum* was the main source for the thirteenth-century *Ancrene Riwle*[45] and was in turn translated into two Middle English versions—one exactly contemporaneous with Chaucer, the other from the mid-fifteenth century.[46] Aelred here invents a type of meditation later adopted by the Franciscans,[47] of placing the reader directly in the biblical narrative, inviting her to see, touch, and hear the sacred events with her own senses. We have already seen Margery Kempe given to this type of Aelredian meditation.[48] Incidentally, Aelred's methods were appropriated in the Renaissance by the Jesuits through St. Ignatius of Loyola's *Spiritual Exercises* and reentered English literature through the seventeenth-century metaphysical poets, notably John Donne.[49] Chaucer, like Rolle and others, prefers in his meditation on the Passion the older form, which avoids direct reader participation in the biblical events, while the author of *Contemplations of the Dread and Love of God* presents his first meditation without it and second (which I have not quoted) with it.

But more important than this distinction is the place Aelred gives to meditation in his sister's moral development. In the fourteenth-century Middle English translation contained in the Vernon Manuscript, he writes:

> De meditacione. Wherfore, dire suster, þat þe swete affeccioun of loue of swete Ihesu mowe wexe in þyn herte, þu most haue þre maner meditacioun: þat is to seyn of þyngges þat ben apassed, of þingges þat beþ present, of þyngges þat beþ comynge. And þerfore, suster, when þyn herte is iclensed fro al vielþe and sten[c] of foule ȝouȝtes by þe excercise of holy vertus, cast þi cliere eȝen abake to þyngges þat beþ asassyd.[50]

After the virtues have overcome the vices, in other words, then meditation may begin. A long meditation follows, charting Christ's life from the Annunciation to the Crucifixion, containing some of the same content as that of both Chaucer and the author of *Contemplations of the Dread and Love of God*:

> and þat fayrest face þat euere was, þe whiche þe cursede Iewes defoyleþ wit here foule spatelyngge, þu whash hit wit terys of þyn eȝen. . . . I am siker, suster, þu miȝt not longe suffre þis, þu miȝt not suffre his comely ryg be so to-torn wit schurges, his gracious face to be bouyd wit bofattes, his wurschipful heed to be corouned wit scharpe thornes to þe brayn, his riȝt hand, þat made heuen and irþe, be dishonest[ed] wit a ryed; I wot uel þu miȝt not longe dure to see þis wit þyn eȝen.[51]

The same Pseudo-Dionysian affirmation and denial operative in Chaucer is at work here—the comely face despised, the worshipful hand that created heaven and earth scorned.

A brief look at the two Middle English manuscripts containing Aelred's text is worthwhile before I make some concluding remarks about Chaucer's role as an author of the devotional prose treatise known as the Parson's Tale. The Vernon Manuscript contains not only the fourteenth-century Middle English version of *De Institutione Inclusarum* but also such items as the *Ancrene Riwle,* miscellaneous works of Richard Rolle, and *Piers Plowman, A-text*.[52] That a "literary" work like Langland's poem is included with these prose devotional treatises is surprising only if we get our Middle English literature from modern edited texts and graduate courses in English departments, where generic distinctions not made in the fourteenth century are tacitly accepted, even sometimes trenchantly enforced. *Piers* and the last of *The Canterbury Tales* are literary works and *Contemplations of the Dread and Love of God,* Aelred's treatise, and the works of Rolle (except his lyrics) are not. But Chaucer and his contemporaries created no such canon.

Bodley Manuscript 423,[53] containing the fifteenth-century translation of Aelred, is a long miscellany including, among other pieces, Latin sermons, the Middle English poem *Stimulus Conscientiae,* John Capgrave's *Solace of Pilgrims, Contemplations of the Dread and Love of God,* selections of the *Revelations of St. Bridget,* or *Liber Celestis* (a text Margery Kempe, as we have seen, knew), various short meditations, and *The Book of Tribulation.* Chaucer's friend Lewis Clifford, as we have also seen, owned a copy of this last text and bequeathed it to his son-in-law, another of Chaucer's friends, Philip de la Vache. Neither manuscript contains the Parson's Tale, but both represent a generic milieu closer to Chaucer than we perhaps often think.

If we thus for a moment imagine a Chaucer who wrote only devotional texts and not those other works, secular in nature "that sownen into synne" (X, 1085), then I suggest we have a surprising figure, someone perhaps of the ilk of Richard Rolle, a layman who dabbled in poetry while writing and translating significant works of devotion. He was a civil servant, but retired near the end of his life doubtless because of religious devotion to the precincts of Westminster Abbey, whose monks, in honor of the prose treatises he wrote, like his *State Super Vias* (i.e., the Parson's Tale), *Boece, Melibeus,* and his poetry like *De Casibus* (i. e., the Monk's Tale), *Legend of St. Cecelia,* and *Legend of the Little Clergeon* (i.e., the Prioress's Tale), buried him within the Abbey church itself. His might even be a fifth name among those of the Middle English mystics—Rolle, Hilton, Julian, Kempe, together with the anonymous *Cloud*-author. But he must be denied this name, for his output of religious devotion is only a part of a larger oeuvre including fabliaux, romances, and "many a song and many a leccherous lay" (X, 1086).

## Pertelote's Dreams and the Reeve's Horse

Before I focus on longer explications of these *Canterbury Tales* that tend toward sin, two short examples will be useful in showing how Chaucer's valorized genre of mystical prose influences even those works where he likely intends no such influence—the Nun's Priest's and the Reeve's Tales.

In the Nun's Priest's Tale, Pertelote interprets Chaucticleer's visionary dream in a modern, scientific way denying authority in the face of experience. Since the days of the patriarch Joseph and the prophets Isaiah and Daniel, dreams, of course, have been associated with mystical experience; they can be God's direct communication to a person about spiritual matters. Chaucer may have gotten most of his ideas about dreams from Macrobius,[54] as any careful reading of the opening lines of *The House of Fame* will indicate, but his older contemporary, the mystic Richard Rolle, was also interested in them and described their types in an almost Pertelotean way. In the *Form of Living,* like both Aelred's *De Institutione Inclusarum* and the *Ancrene Riwle,* a treatise addressed to a female recluse, he writes of dreams:

> Whare-foor, þat þou be noth bigyled with þaim, I wile þat þou witte þat it er sex maners of dremes. Twa er þat na man haly ne other may etchape, þat es: if þair wambes be ouer-tom or ouer-full, þan many vanytese in sere meners byfalles þaim slepand.[55]

This is, of course, Pertelote's explanation: dreams are the result of gastrointestinal disorders. Rolle goes on to catalog the four other, more significant, types, and then we move into Chauntecleer's intellectual environment:

> Þe thryd es of illusyons of our enemy. Þe fierth es of thogth byfoor and illusyon folwand. Þe fyft thurgth reuelacyone of þe haly gast, þat es don on many maners. Þe sext es of thoghtes byfoor þat falles to Cryst or haly kyrke, reuelacion command efter.[56]

Some are warnings sent from God, some delusions sent from the Devil. Rolle concludes on a skeptical note:

> Bot swa mekyle we sal þe latyer gyf fayth til any dreeme þat we may noght sone wit whylke es soth, whylke es fals; whilke es of our enemy, whylke es of þe haly gast. For whar so many dreemes er, þar er many vanytese, and many þai may make to erre: For þai hehth vnquaynt men and swa deceyfs þaim.[57]

We cannot, in other words, tell which dream is true and which is false. Rolle thus eliminates the raison d'être of the chickens' long discourse, and behind his criticism of dreams lies the Pseudo-

Dionysian theory of language: dreams, like words, simultaneously signify and deny signification.

In the Reeve's Tale, the students' horse, so well explicated by V. A. Kolve,[58] gallops loose across the fens, an image of unbridled sexuality.[59] The author of the anonymous devotional work *A Treatise of Ghostly Battle* would agree with Kolve. The first of the battle gear the spiritual warrior must possess is, of course, a horse (not, as we might expect the shield or breastplate of the seemingly unequestrian St. Paul in his letter to the Ephesians); but it must not be an unbridled horse:

> But hit were grete ffoly for any mane to fyghte apone ane horse vnbrydelyde: ffor yeff he be wylde and off euylle condycions, he ys lyke to be hys masters confusyone and to cast hym in to the handes off hys enemyes, and therfore hit ys nedeffulle that he be brydelyde. . . . Thys brydylle ys clepede Abstinence, with the wyche the fflessh shalle be refrayned from flesshly desires.[60]

And later in the Reeve's Tale, when the fighting starts, that same mystical prose authority is useful for an understanding of what the miller and his wife are experiencing:

> Doun ran the blody streem upon his [Aleyn's] brest;
> And in the floor, with nose and mouth tobroke,
> They walwe as doon two pigges in a poke;
> And up they goon, and doun agayn anon,
> Til that the millere sporned at a stoon,
> And doun he fil bakward upon his wyf. . . .
>
> . . . . . . . . . . .
> "Help! hooly croys of Bromeholm," she seyde,
> "*In manus tuas!* Lord, to thee I calle!"
>
> (I, 4276–81, 4286–87)

We grasp the full comedy of this only when we realize that her words are those, taken ultimately from the Psalms, that the author of *The Book of the Craft of Dying* enjoins upon one mortally ill, awaiting death in prayerful patience upon his bed, surrounded by holy people, not by dishonest tricksters pursuing the not-so-gentle art of fisticuffs:

> Þan lat hym sey þis thrise: In manus tuas [domine] commendo spiritum meum, In to thin handis I commyt my soule; and lett the couent sey the same; and if he may not speke lett the couent, or þei þat stont aboute, sey thus: In manus tuas commendo spiritum eius, In thin hon-

dis lord we commend his spirit or his soule. And thus he dyeth surely, and he schal not dye euerlastyngly.[61]

The bed, the onlookers, and the sufferer are all there in Chaucer, but the devout solemnity is transformed into slapstick comedy.

As these short analogues between the writings of the mystics and Chaucer's nondevotional works suggest and as the following longer studies I hope will show, the connection between Chaucer and the mystics was a strong one, transcending intentionality and helpful in explicating many individual passages of *The Canterbury Tales*.

# 3
## Comic Tales

Chaucer may have intended the Parson's Tale as a piece of prose devotion consonant with the genre he would later valorize in his Retraction. He may also have intended that his character the Wife of Bath would have certain similarities to laywomen of a spiritual bent that in turn would generate the significant differences that provide the basis for that character's comic identity. But what of the Nun's Priest's Tale or the Reeve's Tale? Could Chaucer have intended any connection between them and the mystical texts that seem to illuminate occasional passages in them? Intentionality is of course problematic, and critics must guard themselves from reading their own intentions into those of dead authors. Texts exhibit tendencies that we may sometimes discern by using the filter of another text or set of texts. Even the comic, sometimes scatological tales, in short, show similarities to texts of a devotional and mystical nature, and we may learn something by using the filter they offer.

### The Miller's Tale

When Absolon opens his mouth, what occasionally comes out is mystic speech:[1]

> This Absolon doun sette hym on his knees
> And seyde, "I am a lord at alle degrees;
> For after this I hope ther cometh moore.
> Lemman, thy grace, and sweete bryd, thyn oore!
>
> (I, 3723–26)

*Ore,* which occurs in Chaucer only here, is certainly, as some have pointed out,[2] a stereotyped word from the world of courtly love, but it is much more than that. Appropriated by the mystics, *ore* became a metaphor for mystical union.[3] In the anonymous *A Talkyng of þe Loue of God,* for instance, we find:

> Ihesu also þat þou art so feir and so swete, ȝit art þou so louelich and louesum, þat þe holy angeles þat euere þe biholden ben neuere folle to loken on þi face. . . . A Ihesu þin ore, whi haue I likyng In oþer þing þen in þe þat bouȝtest me so deore?[4]

*Ore* surfaces a total of six times in this short treatise. Absolon, in other words, takes a term that the mystics have redirected from earthly to heavenly love and redirects it once more toward its first referent—a Pseudo-Dionysian simultaneous affirmation and denial of meaning.

There are some other interesting connections between *A Talkyng of þe Loue of God* and the Miller's Tale, so much so that they appear to share a common vocabulary, one Pseudo-Dionysian in nature. The Miller's *lemman*[5] ("sweetheart") is a word constantly applied to Christ in the mystical treatise:

> And þerfore ȝif me lykeþ stalworþe lemmon, louen þenne wol I þe louely Ihesu[6]

I will return to this common word in my analysis of the Manciple's Tale, where it is directly connected with the Manciple's attitude toward language.

Absolon's earlier words to Alison are also largely drawn from the mystic speech common to both the Miller's Tale and *A Talkyng of þe Loue of God:*

> "What do ye, hony-comb, sweete Alisoun,
> My faire bryd, my sweete cynamome?
>
> . . . . . . . . . . . . .
> I moorne as doth a lamb after the tete.
> Ywis, lemman, I have swich love-longynge,
> That lik a turtel trewe is my moornynge.
> I may nat ete na moore than a mayde."
>
> (I, 3698–99, 3704–7)

For the author of *A Talkyng of þe Loue of God,* Jesus is

> my derlyng, mi deoring mi louyng, myn hony-brid my swetyng; myn hele & myn hony-ter min hony-lyf min halewy. Swettore art þou þen hony or Milk in Mouþe.[7]

He later speaks of his "loue longyng"[8] towards Jesus, as does the author of *The Abbey of the Holy Ghost:* "for luf-longnge so ferforthe rauesches thorow hertis þat somtyme þay ne wot noght whate þay do."[9] As we shall also see, *ravish* is a particularly mystical word with sexual connotations that the Prioress will appropriate in her Prologue. *A Talkynge of þe Loue of God,* in other words, is a sustained profession of love to Jesus not entirely unlike the one Absolon makes to Alison out in the street.

In contrast, all of Nicholas's actions are done in secrecy and in silence. For the first step in his astrological plot, he retreats into his room "withouten wordes mo" (I, 3408) and carries "ful softe" (I, 3410) enough food and drink for a couple of days. When Robyn knocks and calls to him "he herde nat a word" (I, 3439); when his master joins Robyn in breaking down the door, he "sat ay as stille as ston" (I, 3472) in emphatic contrast to all this noise. The mystics' tendency toward silence, outlined by Pseudo-Dionysius and his followers, is operative here.

The state that Nicholas is in within his silent room is one that bespeaks mystical rapture: "This Nicholas sat evere capyng upright, / As he had kiked on the newe moone" (I, 3444–45). The very location is one of which a writer of a mystical treatise would approve. As the author of *Contemplations of the Dread and Love of God,* for instance, advises, "Whan thou ordeynest þe to praye or haue ony deuocyon founde to haue a preuy place from all maner noyse & tyme of reste w'out ony lettynge."[10] The author of *The Abbey of the Holy Ghost* seems to describe Nicholas when he treats the allegorical figure Meditation:

> Ofte it falles þat þe herte es so ouer-tane and so raueschede in holy meditacyone þat it wote noghte what it dose, heris nor sayse, or seys, so depely es þe herte festenede in god and in his werkes þat wordis hym wanttis: and þe stillere þat he es in slyke meditacione the luddere he cryes in goddis eris. . . . and aftyr þe wyne of swete teris than sendys he þe oyle of consolacione þat gyffes þame sauour & lyghtnes [þaire] knawliggynge, and schewes to þam of his heuenly priuatyse.[11]

Not only is this stillness Nicholas's but that last word, *priuatyse,* as we shall see below, is his particular domain. The *Abbey*-author quickly follows this description with a small example from St. Augustine:

> Sayne Austyne telles of a preste þat, whene he herde any thynge of god þat lykynge ware Ine, he wold be so raueschede in Ioye þat he walde fall downe and lygge als he ware dede.[12]

John the carpenter, responding to Nicholas's feigned ravishments and associating them with stargazing, gives a particularly madcap version of this behavior:

> So ferde another clerk with astromye;
> He walked in the feeldes for to prye
> Upon the sterres, what ther sholde bifalle,
> Til he was in a marle-pit yfalle;
> He saugh nat that. . . .

(I, 3457–61)

Nicholas's ravishment is of course a feigned and private loss of control, yet it is a curious foretaste of the unfeigned and noisy loss of control he suffers at the end of the tale, one I shall return to soon.

Heinrich Suso, as we find out from his autobiography,[13] was accused by his own confreres of the same posture—with the consequent implication of false mysticism—that Nicholas assumes:

> In the chapter meeting two friars sitting next to each other were whispering to each other. The one said to the other derisively, "What a foolish man this prior [i. e., Suso] is, to order us to go to God in our need. Does he think that God will open up heaven and send food and drink down to us?" The other friar said, "He is not the only fool. All of us are fools for choosing him as prior. We all knew beforehand that he is incapable in earthly matters and can only gape up at heaven." There were many scoffing judgments made about him.[14]

In the fourteenth century, in other words, Nicholas's posture was both associated with mysticism and an object of ridicule.

The *Cloud*-author is himself aware of such pretended mystical rapture and complains of it in language oddly reminiscent of Chaucer's:

> bot forþe of oure mater, how þat þees ȝonge presumptuous goostly disciples misunderstonden þis . . . worde UP. For ȝif it so be þat þei ouþer rede, or here redde or spoken how þat men schuld lift up here hertes vnto God, as fast þei stare in þe sterres as þei wolde be abouen þe mone, & herkyn when þei schul here any aungelles synge out of heuen. Þees men willen sumtyme wiþ þe corioste of here ymaginacion peerce þe planetes, & make an hole in þe firmament to loke in þerate. Þees men wil make a God as hem lyst. . . . Þees men wil maken aungelles in bodely licnes, & sel hem aboute ich one with diuerse minstralsie. . . . Somme of þees men þe deuil wil disceyue wonderfully. For he wil seend a maner of dewe—aungelles foode þei wene it be—

as it were cumyng oute of þe eire, & softely & sweetly fallyng in þeire mowþes; & þerfore þei haue it in costume to sitte gapyng as þei wolde kacche flies.[15]

It is not only Nicholas's posture that makes us think of this passage from *The Cloud of Unknowing* but also his interest in astronomy, musical instruments, and angels: John, after all, ascribes his rapture to his astronomical pursuits, and he sings a song about the angel Gabriel to the accompaniment of his psaltery. But far more interesting for our purposes than the similarities of the tale's stage props to those mentioned by the *Cloud*-author is the Pseudo-Dionysian attention to language. Staring "up" as Nicholas does, infers the *Cloud*-author, is a refusal to deny referentiality to that word when it is used in a mystical context. It signifies and fails to signify simultaneously. Nicholas confuses mystic speech with earthly.

Nicholas later counsels John in secret to be silent:

> Fecche me drynke,
> And after wol I speke in pryvetee
> Of certeyn thyng that toucheth me and thee.
>
> (I, 3492–94)

> John, myn hooste, lief and deere,
> Thou shalt upon thy trouthe swere me heere
> That to no wight thou shalt this counseil wreye.
>
> (I, 3501–3)

And John is infected by all this secrecy and silence, asserting,

> I nam no labbe,
> Ne, though I seye, I nam nat lief to gabbe.
> Sey what thou wolt, I shal it nevere telle
> To child ne wyf, by hym that harwed helle!
>
> (I, 3509–12)

This reticence to blab has its complement in Nicholas's stated and John's real reticence to violate God's secrecy; in this they are among the most Pseudo-Dionysian of Chaucer's characters. "Men sholde nat knowe of Goddes pryvetee" (I, 3454), says a John solicitous of the starstruck Nicholas's well-being; "I wol nat tellen Goddes pryvettee"[16] (I, 3558), echoes Nicholas later. *Dionise Hid Divinitee* is the title the *Cloud*-author gave to Pseudo-Dionysius's *Mystical Theology,* and hidden divinity is Nicholas's specialty. That his seemingly endless speech of warning and advice (I, 3492–3610) belies this silence is part of the comedy.

The secrecy and silence of this speech spawns secrecy and silence in action. Nicholas's advice,

> Be wel avysed on that ilke nyght
> That we ben entred into shippes bord,
> That noon of us ne speke nat a word. . . .
>
> (I, 3584–86)

is followed completely:

> And shortly, up they clomben alle thre;
> They seten stille wel a furlong way.
>     "Now, *Pater-noster*, clom!" seyde Nicholay,
> And "Clom!" quod John, and "Clom!" seyde Alisoun.
> This carpenter seyde his devocioun,
> And stille he sit . . .
>
> (I, 3636–41)

Note the connection John makes between silence and religious devotion. His actions preceding this entry into the three kneading-trough arks are infected by Nicholas's secrecy and silence:

> And to his wyf he tolde his pryvetee . . .
>
> (I, 3603)

> He gooth and geteth hym a knedyng trogh,
> And after that a tubbe and a kymelyn,
> And pryvely he sente hem to his in,
> And heng hem in the roof in pryvetee.
>
> (I, 3620–23)

Oddly enough, Absolon, as yet unconnected with any of this secret plot, seems also to have caught this disease of secrecy and silence from Nicholas: he asks a cloisterer in Osney "ful prively" (I, 3662) about John's whereabouts; he later intends to knock "ful prively" at Alison's window (I, 3676); and when he gets there, "softe he cougheth with a semy soun" (I, 3697). Alison, who had earlier climbed down her ladder "ful softe" (I, 3649) to make silent melody in bed with Nicholas, responds to Absolon's soft sounds and laments before her window with whispers not to him but to Nicholas: "And unto Nicholas she seyde stille, / 'Now hust, and thou shalt laughen al thy fille'" (I, 3721–22). Her plot is predicated as much as his on secrecy and silence.

The doings between Nicholas and Alison in John's bedroom, earthly as they are, have some rather unlikely resonances among mystical and devotional texts. The melody they hear in the distance as the friars sing their office can of course call to mind Rolle's valorization of *canor*, "song,"[17] as hallmark of the believer's mystical union with God, and it also recalls the sweetness and song Margery Kempe heard in her own bed. Even the scatological doings, as Alison and Nicholas extend their bottoms to the extended lips of Absolon, are not without analogues among the anonymous works of devotional prose. In *The Vision of William of Stranton*, for instance, St. John leads the visionary William on a tour of purgatorial torments, including some scatalogical fiends:

> Then Sant John lede me to þe fort fyre, and ther I saw many sawlys bondon wyth grett bandys of yrene hoth gloynge, and apon þe savles stode fendys and put þer vggely ersys to þer vysage, me thoght, and kest on them wyth þer erses horrybyl stynke of donge and dyrtte, wyth sparkys of fyre amonge, þat smotte thorow the wrechyd saulys whereuer hytt felle on thame.[18]

Interesting is the connection of the scatalogical activity of these "erses" thrust at the sufferers' visages with great bands of glowing hot iron and sparks of fire—an evocation of the doings of a smith not perhaps unlike the Miller's Gervaise, who provides Absolon with the glowing hot iron of his revenge.

After his misdirected kiss has landed, Absolon is determined to rededicate his befouled lips to the silence that has been attending most of these doings. To the blacksmith Gervaise's raillery, "no word agayn he yaf" (I, 3773), and to Gervaise's direct request for an explanation about why he requires the red-hot coulter, Absolon's reply is Nicholasian in secrecy and silence: "'Therof,' quod Absolon, 'be as be may. / I shal wel telle it thee to-morwe day—'" (I, 3783–84).

This epidemic of silence ends with a fart as loud as "a thonder-dent" (I, 3807) and a loud cry of "Help! Water! Water!" (I, 3815)—uncharacteristic noises from Privy Nicholas—followed by a loud crash as the long-forgotten-John-bearing-kneading-trough ark crashes to the floor. The cries for help, "out" and "harrow," are specifically placed in the least privy and most public of places, "in the strete" (I, 3825). As Bernard Huppé aptly puts it, the Miller's Tale ends in "Babylonic confusion."[19] Nicholas's attempts at controlling things through mystical secrecy and silence prove in the end as ineffectual as John's jealousy and Absolon's serenades.

There is a connection, I would argue, between this pseudomysti-
cal silence and authorial control. The authorial control the Miller
exerts belies this confusion at the end.[20] His tale is full of learned
allusion[21] and word play,[22] and its two plots merge with the grace
of ballet dancers.[23] Charles Muscatine perhaps best sums up its
consummate narrator's art:

> Where the typical fabliau brings in properties and explanations only
> as needed, the *Miller's Tale* seems to explain everything. That the town
> is Oxford explains—overpoweringly explains—the presence of a clever
> clerk. That Absolon is named Absolon "explains" his blond beauty
> and his femininity. That John the carpenter is made a "rich gnof"
> in the very first statement explains his securing a pretty, young
> wife. . . . The boarder's two days' self-confinement is silently prepared
> for in the eighteenth verse (3204); he rooms "allone, withouten any
> compaignye."[24]

I would suggest that Muscatine's operative word here is *silently*—
that the Miller succeeds in control where Nicholas fails because
of his use of silence. Not only do these small, silent traces explain
things, but the larger plot succeeds because of the Miller's privy
doings: his long silence about the sleeping John creates the stirring
climax as the word *water* awakens both him and us.

The Miller's silence extends to his conception of what the genre
is of the tale he is telling. He himself explains before beginning
that "I wol telle a legende and a lyf / Bothe of a carpenter and of
his wyf" (I, 3141–42). Saints' Legends, of course, were the staple
of mystical literature throughout the late Middle Ages. But the
Miller's Tale is certainly not hagiography:[25] most if not all critics
label it a fabliau instead. Yet Helen Cooper reminds us that fabliaux
have morals at the end, where the Miller provides us only with a
recapitulation.[26] That he prefers silence to a moral and that the
trace of a moral that he leaves dismantles the genre of hagiography
make him as uncontrollable to literary critics as he is to Harry
Bailly. It may be that all we can do with him is sidestep the link
he dominates and speak of the tale's narrative voice instead of the
Miller,[27] refer to "the no man's land that exists between [him and]
the poet Chaucer,"[28] or observe that his presence "fades rapidly"
in the tale.[29] That he creates a character named Robyn for his Tale
where his own name is Robyn[30]—in the framework of a larger
poem written by Chaucer containing a character named Chaucer—
might indicate to the contrary: that his presence controls his poem
to a greater degree than it appears Chaucer himself is silent on
this point. But Chaucer has called the Miller a goliard in the Gen-

eral Prologue (I, 560): any reader of the *Carmina Burana* knows
that goliards, drunk or not, could write good poetry.


## The Friar and the Summoner

Both the Friar[31] and the Summoner seek control over each other
through their tales, eschewing the technique of control by silence
that was developed by Nicholas and, as shall be seen, perfected by
the Man of Law's Custance. Their insults are effective, occasioning
generations of teachers of English literature given to solemn con-
demnations of both vocations. Of greater interest, however, is how
the tales of each control the teller, erasing his meaning and sucking
him inexorably from the framework reality of *The Canterbury Tales*
and into their tales themselves.[32] This is particularly true, I suggest,
of the second teller, the Summoner, who recognizes this tendency
in the tale of his nemesis yet cannot avoid it in his own.

Almost unanimously, critics of the Friar's Tale lament his summoner's stupidity at not recognizing danger when the yeoman announces his demonic nature:[33]

> "Brother," quod he, "wiltow that I thee telle?
> I am a feend; my dwellyng is in helle. . . .
>
> . . . . . . . . . . . . . . .
> "A!" quod this somonour, "benedicite! What sey ye?
> I wende ye were a yeman trewely.
> Ye han a mannes shap as wel as I;
> Han ye a figure thanne determinat
> In helle, ther ye been in youre estat?"
>
> (III, 1447–48, 1456–60)

The summoner's blind curiosity, goes the standard interpretation,
is pure stupidity:[34] where the proper response is a sign of the cross
on the forehead and a judicious flight, the summoner stays, pro-
longing this friendly chat with the fiend—to his eternal damnation,
both literal and literary.

I suggest that the situation is rather more complex. The narrator
has earlier classified the discourse between fiend and summoner
with words unusual in context:

> Everych in ootheres hand his trouthe leith,
> For to be sworne bretheren til they deye.
> In daliance they ryden forth and pleye.
>
> (III, 1404–6)

*Daliance* is a word most often used in Middle English literature in the context of courtly love and is roughly equivalent to our modern word *flirtation*.[35] That the Friar applies an overtly sexual word to his Tale's summoner might be an oblique reference to the Summoner's possible and critically notorious homosexual friendship with another travelling companion, the Pardoner, who sings "Com hider, love, to me!" while the Summoner bears him "a styf burdoun" (I, 672–3). Whether the flirtation is real or metaphorical in the Friar's Tale, it nevertheless requires a mode of conversation given to irony and repartee—or to use the narrator's other word, *pleye*. The tale's summoner, in other words, is likely responding playfully to an assertion he takes as playfully nonliteral and is not necessarily as abysmally stupid as most would make him. What damns him instead is his tendency to deflect things from himself, not to take things personally, to consider himself secure from all danger, to persist in playing when the game has long been over. In other words, he reacts to the situation naturally, as any of us would if an interlocutor playfully announced, "I'm a devil, you know." But the Friar has changed the rules on his character by shifting things onto a supernatural plane.

His summoner, of course, is traveling in the woods when he encounters a yeoman dressed in green and black who turns out to be a devil. The summoner calls himself a "bailly," doubtless in very shame of his own profession. The yeoman/Devil and the bailly/summoner engage in friendly conversation, calling each other "brothers," which, strictly in a biological or ecclesiastical sense, they are not. The devil then playfully reveals his true nature, and the summoner questions him about life down in hell. They finally agree to share their winnings, until an old woman whom the summoner attempts to bribe condemns him to hell, and the Devil, once he is sure of the condemnation, accepts the soul of the summoner himself as his earnings.

In an anonymous Middle English mystical text, *The Remedy against the Troubles of Temptation*,[36] we have what amounts to a very similar story, with the main difference the emphasis on salvation, not damnation: A squire by the name of John Holmes, who has fallen into despair over his chances for salvation, was once out walking in a wood, where "an aungell came to hym in fourme of a man"[37] and engages him in conversation, desiring to know why he is so downcast. Holmes tells him the cause, and the man/angel attempts to dissuade him about the inevitability of his damnation. When Squire Holmes persists in his despair, the man/angel proposes a game: they will throw dice to resolve the question, and if

Holmes throws the higher, he will be saved. Still a doubter, the squire reluctantly agrees and watches the man/angel throw three sixes and despairingly wishes to give up the game. "But," says the anonymous author,

> so specyally the aungell desyred and spake that at the last the squyer threwe the dyce and in throwynge by the gracyous myght and power of god euery dyce dewyded in two & on euery dyce was the numbre of syxe and so he had the double that the aungell had. And as he was meruaylynge therupon the aungell vanysshed out of his syght wherfore he thought veryly that it was an aungell sente from god to brynge hym out of his sorowe.[38]

Chaucer's Friar and the anonymous author of *The Remedy against the Troubles of Temptations* plainly live in the same ideological universe. The supernatural is there ready to break into the natural in disguise when ultimate questions like those about salvation and damnation are to be answered. Older historicists might be tempted to posit monodirectional influence of one story upon the other. New Historicists, however, would point out that the stories arise as much from cultural intentionality as from the intentionality of the authors. Both stories are by very nature hierarchical: both games presuppose that someone is in control—that dice do not lie, that the rules of sharing extend beyond the quotidian into the spiritual. A hierarchical church and a hierarchical monarchy validate such exchanges as legitimate power transactions.

More important, perhaps, is the Pseudo-Dionysian simultaneous affirmation and denial of language: the yeoman is not really a yeoman but a devil, the bailly is not really a bailly but a summoner, the man is not really a man but an angel. And the very homely milieu of each story—a walk in the woods—is an entry into the exceptional, the supernatural. The message, moreover, dismantles, for on the one hand it is possible to posit as "meaning" for each of these stories a moral something like: God/the Devil can intercede into everyday affairs bringing salvation/damnation. Yet on the other the fact that each story was deemed worthy of being written down belies that very meaning: this is an exceptional story precisely because God and the Devil do not daily act in this manner.

The tale's summoner, moreover, cannot be more different from the Summoner of the framework pilgrimage, the Friar's nemesis, for he is a man who does not deflect things away but toward himself. The Friar's Tale for him is a personal insult:

For thogh this Somonour wood were as an hare,
To telle his harlotrye I wol nat spare;
For we [Friars] been out of his correccioun.
They han of us no jurisdiccioun,
Ne nevere shullen, terme of alle hir lyves.
    "Peter! so been wommen of the styves,"
Quod the Somonour, "yput out of oure cure!"
    "Pees! with myschance and with mysaventure!"
Thus seyde oure Hoost, "and lat hym telle his tale.
Now telleth forth, thogh that the Somonour gale;
Ne spareth nat, myn owene maister deere."
"This false theef, this somonour," quod the Frere.

(III, 1327–38)

Harry Bailly's word of control, *pees,* also a word of silence, is rapidly becoming his only desperate means by which to regain control over *his* game (cf. III, 1298). The larger point, though, is that the tale's summoner, as similar as he is to the "real" Summoner in other matters like bribery, simply does not "gale," interrupt, or take things personally—to his everlasting detriment. The Friar, in other words, re-creates the Summoner along radically different lines, a re-creation doubtless underscored by a pointing gesture when he resumes his tale: "*This* false theef, *this* somonour."[39]

But the re-creation is in the Friar's own image—perhaps an ironic[40] maneuver by Chaucer leading to an unintentional erasure by the Friar of his own text.[41] The first instance of self-imaging occurs in the passage just quoted, where the Friar announces that the subject of his tale will be his summoner's "harlotrye" (III, 1328). Chaucer indeed implies in the General Prologue that this was one of the Summoner's characteristic failings:

> In daunger hadde he at his owene gise
> The yonge girles of the diocise,
> And knew hir conseil, and was al hir reed.

(I, 663–65)

But a much less ambiguous indictment for harlotry is leveled there at the Friar himself:

> In alle the ordres foure is noon that kan
> So muchel of daliaunce and fair langage.
> He hadde maad ful many a mariage
> Of yonge wommen at his owene cost.
> Unto his ordre he was a noble post.

(I, 210–14)

Note the use of the word *daliaunce* now to describe the Friar himself, not the summoner he later creates. Harlotry, of course, was a grave sin for a cleric. As the author of *A Revelation of Purgatory* writes:

> Bot amange al þe peynes þat I sawe of al men and wommen, me thoȝt prestes þat had bene lecherous in har lyfes, and har wommen with ham—wheþer þay wer religious men and wommen or seculers—men and wommen of ordyr me thoȝt in þat syȝt [of purgatory] had moste peyne.[42]

That his tale contains no further mention of his summoner's sexual vices is either an indication that the Friar has decided to avoid a subject that presents more dangers to himself than to his nemesis or that he has lost control of his own subject matter in his anger at the Summoner's interruption.

When the tale's fiend announces, "For sothe, I take al that men wol me yive" (III, 1430), it is clear that he too is a creation in the Friar's own image, for such pecuniary aggression is one of his own main characteristics. As Chaucer says in the General Prologue about Brother Hubert:

> And over al, ther as profit sholde arise,
> Curteis he was and lowely of servyse.
>
> .  .  .  .  .  .  .  .  .  .  .  .  .
> For thogh a wydwe hadde noght a sho,
> So plesaunt was his "*In principio*,"
> Yet wolde he have a ferthyng, er he wente.
>
> (I, 249–50, 253–55)

This widow of the General Prologue bears, of course, strong similarities to old Mabely, the Friar's summoner's intended victim.

The constant form of address, moreover, that fiend and summoner alike use for their social intercourse in the Friar's Tale has an extended range of use inclusive of friars:

> "Brother," quod he, "where is now youre dwellyng"
>
> "Brother," quod he, "fer in the north contree"
>
> "Now, brother," quod this somonour . . .
>
> "Now, by my trouthe, brother deere," seyde he
>
> (III, 1410, 13, 17, 24)

"Brother," of course, is English for "friar."[43]

In addition, in the thirteenth and fourteenth centuries friars dominated the universities. From Thomas Aquinas and Bonaventure in Paris to Roger Bacon and Duns Scotus in Oxford, the great Scholastic thinkers were friars, either Dominican or Franciscan.[44] Curiously, the Friar's summoner seems to be preparing for such an academic appointment at the end of the tale:

> "Now, brother," quod the devel, "be nat wrooth;
> Thy body and this panne been myne by right.
> Thou shalt with me to helle yet tonyght,
> Where thou shalt knowen of oure privetee
> Moore than a maister of dyvynytee."
>
> (III, 1634–38)

The Summoner's silence instead of repentance will lead to this most scholastic knowledge of hell's "privetee." We are back in the scholastic universe of Privy Nicholas.

Finally, the Friar becomes so caught up in his tale that he begins to imitate the emotions and words of even its third character, the widow Mabely, who responds to the summoner's accusations with the exclamation, "thou lixt!" (III, 1618). As the Summoner begins his tale of requital, the Friar interrupts with Mabely's words: "Nay, ther thou lixt, thou Somonour!" (III, 1761). Simultaneously, of course, he imitates the Summoner, who had, as we have seen, interrupted him at the beginning of his own tale.

In short, all these identifications between friars and the Friar with characters in his own tale are the signs that show how his tale dismantles, for it damns himself in its purported attempt to damn the Summoner.

The Summoner, I suggest, understands this self-damnation and frames his tale as much as criticism of the Friar's text as of his person. The Summoner's Tale not only re-creates an exact replica of the framework's Friar—from his greed right down to his lisp[45]— it also re-creates the Friar's textual proclivity to damn himself with his own words.[46] But like a Master of Divinity, the Summoner creates a rather more theological framework for his friar's self-damnation.

Before a discussion of the theological structure the Summoner uses to damn his friar, it is worth noting that his vision of that damnation that begins his tale has analogues among the anonymous prose texts of devotion. The Summoner's mystical vision of hell is scatalogical in nature:

This Frere bosteth that he knoweth helle,
And God it woot, that it is litel wonder;
Freres and feendes been but lyte asonder.
For, pardee, ye han ofte tyme herd telle
How that a frere ravysshed was to helle
In spirit ones by a visioun;
And as an angel ladde hym up and doun,
To shewen hym the peynes that ther were,
In al the place saugh he nat a frere;
Of oother folk he saugh ynowe in wo.
Unto this angel spak the frere tho:
"Now, sire," quod he, "han freres swich a grace
That noon of hem shal come to this place?"
"Yis," quod this angel, "many a millioun!"
And unto Sathanas he ladde hym doun.
"And now hath Sathanas," seith he, "a tayl
Brodder than of a carryk is the sayl.
Hold up thy tayl, thou Sathanas!" quod he;
"Shewe forth thyn ers, and lat the frere se
Where is the nest of freres in this place!"
And er that half a furlong wey of space,
Right so as bees out swarmen from an hyve,
Out of the develes ers ther gonne dryve
Twenty thousand freres on a route,
And thurghout helle swarmed al aboute,
And comen agayn as faste as they may gon,
And in his ers they crepten everychon.
He clapte his tayl agayn and lay ful stille.
This frere, whan he looked hadde his fille
Upon the tormentz of this sory place,
His spirit God restored, of his grace,
Unto his body agayn, and he awook.
But natheles, for fere yet he quook,
So was the develes ers ay in his mynde,
That is his heritage of verray kynde.

(III, 1672–1706)

We have already encountered such scatology in *The Vision of William of Stranton,* where souls suffer from glowing hot iron and asses extend toward their visages—punishments used to comic effect in the Miller's Tale.

In that same vision scatology is also reserved for those who have taken religious vows:

And þan I saw the fendes turnyng here arses toward þe sowles, shytyng vppon hem, the which dirt stonk so fowle þat it was a passyng payn. And into þat hous come grete passyng haulstones owt of þe eyr, smytyng summe of þe sowles, summe on þe hedes, and summe on þe bodies, and al tobrosid hem. Then Seint John said, "Þese ben þe sowles of men of holy chirch, as persones, vicaries, and other prestes, þat shuld haue tawght good doctrine, and good exemple haue yevyn to þe comen people[47]

This punishment is reserved for those who have refused to take care of the poor; it is reminiscent of the Friar in the General Prologue, who "knew the tavernes wel in every toun / And everich holstiler and tappestere / Bet than a lazar or a beggestere" (I, 240–42).

First, it is good textbook practice to visit the sick with moral and spiritual advice, as does the Summoner's friar. As *The Book of the Craft of Dying* puts it,

Wherfor euery sikman, & euery other man þat is in ony perill, shuld be diligently inducid & exhortid þat he make hym-selfe be-fore all oþer þingis pes with god, resseyving spiritual medicins, þat is to seye takynge the sacramentis of holy church, ordeynyng and makynge his testament, & laufully disposynge for his household & other nedis if he haue any to dispose for.[48]

The attempted redirection of this disposal from the household toward the friary is, of course, the object of the friar's inducement and exhortation. But of more interest than that simple irony is the theological framework the friar erects for his inducements.

As readers of Dante's *Divine Comedy* or of the Parson's Tale—and indeed of that tale's major source, the *Summa Virtutum de Remediis Anime,* or any similar Middle English treatise—know, medieval moral theologians were fond of dividing human misconduct into classifications, the most famous of which was the Seven Deadly Sins. As *Saint Edmund's Mirror* explains, "Þir are þe seuen dedly synnes:—Pryde and Envy, Ire, Slouth, Couetyse, Glotony and Lechery."[49] Or as *Jon Gaytrygge's Sermon* puts it,

Þe sexte thynge, and þe laste [of his topics] . . . es, þe Seuen heuded or dedly synnes þat ilke a man and woman awe for to knawe to flee and forhewe, For folkes may noght flee þam bot þay knawe thaym. Pride and Enuye, Wreth and Glotonye, Couetyse and Slouthe, and Lecherye. And for-þi er þay called Seuen heuede Synnes, for þat all oþer commes of thaym; and for-þi er þay callede dedely synnes, for þay gastely slaa ilke manes & wommanes saule þat es haunkede in alle or in any of thaym. Whare-fore þe wyese man byddes in his buke "als fra þe face of þe neddyre, fande to flee syn." For als þe venym of þe neddire slaas manes body, Swa þe venym of syn slaas manes saule.[50]

The *Tretyse of Loue* thus contains a section usually titled "Remedies against the Seven Deadly Sins." One sin to which Dante devotes a particularly large portion of his *Inferno* is Ira, wrath. It is the sin, moreover, to which Thomas in the Summoner's Tale seems particularly given. His wife speaks to the tale's friar:

> "Now, by youre leve, o deere sire," quod she,
> "Chideth him weel, for seinte Trinitee!
> He is as angry as a pissemyre,
> Though that he have al that he kan desire;
> Though I hym wrye a-nyght and make hym warm,
> And over hym leye my leg outher myn arm,
> He groneth lyk oure boor, lith in oure sty.
> Oother desport right noon of hym have I;
> I may nat plese hym in no maner cas."
>
> (III, 1823–31)

Anger, it seems, drives out of Thomas another of the Deadly Sins: Luxuria, lust. That Chaucer/the Summoner have in mind wrath in its guise as one of the Seven Deadly Sins is of course evident in line 2005: "Ire is a synne, oon of the grete of sevene." The obliging friar is quick to begin a long and, admittedly, muddled sermon to Thomas on the subject of wrath, but straying on more than one occasion toward another of the Deadly Sins, gluttony (III, 1915–17, 2043–55.). The greatest of the seven, pride, is not the friar's concern.

This willful ignoring of pride is, I suggest, a sign or code by which we may begin to understand the Summoner's reading of the Friar's text, for pride is the tale's friar's particular flaw. His pride is, in accord with the rather vocational argument between friars and summoners, in his order rather than in himself:

> For, sire and dame, trusteth me right weel,
> Oure orisons been moore effectueel,
> And moore we seen of Cristes secree thynges,
> Than burel folk, although they weren kynges.
>
> (III, 1869–72)

The friar shares something here with Nicholas, who also knows God's secrets. The pride is, of course, unfounded, as the friar unwittingly indicates:

> "For who kan teche and werchen as we konne?
> And that is nat of litel tyme," quod he,

> "But syn Elye was or Elise,
> Han freres been—that fynde I of record—
> In charitee, ythanked be oure Lord!"
>
> (III, 2114–18)

Elijah ("Elye"), not Elisha ("Elise"), was the legendary founder of the Carmelite Friars;[51] the Summoner's friar is not sure which, indicating that his claim to excellence in teaching is suspect. Incidentally, the Summoner is ambiguous about which type of friar his hero is: his emphasis on preaching seems to associate him with the Dominicans (the Order of Preachers); this passage associates him with the Carmelites; yet the "real" Friar of the framework, his nemesis, seems to be a Fransiscan, given Chaucer's barb in the General Prologue about Brother Hubert's avoidance of lepers (I, 244–45)—St. Francis, as the famous story goes, kissed a leper on the mouth and enjoined his followers to care for those afflicted with the disease—an action, as we have seen, Margery Kempe imitates. Either the Summoner is muddled on this point, or, as I think more likely, it is an offhand slur: all friars look alike.

Not only is the tale's friar given to the chief sin of pride, he is subject to the other six as well. He is slothful (Accidia, the besetting sin of religious orders), neglecting to do good by erasing from the slate he carries with him the names of those whose money has just purchased prayers:[52]

> Oure suster deere—lo! Heere I write youre name.
> .  .  .  .  .  .  .  .  .  .  .  .  .  .  .  .  .  .
> And whan that he was out at dore, anon
> He planed awey the names everichon.
>
> (III, 1752, 1757–58)

He is lustful (Luxuria, a violation of his vow of chastity):

> The frere ariseth up ful curteisly,
> And hire [Thomas's wife] embraceth in his armes narwe,
> And kiste hire sweete, and chirketh as a sparwe
> With his lyppes. . . .[53]
>
> (III, 1802–5)

He is gluttonous[54] (Gula, the sin that diverts him from his proper subject during his long sermon):

> "Now, dame," quod he, "now *je vous dy sanz doute,*
> Have I nat of a capon but the lyvere,
> And of youre softe breed nat but a shyvere,
> And after that a rosted pigges heed—"

(III, 1838–41)

The delicacy, not quantity, of food consumed by the glutton was often more of a concern of those treating the Seven Deadly Sins. As the anonymous Middle English poem, "The Lamentation of a Dying Sinner," a verse descant on the Seven Deadlies, puts it:

> In deligat metys I had gret delytt
>     So had I wyne on-to my pay:
> Þat garres þes wormes on me to byt,
>     And euer þer sang ys "wyllossay!"

(49–52)[55]

The friar is, of course, also greedy (Avaricia, a violation of his vow of poverty): "Yif me thanne of thy gold, to make oure cloystre" (III, 2099). He is wrathful (Ira, the subject of his long sermon), for after he grasps in both sense Thomas's fart,

> The frere up stirte as dooth a wood leon—
> "A! false cherl," quod he, "for Goddes bones!
> This hastow for despit doon for the nones.
> .  .  .  .  .  .  .  .  .  .  .  .  .  .  .
> He grynte with his teeth, so was he wrooth.

(III, 2152–53, 2161)

Here wrath causes him to swear blasphemously, the particular sin both Margery Kempe and the Parson decry; grinding of teeth is, along with weeping, the biblical sign of damnation (see, for instance, Matt. 8:12, 13:42, 22:13, 24:51, 25:30, and Luke 13:28). There is even evidence that he is envious (Invidia). Although his own words and actions do not convict him of this sin, Thomas, at least, alludes to it: "'Nay,' quod the sike man, 'by Seint Symoun! / I have be shryven this day at my curat'" (III, 2094–95). The envy between friars and the secular clergy is, in fact, the origin of much of the pro- and antifraternal polemic of the fourteenth century.[56] Richard FitzRalph, Archbishop of Armagh and an older contemporary of Chaucer, was famous as the author of the polemical tract "Defense of the Curates," perhaps the most virulent antifraternal treatise of the era.[57]

In short, the Summoner invests his friar with not one or two but all the Deadly Sins—a surer method of damnation than a happen-stance meeting in the woods with a fiendish yeoman. In doing so, the Summoner reveals himself as an acute reader of his nemesis's text. As the Friar has unwittingly saturated his text with signs that dismantle its meaning, thus becoming himself the damned sum-moner by investing his character with qualities general to his order and specific to himself, the Summoner responds by creating a friar who does the same. His insult, in other words, is simultaneously an act of parodic literary criticism.

But he cannot escape his own trap. He himself was, of course, prompted to this act by the same sin of wrath that looms so impor-tantly in his tale. After being silenced by the Host and enduring his enemy's insulting tale,

> This Somonour in his styropes hye stood;
> Upon this Frere his herte was so wood
> That lyk an aspen leef he quook for ire.
>
> (III, 1665–67)

We think not only of his friar's teeth grinding, but also of Thomas:

> This sike man wax wel ny wood for ire;
> He wolde that the frere had been on-fire,
> With his false dissymulacioun.
>
> (III, 2121–23)

These lines, even disregarding the Summoner's own sickness (see I, 629–35), are as accurate a description of him as of his character. When we remember that Chaucer used the same metaphor of a sparrow to describe him as he uses to describe his Friar ("As hoot he was and lecherous as a sparwe" [I, 626]; "And kiste hire sweete, and chirketh as a sparwe" [III, 1804]), we realize that, like his enemy the Friar, he is sinking into his own text.

One final nail secures him in the coffin of his own making. As the gentlefolk of his tale debate how to divide a fart like Thomas's into twelve, the lord of the manor comments:

> The rumblynge of a fart, and every soun,
> Nis but of eir reverberacioun,
> And evere it wasteth litel and litel awey.
> Ther is no man kan deemen, by my fey,
> If that it were departed equally.
> What, lo, my cherl, lo, yet how shrewdly
> Unto my confessour to-day he spak!

I holde hym certeyn a demonyak!
Now ete youre mete, and lat the cherl go pleye;
Lat hym go honge hymself a devel weye!

(III, 2233–42)

This chop logic might well be a parody of the academic discourse of friars teaching at big universities, but the betaking of Thomas to the Devil is an unfortunate link with the climax of the Friar's Tale, where the summoner is also given over to the fiend. Insulters of friars, the Summoner as well as Thomas, are—in the Summoner's own words—the devil's property. In short, both the Summoner and Friar seek to control their adversaries with words, lose control of their own tales, and sink into them toward damnation.

# 4

## The Prioress's Tale

The anonymous writer of *The Vision of William of Stranton* had, it seems, a low view of the office of prioress. Almost at the end of the *Vision* we see a prioress not unlike that of Chaucer's General Prologue undergoing her last judgment:

And þou schall see an examynacion of a prioresse, for hyr saule is cummyn hether now to haue hyr jugement. And wyth þat þe besschoppe and all þe cumpany wentt forthe vnto a hyghe hyll wher the savle was abydynge, and I felowde after. And trevly þer were many fendes abowt þat saule. And then on of þe monkys that cam wyth þe byschoppe opynde a boke of all evyll dedes þat sche hade done, and sche was examynde how sche hade gouernyde hyrselfe and hyr coventt. And trevly, þer was a straytt examynacion, bott sertenly, agayn hyr owne person he hade bott lytyll gylte. And then þe fendys accusyde hyr and sayde þat sche cam to þe religeon all for pomppe and pride, and forto have abundance of wardely esee and riches, and nott for devocyon nor mekenes and lawnes of hertt, as relygion askys to doo, bothe of men and of wemen. And ȝett sayde þe fendys that hytt is well knowne to God and all þe angellys of hevyn, and to men dwellynge in þat cuntre where sche wonnyde, and to all þe fendys of helle, þat sche agayne hyr ordyr was of mysgouernance, in werynge of pelleure, and gyrdyllys of syluer, and goled rynges on hyr fyngyrs, and sylluer bokyllys on hyr schone; and lyggynge on nyghttys lyke a quene or an emperyce, nothynge dessyrynge bott eese and reste, and not rysyng on nyghttys to God seruice; and wyth all delycate mettys and drynkys sche was fede.[1]

Like Madam Eglentine she likes pomp and worldly ease and delicate things to eat and drink. On this evidence it might be tempting to leave the Prioress in purgatory, turn the leaf, and choose another chapter. But there is more, I argue, to her complex spirituality than that.

## The Prioress and the Women Mystics

The recent work of historians interested in female spirituality in the Middle Ages, particularly that of Caroline Walker Bynum and Rudolf M. Bell,[2] tells us, of course, much about medieval women, but it can, I think, tell us some interesting things about medieval literature as well. The New Historicists[3] have demonstrated that "history" and "literature" have a more complex relationship than the old historicists assumed; that is, occurrences in "real life" in former ages did not simply leave their imprint on contemporaneous literature. Often it was the other way around: often "history" and "literature" engaged in a dialectic with each affecting the other, often the barriers dividing "literary texts" from "nonliterary texts" broke down, and always "history" was itself a text in the process of being written.

An interesting example of this frequently symbiotic relationship is that of Chaucer's *Canterbury Tales* and the particularly female spirituality outlined by Bynum, Bell, and others. Late medieval England was an age of devotional literature, much either by or about women. Julian of Norwich and Margery Kempe are, given the anonymity of earlier texts, arguably the language's first women writers, and Middle English versions were made of the *Dialogue* of St. Catherine of Siena and of the *Liber Celestis* of St. Bridget of Sweden. Lives of female saints were enormously popular;[4] Chaucer's Second Nun's Tale of St. Cecelia is only one of many examples of that genre. Thus that female spirituality and Chaucer's text have an important relationship is perhaps to be expected. In fact, an understanding of that relationship can help us construct a possible medieval reader's response to one of *The Canterbury Tales* that has struck many as problematical—that of the Prioress.

The Prioress is, of course, interested in virginity, for she addresses her tale to the Virgin Mary ("O mooder Mayde, O mayde Mooder free! [VII, 467]). After the murder of her tale's hero, the little clergeon, she places him in the company of the virgin martyrs of Apocalpyse 14:1–5:

> O martir, sowded to virginitee,
> Now maystow syngen, folwynge evere in oon
> The white Lamb celestial—quod she—
> Of which the grete evaungelist, Seint John,
> In Pathmos wroot, which seith that they that goon
> Biforn this Lamb and synge a song al newe,
> That nevere, flesshly, wommen they ne knewe.

(VII, 579–85)

It is appropriate here to see what virginity might have meant to a woman saint, mystic, or religious of the late Middle Ages, for it was less an abstract theological topic than a graphically physical reality.

Perhaps it is best to start a selective list of examples with that of Margery Kempe. I am not, of course, anachronistically claiming her direct influence on Chaucer, even if their lives did overlap somewhat; my intent is to describe behavior that was common in the twelfth through fifteenth centuries and thus available to Chaucer's readers for pertinent comparisons and contrasts when they either read or heard the Prioress's Tale. An early topic of Kempe's in the opening sections of her *Book,* as we have seen, concerns her relationship with her husband. Through her amanuensis, she writes about her experiences in the third person:

> Than þis creatur, of whom thys tretys thorw þe mercy of Ihesu schal schewen in party þe leuyng, towched be þe hand of owyr Lord wyth grett bodyly sekeness, wher-thorw sche lost reson & her wyttes a long tym tyl ower Lord be grace restoryd her a-geyn as it schal mor openly be schewed aftyrward. Her werdly goodys, whech wer plentyuows & abundawnt at þat day, in lytyl whyle after wer ful bareyn & bare. . . . Þei þat be-forn had worshepd her sythen ful scharply repreuyd her. . . . And in schort tyme ower mercyful Lord vysytyd þis creatur wyth plentyuows teerys of contricyon day be day, in so mech þat sum men seyden sche mygth wepen whan sche wold & slawndered þe werk of God.[5]

A pattern here in its early stages is clearly already discernible—a sickness and consequent inertia leading to loss of earthly goods, criticism from family and friends, and copious tears. This passage recounts the beginning of Kempe's mystical experiences, which were soon to have a focus—the virtual elimination of her husband.[6]

Married at about the age of twenty, she quickly bore a child. She describes the great sickness and depression childbirth caused her:

> Whan þis creatur was xx ʒer of age or sumdele mor, sche was maryed to a worshepful burgeys and was with chylde wyth-in schort tyme, as kynde wolde. And, after þat sche had conceyued, sche was labowrd wyth grett accessys tyl þe chyld was born, & þan, what for labowr sche had in chyldyng & for sekenesse goyng beforn, sche dyspered of hyr lyfe, wenyng sche mygth not leuyn.[7]

Thus, seeking absolution, she sends for a priest, who gives her such a harsh penance that she goes mad, having visions of hell.[8]

Her madness focuses on those close to her, particularly her husband: "Sche slawndred hir husbond, hir frendys, and her owyn self."[9] Christ heals her, and she recovers, channeling the energy she later admits she should have channeled toward spiritual matters toward business enterprises instead—a brewery and a mill.

After her sickness and post partum depression, the next meaningful spiritual experience she has occurs when she is in her husband's bed:

> On a nyght, as þis creatur lay in hir bedde wyth hir husbond, sche herd a sownd of melodye so swet & delectable, hir þowt, as sche had ben in Paradyse. . . . [The sweet melody] caused þis creatur whan sche herd ony myrth or melodye aftyrward for to haue ful plentyuows & habundawnt teerys of hy deuocyon. . . . And aftyr þis tyme sche had neuyr desyr to komown fleschly wyth hyre husbonde, for þe dette of matrimony was so abhominabyl to hir þat sche had leuar, hir thowt, etyn or drynkyn þe wose, þe mukke in þe chanel, þan to consentyn to any fleschly comownyng saf only for obedyen.[10]

Here the tears of the mystic are directly related to, even the cause of, a desire to avoid sexual contact. She consequently requests her husband to allow her to live with him chastely; for a long time he refuses, and the weapon she uses against him, one suggested in a vision by Christ himself,[11] is fasting:

> Anoþer tyme, as þis creatur prayd to God þat sche myt leuyn chast be leue of hir husbond, Cryst seyd to her mende, "Þow must fastyn þe Fryday boþen fro mete & drynke, and þow schalt haue þi desyr er Whitsonday, for I schal sodeynly sle þin husbond."[12]

As we noticed earlier in our discussion of the connections between Kempe and the Wife of Bath, one is reminded of St. Cecelia's pugnacious angel in the Second Nun's Tale, who would slay Valerian if he would not consent to a chaste marriage (see VIII, 141–61). Christ, mercifully, does not do this to John Kempe, but significant is the addition here of fasting to tears as a means to avoid an earthly husband. Food, in other words, has something to do with her desire for if not virginity at least a chaste marriage. At age forty, her long struggle ended when she finally persuaded her husband to allow her a chaste marriage.[13] By that time she had borne him fourteen children. Her career as a mystic could now begin.

The main impulse behind this avoidance of sexual contact in Margery Kempe and many another mystic is doubtless the

Church's valorization of virginity. Paul, after all, says: "Dico autem non nuptis, et viduis: bonum est illis si sic permaneant, secut et ego" ("There is something I want to add for the sake of widows and those who are not married: it is a good thing for them to stay as they are, like me") (1 Cor. 7:8–9). Supported by the celebate—and literate—clergy, virginity throughout the Middle Ages was privileged as the way of life most pleasing to God. A formidable literature of virginity quickly grew throughout Western Europe in the Middle Ages, particularly in England.[14]

The Anglo-Saxon Aldhelm, for instance, wrote a lengthy prose tract, *De Virginitate,* defending the virtue as—surprisingly, considering the rival claims of the Pauline faith, hope, and love—the chief. He writes:

> Therefore, if the glory of holy virginity is believed to be next kin to angelic beatitude, and the beauteous company of the heavenly citizens wins praise for the merit of chastity, it ought to be extolled with the acclaim which is its due, since among the other ranks of the virtues it is singled out to wield the scepter of the highest sovereignty and the sway of government; since, indeed, just as the taste of honeyed sweetness quite incomparably excels everything that is experienced as pleasing and delectable when brought to human mouths and the palates of mortals, so the divine majesty—though I speak however with the peace and indulgence of those saints once bound by the ties of matrimony—set the special attribute of virginity before all the ranks of virtues in general which are enumerated in the list of the gifts (of the Holy Spirit).[15]

Even so early on, a few centuries before the time Bynum and Bell study, we have the metaphorical connection between virgin sanctity and food. The sweet taste in the virgin's mouth, as I shall show when I discuss in full the Prioress's little clergeon and her use of St. John's Apocalypse, is still as operative an image in the fourteenth century as it was in the seventh. Aldhelm's treatise, though, together with so many medieval treatments of virginity, nods in the direction of marriage: it is possible to be saintly in the married state, implies Aldhelm, but virginity is even better, making salvation all the more likely.

In the late twelfth century, Aelred of Rievaulx, in his *De Institutione Inclusarum,*[16] begins with praise of virginity: "Þys vertu, þat is to seye of maydenhood or chastite, hit is a wylful sacryfyse and an offryngge to God vre and liberal."[17] Again, the virtue is presented with an over-the-shoulder glance at earthly sexual relations:

Þyse beþenkyngge, an holy womman loke hy kepe wit al diligence and drede þilke precious tresour of maydenhood, which so profitable is ihad, and ilost wit-oute recouerer. Be-þenke heo heore continuelly to whos chaumbre heo is imaad gay, to whos cleppynge heo is agreyþed.[18]

In other words, the virgin is the bride pledged to Christ alone and destined for his bed. An earthly husband of a would-be mystic is thus, simply, evil—a usurper of Christ's prerogatives, an adulterer of the worst sort.

The author of the thirteenth-century *Ancrene Riwle,* who is greatly indebted to Aelred in this and most other matters, agrees:

streche þi luue to Iesu Crist; þu hauest him iwunnen. Rin [touch] him wið ase much luue. as þu hauest sum mon sum chearre. he is þin to don wið al þı tu wilnest.[19]

The sexual language here is noteworthy: the virgin recluse has won Christ's love and thus may touch him with the love she sometimes feels for an earthly man: she may do with him what she wills. Thus Margery Kempe can record the vow that Christ makes to her:

I take þe, Margery, for my weddyd wyfe, for fayrar, for fowelar, for richar for powerar. . . . And þan þe Modyr of God & alle þe seyntys þat wer þer present in his sowle preyde þat þei myth haue mech joy to-gedyr.[20]

And this marriage, at least in Kempe's mind—and those of some other mystics like the German Mechthild of Madgeburg, with whom she shares some graphic language[21]—is decidedly sexual. Christ again speaks to Kempe: "þu mayst boldly, whan þu art in þi bed, take me to þe as for þi weddyd husbond,"[22] and again: "þu mayst boldly take me in þe armys of þi sowle & kyssen my mowth, myn hed, & my fete as swetly as thow wylt."[23]

The literature of virginity in the Middle Ages, in short, is best looked at as a rechanneling of sexual energy, not a suppression of it. But such redirection requires condemnation of the place from which the energy has been redirected. Thus for the author of the thirteenth-century *Hali Meiðhad* (holy maidenhood), sexual desire within marriage is evil:

þet ilke unhende fleshches brune, þet bearninde ʒeohðe of þet licomliche lust biuore þet wleatewilc werc, þet bestelich gederunge, þet scheomelese sompnunge, þet ful of fulðe, stinkinde ant untohe dede.[24]

Burning, beastly, filthy, stinking—the author of *Hali Meiðhad* is admittedly an extreme case, but his level of vituperation against earthly sex is still well within the orthodox.

Virginity was, in other words, a sexually charged encounter with Christ that absolved the female saint, mystic, or religious from the social circumscriptions attending physical contact with an earthly husband.[25] Thus by extension the little clergeon's analogous movement away from his own social circumscriptions may be understood. Like Chaucer's exact contemporary, Catherine of Siena,[26] who cut off her hair at an early age to avoid marriage and refused consistently to do her allotted daily chores about her parents' household, the little clergeon prefers religious devotion to his normal social responsibilities:

> "And is this song maked in reverence
> Of Cristes mooder?" seyde this innocent.
> "Now, certes, I wol do my diligence
> To konne it al er Cristemasse be went.
> Though that I for my prymer shal be shent
> And shal be beten thries in an houre,
> I wol it konne Oure Lady for to honoure!"
>
> (VII, 537–43)

St. Catherine of Siena and other women mystics were beaten as children for refusing the duties that society had given them, including household chores, in favor of the religious duties they would impose upon themselves. The clergeon here, of course a male, is avoiding neither housework nor an unwanted marriage, but the pattern of preferring his own idiomatic version of religion to that prescribed for him by others is nevertheless one borrowed from the women mystics.

But it is with the centrality of food in the little clergeon's world and not his rejection of social roles that he has most to share with the women mystics. Given the intense physicality of the women mystics' version of virginity, moreover, the physicality of other aspects of the Prioress's Tale is hardly surprising.

As a nun, the Prioress would have lived in the monastic environment of holy reading, the *lectio divina* that has been, since the time of St. Benedict and before, the main staple of the mental diet of the religious. The constant ingestion, if you will, of texts is important for understanding the Prioress's female spirituality. St. Benedict's rule enjoins the religious "to listen freely to holy lessons" ("lectiones sanctas libenter audire"),[27] and the whole of its Chapter 38 is devoted to explaining what this means:

Mensis fratrum edentium lectio deesse non debet; ne fortuitu casu
qui arripuerit codicem legere audeat ibi, sed lecturus tota ebdomada
dominico die ingrediatur. Qui ingrediens, post missas et communionem
petat ab omnibus pro se orari, ut avertat ab ipso deus spiritum ela-
tionis. Et dicatur hic versus in oratorio tertio ab omnibus, ipso tamen
incipiente: Domine labia mea aperies, et os meum adnuntiabit laudem
tuam. Et sic accepta benedictione, ingrediatur ad legendum. Sum-
mumque fiat silentium ad mensam ut nullius musitatio vel vox: nisi
solius legentis ibi audiatur. Que vero necessaria sunt comedentibus et
bibentibus, sic sibi vicissim ministrent fratres ut nullus indigeat petere
aliquid. Si quid tamen opus fuerit sonitu cujuscumque signi otius peta-
tur quam voce. Nec presumat ibi aliquis de ipsa lectione aut aliunde
quicquam requirere.[28]

There shall be reading during meals. The reader shall not be anyone,
whoever happens to pick up the book: one person shall read for a
week, beginning on Sunday. As he enters on his week, after the office
and the Communion, he shall ask everyone for prayers that God may
preserve him from the spirit of vanity. In the oratory he shall begin the
verse: "O Lord, open thou my lips, and my mouth shall show forth
thy praise" and everyone shall repeat it three times. Then he shall
receive the blessing and so enter upon his office. Complete silence
shall be kept during meals. There shall be no whispering: no one is to
say anything except the reader. The brothers are to supply each other
with what they need in the way of food and drink, so that no one needs
to ask for anything. If anything is lacking, they are to ask for it by a
sign, not by speaking. No one is to ask questions about what is read
or about any other subject, so that no one will have to answer.[29]

Notice the emphasis on opening one's mouth. Normally at meals
such actions initiate the process of ingesting food; here they emit
texts as part of the process of ingesting spiritual wisdom.

Thus in the anonymous Middle English devotional text, *The Abbey of the Holy Ghost,* a personification allegory translated from
the French in which the various theological virtues establish a
convent of nuns in the reader's soul, Sobriety has the office of
lector:

Sobirnes redis at the borde the lyues of the haly ffadirs, and synges
and reherces whate lyfe þat þay lede, for to take gud ensampille to do
als þay dyd, and þere-thorowe slyke mede to myne als þay now hafe.[30]

In a monastic context, in other words, reading and eating are component parts of a single entity, and lives of the saints, intended as
examples for moral nurture, are the basic diet.

How complete was this identification between food and the text in Chaucer's world may be seen in a passage from a work that we know Chaucer read, Guillaume de Deguileville's *Le Pelerinage de la vie humaine*. Chaucer's earliest poem, "An ABC," was a translation of the alphabet poem in praise of the Blessed Virgin that comes near the end of Deguileville's third part. In the fourth part, the allegorical dreamer-pilgrim finally escapes from his torment from the personifications of Sloth, Pride, Anger, and the like, and enters into an allegorical monastery where the virtues are cloistered. In the Middle English prose translation, his guide, Grace Dieu, describes to him one of the nuns:

> The ladi þat þou hast seyn goo bi þe cloistre and bere mete upon parchemyn is pitaunceere of heerinne, and suthselerere. She yiveth mete to þe soule, and feedith it þat hungre nouht. She fillethe þe herte, with hire goode and sweete mete, nouht þe wombe. She is also cleped Lessoun and Studie bi hire rihte name.[31]

The parchment upon which texts are written is like the platter upon which food is served. The written food sustains not the body but the soul. In Deguileville's second French version, moreover, Lesson is accompanied by Hagiography[32]—indication of what sorts of lessons the nuns are to ingest. We are, to a great extent, what we read, particularly the lives of the saints.

Deguileville was a Cistercian, the anonymous author of the French original that stands behind the Middle English *Abbey of the Holy Ghost* probably a Carthusian, Benedict of course the first Benedictine. Yet this association between texts and food was extracloistral as well.

For a saintly layman like Charles of Blois, against whose efforts to gain the dukedom of Brittany Chaucer's king Edward III maneuvered, food and hagiographical texts could merge. As Richard Kieckhefer puts it," at mealtime he related tales of the saints with such animation that he often neglected his food altogether."[33] And Peter of Luxembourg, the scion of a noble house who became a cardinal while a teenager yet lived a saintly life, preferred to read from his prayerbook while at meals.[34] For some of Chaucer's contemporaries, in other words, the holy text became indistinguishable from food.

Not only was this connection between food and text available to Chaucer through the experience of his contemporaries, it was also his through the authority of other texts. Often those Saints' Lives contain details about food—miraculous feedings and food distribution miracles, for instance. There is even an occasional startling detail involving food, like St. Christina's offering her own flayed flesh as food to her evil father, Urban, who is in the process of torturing her. As the midfifteenth-century English Life of St. Christina done by Osbern Bokenham has her exclaim to her father,

> O ould shreu of yll dayis þat pace,
> Syth þou desyryst flessh for to eet,
> Seke no forthere nere in noon oþer place.
> Haue of þine own & faste gyne to frete.[35]

More to our point, however, is the Life of St. Mary of Egypt. She was a prostitute, as the legend goes, who went on a pilgrimage to the Holy Land to gain business, not spiritual merit, but was miraculously converted and then fled into the trans-Jordanian wilderness to live alone in penance. For thirty-seven years she sees no one and fasts. As the early fourteenth-century Life in the *South-English Legendary* puts it,

> ðeot heo leouede twenti ȝer after þe seuentene bi-fore
> Þat heo ne et no mannische mete bot weodes and wilde more.[36]

Then a Monk named Zosimus happens upon her, as the Life points out, to write down her Life:

> A Monuk cam to hire, are heo deide as þe bok us doth lere—
> For ore louerd wolde þat hire lijf a-mong Men i-kud were.[37]

She recounts the story of her life and ends with the request that he respond by bringing her food—that of the Eucharist:

> For i nas neuereft I-hoseled sethþe ich passede þe flum Iordan,
> Þat is nouþe seuene-and-þritti ȝer þat I-ne sayȝ neuereft man.
> Do þat ich þe habbe i-bede mi leoue fader Zosime,
> And blesse me, for ich mot heonne wende for it is nouþe al time.[38]

He returns at the appointed Holy Thursday of the next year with the bread and wine. His subsequent visit the following year confirms this interchange of food and text, for he finds her lying dead, face turned toward the East, with a nearby parchment written in her hand explaining the circumstances of her death, which has happened immediately after her ingesting food:

> Bi-side hire he saiȝligge a writ and he it nam up on is hond.
> Þeos wordes, þat ich ou wolle nouþe telle þaron i-write he fond:

"Frere Zosime, bure þat bodi of þis wrechche wommane Marie,
And prey to god þat he hire for-ȝiue hire sunnes and hire folie,
Þat deide anon-riȝt after hire hosel. . . .[39]

This relationship between food and text is particularly evident
in the one text Chaucer alludes to directly in the Prioress's Tale:
The Prioress addresses her newly slain clergeon by locating him
in a prior text, that of St. John's Apocalypse:

> O martir, sowded to virginitee,
> Now maystow syngen, folwynge evere in oon
> The white Lamb celestial—quod she—
> Of which the grete evaungelist, Seint John,
> In Pathmos wroot, which seith that they that goon
> Biforn this Lamb and synge a song al newe,
> That nevere, flesshly, wommen they ne knewe.

> (VII, 579–85)

The reference is to the virgin martyrs of Apocalypse 14:1–5:

Et vidi: et ecce Agnus stabat supra montem Sion, et cum eo centum
quadraginta quatuor millia, habentes nomen eius, et nomen Patris eius
scriptum in frontibus suis. Et audivi vocem de caelo, tanquam vocem
aquarum multarum, et tanquam vocem tonitrui magni: et vocem, quam
audivi, sicut citharoedorum citharizantium in citharis suis. Et canta-
bant quasi canticum novum ante sedem, et ante quatuor animalia, et
seniores: et nemo poterat dicere canticum, nisi illa centum quadraginta
quatuor millia, qui empti sunt de terra. Hi sunt qui cum mulieribus
non sunt coinquinati: virgines enim sunt. Hi sequuntur Agnum quo-
cumque ierit. Hi empti sunt ex hominibus primitiae Deo, et Agno: et
in ore eorum non est inventum mendacium: sine macula enim sunt
ante thronum Dei.

Next in my vision I saw Mount Zion, and standing on it a Lamb who
had with him a hundred and forty-four thousand people, all with his
name and his Father's name written on their foreheads. I heard a sound
coming out of the sky like the sound of the ocean or the roar of thunder;
it seemed to be the sound of harpists playing their harps. There in
front of the throne they were singing a new hymn in the presence of
the four animals and the elders, a hymn that could only be learnt by
the hundred and forty-four thousand who had been redeemed from the
world. These are the ones who have kept their virginity and not been
defiled with women; they follow the Lamb wherever he goes; they have
been redeemed from amongst men to be the first-fruits for God and for
the Lamb. They never allowed a lie to pass their lips [lit., "no lie was
found in their mouths"] and no fault can be found in them.

Here we have the same grouping as in Chaucer of virginity, of singing a new song (with emphasis on the process of learning it), and of things found in the mouth.

But even more important for our purposes is a passage somewhat earlier from the Apocalypse in which we find a central image of the text as food:

> Et audivi vocem de celo iterum loquentem mecum, et dicentem: Vade, et accipe librum apertum de manu angeli stantis super mare, et super terram. Et abii ad angelum, dicens ei, ut daret mihi librum. Et dixit mihi: Accipe librum, et devora illum: et faciet amaricari ventrem tuum, sed in ore tuo erit dulce tanquam mel. (Apoc. 10:8–9)

> Then I heard the voice I had heard from heaven speaking to me again. "Go," it said, "and take that open scroll ["book" in the Vulgate] out of the hand of the angel standing on sea and land." I went to the angel and asked him to give me the small scroll, and he said, "Take it and eat it; it will turn your stomach sour, but in your mouth it will taste as sweet as honey."

As in the passage to which the Prioress alludes, here too we find an emphasis on what is in the mouth. In the pertinent section of Bede's influential *Commentary on the Apocalypse*,[40] the connections made in this second passage between food and text are clear:

> *Et abbi ad angelum, dicens ei ut daret mihi librum.* Accedat ad Dominum qui velit docendi percipere sacramenta. *Et dixit mihi: Accipe librum, et devora illum.* Id est, insere tuis visceribus, et describe in latitudine cordis tui. *Et faciet amaricare ventrum tuum,* etc. Cum perceperis, oblectaberis divini eloquii dulcedine, sed amaritudinem senties, cum praedicare et operari coeperis quod intellexeris. Vel certe juxta Ezechielem intelligendum, qui cum librum se devorasse diceret, adjecit, *Et abii amarus in indignatione spiritus mei. Et dixit mihi: Oportet te iterum prophetare populis et gentibus.* Quid liber comestus, et amaritudini mista dulcedo significaret, exprimit, quod, videlicet, ereptus exsilio, gentibus esset Evangelium praedicaturus, amore quidem dulce, sed tolerandis persecutionibus amarum.[41]

> *Give.* Let him come to the Lord who wishes to receive the sacraments of teaching. *Take.* That is, place it in your inward parts, and write it down in the breadth of your heart. *Bitter.* When you have received it, you will be delighted by the sweetness of the divine oracle; but you will perceive a bitterness on beginning to preach, and to practise what you have learned, or, at least, it is to be so understood according to Ezekiel, who, when he said that he had eaten the book, added, "And

I went away in bitterness, in the indignation of my spirit." *Prophesy.* He shows what was signified by the book eaten up, and the sweetness mingled with bitterness, namely, that he was to be delivered from banishment, and was to preach the Gospel to the nations, which is sweet indeed through love, but is bitter through the persecutions that are to be endured.[42]

The sacrament—that is, the Eucharist—is here related allegorically to teaching and prophesying, becoming a literal text, as Chaucer's little clergeon does, preaching to the unconverted. Christ the *Word,* in other words, is a text ingested sacramentally.

In the fourteenth-century English illuminated manuscript the *Cloisters Apocalypse,*[43] it is possible to see what an artist, exactly conational and contemporary with Chaucer, makes of this passage. On folio 16v (fig. 1), we see St. John approach the angel to receive and eat the book. The angel stands half on the sea and half on the land, just as the book is in a similarly liminal state, partly eaten, partly not. What is perhaps most interesting about this miniature, though, is St. John's placement in it. Usually he is an observer of the events taking place, as he is on folio 25v (fig. 2), the depiction of the actual passage the Prioress alludes to. There the visionary apostle is seated on the lower left, below the Mount Sion that holds the virgin martyrs, grasping his book in his lap and gazing in detached visionary ardor upon the events that will form the subject of that book. In a great many other miniatures in the *Cloisters Apocalypse* he is actually outside the frame, looking in, always holding his book. But when he accepts the book to eat it, he is central, himself having become the text which he now eats. As Bede points out, he actually becomes his own text by living through the persecutions he describes and preaching the word that he has eaten through his own, living mouth.

One further miniature is worth seeing in this connection, particularly in its structural relationship to the Prioress's Tale. On folio 2v, part of prefatory material not yet depicting events recounted in the Apocalypse, we find a double miniature representing the Massacre of the Innocents and the Flight to Egypt (fig. 3). In the lower portion, as in the Prioress's Prologue, there is the same emphasis on the Virgin Mary and a child at the breast. In the upper, we see grieving mothers and murdered children, one of whom suffers a wound to the lower extremity of his alimentary canal.

The association between virgin martyrs, food, and text is certainly a complex and rich one, but more than just the prayers to the Blessed Virgin and the emphasis on motherhood, in other words,

Fig. 1. *Apocalypse in Latin: John eats the Book and is Commanded to Prophesy.* Ca. 1320. Paint, gold, silver, and brown ink on vellum. 12⅛″ × 9″. The Metropolitan Museum of Art, The Cloisters Collection, 1968. (68.174 fol. 16 V)

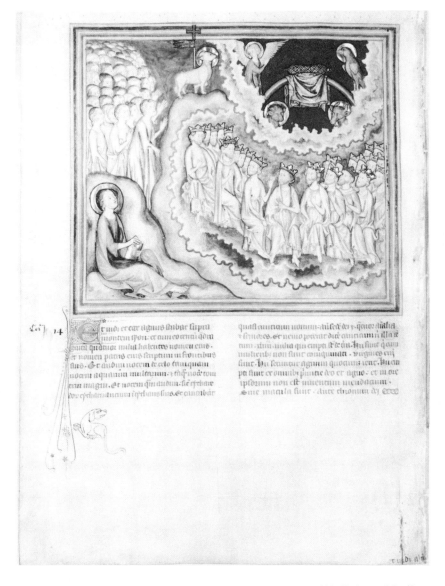

Fig. 3. *Apocalypse in Latin: The Massacre of the Innocents and the Flight into Egypt.*
Ca. 1320. Paint, gold, silver, and brown ink on vellum. 12⅛" × 9". The Metropolitan
Museum of Art, The Cloisters Collection, 1968. (68.174 volio 2 verso)

connect the Prioress's Tale to spiritual matters.[44] In it we see an emphasis on mouths and throats and things that either pass through them or are placed in them. As Bynum points out, ingesting and distributing food was as central to female spirituality in the Middle Ages as refusing it in a fast:

> Not only was food a more significant motif in late medieval spirituality than most historians have recognized, food was also a more important motif in women's piety than in men's. For certain late medieval women, fasting became an obsession so overwhelming that modern historians have sometimes thought their stories preserve the earliest document-able cases of anorexia nervosa. Women all over Europe served Christ by feeding others, donating to the poor the food that husbands and fathers felt proud to be able to save and consume.[45]

Often the women mystics who starved themselves survived for periods by ingesting the Eucharist alone. St. Catherine of Siena, for instance, fed others to the point of alienating her father and subsisted solely on the Eucharist near the end of her life. Her extant writings frequently refer to food, usually as metaphors.[46]

The Prioress's language is similarly imbued with this metaphori-cal use of food. To start her Tale she depicts the town where the miracle occurs almost as if it contained the throat and alimentary canal necessary for ingesting food:

> Ther was in Asye, in a greet citee,
> Amonges Cristene folk a Jewerye.
>
> . . . . . . . . . . .
> And thurgh the strete men myghte ride or wende,
> For it was free and open at eyther ende.
>> (VII, 488–89, 493–94)

The clergeon's last passage through the city ends in the nasty place that completes the alimentary metaphor:[47]

> This cursed Jew hym hente, and heeld hym faste,
> And kitte his throte, and in a pit hym caste.
>
> I seye that in a wardrobe they hym threwe
> Where as thise Jewes purgen hir entraille.
>> (VII, 570–73)

The little clergeon thus himself metaphorically becomes food—a transformation that was common among women mystics—and it is miraculous food at that, considering his post mortem career.

The Eucharistic (even cannibalistic) elements here are strong,[48] but more to my purpose is the close identity many women mystics made between themselves and food. Often the women mystics envisioned themselves as miraculous food, capable of bringing salvation or at least physical satiety or well-being to those about them[49]—an inversion, in fact of the story of St. Mary of Egypt and Zosimus, her clerical provider of food. In one of her visions, for instance, Mechthild of Magdeburg speaks of the necessity to feed the souls in purgatory with her own blood, thus contributing to their eventual release.[50] More common than blood in such cases of mystical feeding was, of course, milk.[51] The thirteenth-century Christina Mirabilis, for instance, escaped from her hostile family into the wilderness and fed herself for two months with her own milk.[52] Lidwina of Schiedam occasionally fed others just as miraculously with her own milk, including her male confessor.[53] She also suffered a serious accident while skating, and in her resulting bodily deterioration, she shed skin and bone which, once shed, smelled sweet.[54] In such a context, the Prioress's reference to the little clergeon's entombment has a simultaneously sensory and spiritual implication that modern readers are likely to miss: "And in a tomb of marbul stones cleere / Enclosen they his litel body *sweete*" (VII, 681–82, emphasis mine).

A further corporealizing occurs in her Prologue, where she quotes Psalm 8 to introduce her particular themes of childhood, motherhood, and innocence.[55] In the Vulgate the appropriate verses read:

> Domine, Dominus noster,
> Quam admirabile est nomen tuum in universa terra!
> Quoniam elevata est magnificentia tua super caelos.
> Ex ore infantium et lactentium perfecisti laudem.

Oh Lord, our Lord, how admirable is your name throughout the earth, for your magnificence is elevated above the heavens. From the mouths of babes and those unweaned your praise is perfected.[56]

The Prioress translates these lines fairly literally but with an increased physicality that emphasizes the lactation:

> O Lord, oure Lord, thy name how merveillous
> Is in this large world ysprad—quod she—
> For noght oonly thy laude precious
> Parfourned is by men of dignitee,
> But by the mouth of children thy bountee

Parfourned is, for on the brest soukynge
Somtyme shewen they thyn heriynge.

(VII, 453–59)

The rather colorless *lactentium* is replaced by the more sensory
image of infants "on the brest soukynge." "Mouth" of course is
present in the Latin, as it is in the very song the clergeon learns
to sing, *Alma Redemptoris Mater,* where the Annunciation comes
"from the mouth of Gabriel," or as the fourteenth-century translation done by the friar William Herebert has it, "Of Gabrieles
mouþe / ou vonge þilke 'Ave'"[57] But it gains emphasis in the Prioress's Tale through the parallel actions of the suckling babe, the
*Alma* proceeding through the clergeon's throat, and the miracle of
his postmortem singing:

> O grete God, that parfournest thy laude
> By mouth of innocentz, lo, heere thy myght!
> This gemme of chastite, this emeraude,
> And eek of martirdom the ruby bright,
> Ther he with throte ykorven lay upright,
> He *Alma redemptoris* gan to synge
> So loude that al the place gan to rynge.

(VII, 607–13)

The Prioress's rather abrupt reference to St. Nicholas (VII, 514)
is even more explainable in this context than in that of Chaucer's
visit to Lincoln Cathedral, which had a St. Nicholas window, as
has been suggested recently,[58] for among St. Nicholas's many miracles was his ability, as a suckling child, to abstain from his
mother's milk except for Wednesdays and Fridays.[59]

The antiphon *Alma Redemptoris Mater,* moreover, is not so
much sung as ingested or regurgitated:

> His felawe taughte hym homward prively,
> Fro day to day, til he koude it by rote,
> And thanne he song it wel and boldely,
> Fro word to word acordynge with the note.
> Twies a day it passed thurgh his throte,
> To scoleward and homward whan he wente;
> On Cristes mooder set was his entente.

(VII, 544–50)

The song passes through his throat as he passes daily back and
forth through the Jewry. His throat will, of course, be cut—an

attempt by the Jews to silence him and a detail found frequently
in the Lives of female saints like Cecelia and Lucy—yet the song,
like the food of the female mystics, continues its progress through
miracle rather than nature:

> "My throte is kut unto my nekke boon,"
> Seyde this child, "and as by wey of kynde
> I sholde have dyed.
>
> . . . . . .
> Yet may I synge *O Alma* loude and cleere."
>
> (VII, 649–51, 55)

Given the particularly female interest in food in the Middle Ages
and given the particularly feminine meaning of the song, whose
English title, of course, is "O Foster Mother of the Redeemer," the
alimentary metaphor is hardly surprising.[60] The voice of the Tale
is not just that of late medieval pathos,[61] but, more precisely, that
of a particular kind of female spirituality.[62]

The little clergeon, male though he is, has as well a relationship
with the abbot who interrogates and finally buries him that is similar in some important ways to that between both female saints and
their judges and women mystics and their confessors/biographers.

In the Lives of women saints, especially those who suffered
under the early persecutions of the Church, male judges often take
on the role of interrogators and engage in dialogues with the
women saints where they gradually, as it were, lose the contest, as
their victims gain confidence in their skills as debaters and prove
the folly of worshiping idols. Of course the closest of such Lives
to Chaucer is the one he himself translated from Jacobus of Voragine's Latin *Golden Legend* and included in *The Canterbury Tales*
as the Second Nun's Tale—the Life of St. Cecelia.

We shall return later to the conflict between St. Cecelia and her
male judge. But in some ways an even better example of this role
reversal may be found in the Life of St. Katherine of Alexandria.
There the Emperor Maxentius accuses the girl, who is a king's
daughter famous for her accomplishments in the seven liberal arts,
of failure to worship the state idols. Cecelia-like, she confounds
him, so he summons his fifty philosophers, who attempt an academic debate with her. They also fail, and in the version of her
Life contained in the *South English Legendary,* an exasperated
Maxentius complains to the professors in language that in a later
age could be accused of gender stereotyping:

Þo seide þe Aumerrur In grete wrathþe: "nis non of eov þat
   can—
A-mong so manie grete Maistres—answereie a fol womman?"[63]

They defensively reply with words not only indicating a role reversal but also emphasizing the alimentary location of her wisdom:

"Certes, sire," þis Maistres seiden: "so gret clerk nov nis
þat scholde to hire reson ȝiue answere for her seith so i-wis,
We seggeth, þe holie gost is with hire and In hire mouþe,
þat we ne conne hire answerie nouȝt. . . ."[64]

The philosophers decide to take on her role by themselves convert-
ing to Christianity.

Women mystics in the Middle Ages, awash Constance-like not
so much in a sea of male judges but of male clerics, often were
dependent on their male confessors and/or biographers to interpret
for themselves the meaning of their visions and spiritual experiences. The twelfth-century Hildegard von Bingen, for instance,
diffident about her skills as a Latinist, relied on the monk Volmar
for rhetorical and grammatical help;[65] Margery Kempe, illiterate,
needed the help of her local priest.

As in so many other areas, Chaucer's contemporary Catherine
of Siena provides a definitive example of a woman mystic's relationship with her confessor.[66] The Dominican friar Raymond of
Capua, who later became master general of his order, was an academic theologian trained at the University of Bologna. He became
Catherine's confessor and spiritual director, advising her on matters theological and mystical. Catherine was illiterate, and she began to dictate her long *Dialogue* to him; after her death he wrote
her biography, translated part of the *Dialogue* into Latin, and
worked for her canonization. Their relationship, like those of some
of the other women mystics and their confessors, was close and
cordial, but the interesting detail is that the male teacher/director
soon became the pupil/directee: Catherine was quickly addressing
him as "son" and giving him spiritual advice based on her ascetic—
that is, essentially passive—experiences of suffering and inedia. It
is she—and not he—who has been officially named by the Vatican
as a doctor of the church.

Many other women mystics, of course, shared this pattern. The
late- thirteenth-century Angela of Foligno,[67] for instance, was an
illiterate who dictated her *Book of Divine Consolation* to her confessor, a Franciscan friar and relative named Arnaldo; often she

reversed the normal ecclesiastical gender roles, advising local friars about spiritual matters and calling them her "sons." Similar
authoritative roles were adopted by Lutgard of Aywieres and Mary
of Oignies.[68]

The pattern—where the male power-figure reverses roles with
the powerless (and thus, paradoxically, authoritative) woman mystic—becomes the norm, one discernible in the Prioress's Tale.
After the little clergeon is found dead but still singing his antiphon,
he is brought to the local abbey and is presented to the abbot for
interrogation:

> This abbot, which that was an hooly man,
> As monkes been—or elles oghte be—
> This yonge child to conjure he bigan,
> And seyde, "O deere child, I halse thee,
> In vertu of the hooly Trinitee,
> Tel me what is thy cause for to synge,
> Sith that thy throte is kut to my semynge?"
>
> "My throte is kut unto my nekke boon,"
> Seyde this child, "and as by wey of kynde
> I sholde have dyed, ye, longe tyme agon.
> But Jesu Crist, as ye in bookes fynde,
> Wil that his glorie laste and be in mynde,
> And for the worship of his Mooder deere
> Yet may I synge O Alma loude and cleere."
>
> (VII, 642–55)

Like Catherine of Siena and the others, the little clergeon is illiterate ("Noght wiste he what this Latyn was to seye." [VII, 523]),
and like them he inverts the normal relationship he should have
with the powerful male ecclesiastic: he begins to lecture him about
what he may find in books.

Further evidence of this role reversal comes after the abbot re-
moves the miraculous grain from his mouth:

> This hooly monk, this abbot, hym meene I,
> His tonge out caughte, and took awey the greyn,
> And he yaf up the goost ful softely.
> And when this abbot hadde this wonder seyn,
> His salte teeris trikled doun as reyn,
> And gruf he fil al plat upon the grounde,
> And stille he lay as he had ben ybounde.
>
> (VII, 670–76)

Like Raymond of Capua, who reports Catherine's inedia and food
miracles, the abbot is interested in what goes in and out of the

little clergeon's mouth. At the end of their relationship the abbot assumes a posture by nature (compare "by wey of kynde" [VII, 650]) the little clergeon's and not his own: he lies still, that is, silently, on the ground—the very posture that, presumably, the boy's murderer wished unsuccessfully to produce. But the act here of course signals reverence and humility, the awed subordination of the abbot, a man of such high, prelatical dignity, to a little, illiterate child: even "*hym* mene I," even an abbot. The relationship is again reminiscent of Raymond of Capua, the future master general of the Dominicans, submitting to the spiritual direction of an illiterate young woman.

Chaucer's Prioress's Tale thus grows out of and contributes to the ideology of female spirituality in the Middle Ages. To borrow again Stephen Greenblatt's phrase,[69] it is best read in terms of the circulation of social energy that simultaneously it produces and in turn produces it. If, in other words, a Saint's Life as text is analogous to food ingested, then the text becomes a staple of life. Thus it should come as no surprise that so many female saints prefered the text of holiness to the food that would nourish the bodies that they had dedicated in perpetual virginity to Christ as bridegroom. A concatenation of saints in reverse chronological order should make this point clear. The late-seventeenth-century nun and saint Orsola Mancini, who took the name Veronica with her veil, patterned her life after reading the hagiographical account of Rose of Lima, who herself had imitated St. Catherine of Siena after reading her Life.[70] All three refused to eat for long periods. Would Veronica and Rose have starved themselves had they not ingested the text of Catherine? When the Prioress invests her "saint's life" with the food metaphor and role reversal we know circulated in and out of women's lives and their Saints' Lives, she is responding both as a reader of texts and an author of one.[71] With her careful table manners and courtly proclivities outlined in the General Prologue, she may not herself follow the pattern of the martyred virgin, the anorectic medieval woman saint, the recluse, or the religious, but her tale nevertheless speaks in a voice that shares some of the sensibility of late medieval female mysticism.

### Doubled Language and a Grain on the Tongue

The Prioress's Tale, moreover, exhibits so strong a connection with the mystics' language theories outlined by Pseudo-Dionysius and his followers that several other aspects of her tale are worth considering in further detail. The Prioress's little clergeon, for instance, is much more vulnerable than his counterpart among the more than thirty close analogues Carleton Brown identifies for her tale.[72] The little boy is, to use the Prioress's own word, more "litel" than the other murdered children and seems to possess less power over the world about him.[73] The list of what the little clergeon cannot do is impressive. He does not, for instance, understand Latin ("noght wiste he what this Latyn was to seye, / For he so yong and tendre was of age" [VII, 523–24]). When he does learn to sing the Latin antiphon *O Alma Redemptoris Mater,* the narrator significantly expresses the accomplishment in language of debility rather than ability:

> As I have seyd, thurghout the Juerie
> This litel child, as he cam to and fro,
> Ful murily than wolde he synge and crie
> *O Alma redemptoris* everemo.
> The swetnesse hath his herte perced so
> Of Cristes mooder that, to hire to preye,
> He kan nat stynte of syngyng by the weye.
>
> (VII, 551–57)

The use of theological words cut off from meaning is, of course, Pseudo-Dionysian. And indeed the little clergeon cannot protect himself from his murderer, who takes him to "a privee place"[74] to kill him—a place of silence that engulfs, at least momentarily, the song he cannot stop in the language he cannot understand. He is a victim totally out of control.

His inability to keep quiet in a language he does not know and is thus divested of meaning, of course, is reminiscent of the apostles on the day of Pentecost, who, filled with the Spirit, run out into the streets, unable to stint the unknown languages controlling their tongues (see Acts 2:1 47). The result of the apostolic glossolalia is widespread conversion; the result of the little clergeon's is not. In fact most of the analogues to the Prioress's Tale end in the conversion of the Jews, while hers ends in their rather viscous execution:[75] "Therfore with wilde hors he dide hem drawe, / And after that he heng hem by the lawe" (VII, 633–35). We must think here of the unbridled horse of the Reeve's Tale, for these wild horses are every bit as much an image of the uncontrolled. What in the analogues and in the Bible, in other words, leads to the growth of the Church here leads to fragmentation: the Jews are torn apart literally as they are torn forever from the Church figuratively.

Fragmentation, in fact, controls the Prioress's Tale. The motherhood that is so important in the tale, for instance, is finally a relationship to be broken in death as the little boy's throat is severed. More importantly, those familiar with the many analogues to the tale experience it as fragmented, for in most,[76] the clergeon is restored to life by the end. The Prioress thus denies her tale the expected ending. With no healing at the end, no resurrection, no conversion, we experience her Tale as somehow truncated.

What is curious about the Prioress's ending is that even the death of the little clergeon is somehow incomplete, unresolved:

> O grete God, that parfournest thy laude
> By mouth of innocentz, lo, heere thy myght!
> This gemme of chastite, this emeraude,
> And eek of martirdom the ruby bright,
> Ther he with throte ykorven lay upright,
> He *Alma redemptoris* gan to synge
> So loude that al the place gan to rynge.
>
> (VII, 607–13)

Even in death he cannot be silent, and as a result this gem of vulnerability becomes the archcontroller of his own tale, managing the plot, bringing about the final ending. His singing leads first his mother and later the Christians led by the abbot of a nearby monastery to expose the criminals (who somehow have proliferated from the third person singular to the third person plural, as is the way with most anti-Semitic uprisings), and his postmortem loquaciousness also is the means whereby the narrator explains the marvelous doings of her plot:

> "My throte is kut unto my nekke boon,"
> Seyde this child, "and, as by wey of kynde
> I sholde have dyed, ye, longe tyme agon.
> But Jesu Crist, as ye in bookes fynde,
> Wil that his glorie laste and be in mynde,
> And for the worship of his Mooder deere
> Yet may I synge *O Alma* loude and cleere."
>
> (VII, 649–55)

The little clergeon who could not construe Latin has, as we have seen, now become a full-blown clerk, lecturing to a prelate about what he may find in books. It is not until the magical grain—a detail unique to the Prioress's Tale among the extant versions—is removed from his mouth that the clergeon becomes silent. This silence generated by the little clergeon in death spreads inexorably outward from him, engulfing the Abbot. Two stanzas later the Prioress concludes with an "Amen" (VII, 690) and is forever silent.

Helen Cooper provocatively explains this grain, which Chaucer evidently picked up from a reference in the second Vespers of the Eve of Holy Innocents Day,[77] as the clergeon's "spiritual understanding beyond the 'chaff' of words."[78] There is support for this idea beyond what Cooper or other explicators of the mysterious grain have yet developed. The Book of Jeremiah defines *grain* as the word of the Lord given to the prophet in mystical vision in opposition to the chaff of the false prophets:

> Audivi quae dixerunt prophetae
> Prophetantes in nomine meo mendacium,
> Atque dicentes: Somniavi, somniavi.
>
> . . . . . . . . . . .
> Narret somnium;
> Et qui habet sermonem meum,
> Loquatur sermonem meum vene
> Quid paleis ad triticum? dicit Dominus.
>
> (Jer. 23:25, 28)

"I have heard what the prophets say, the prophets who speak lies in my name and cry, "I have had a dream, a dream!" . . . If a prophet has a dream, let him tell his dream; if he has my word, let him speak my word in truth. What has chaff to do with grain? says the Lord.

When the circumstances of the prophet Jeremiah's vocation are recalled, the similarity between this passage and Chaucer's becomes apparent:

> Et factum est verbum Domini ad me, dicens:
> Priusquam te formarem in utero, novi te,
> Et antequam exires de vulva, sanctificavi te,
> Et prophetam in gentibus dedi te.
> Et dixi: A, a, a, Domine Deus, ecce nescio loqui,
> Quia puer ego sum.
> Et dixit Dominus ad me:
> Noli dicere: Puer sum;
> Quoniam ad omnia quae mittam te ibis,
> Et universa quaecumque mandavero tibi loqueris.
> Ne timeas a facie eorum,
> Quia tecum ego sum ut ernam te,
> Dicit Dominus.
> Et misit Dominus manum sum, et tetigit os meum, et dixit Dominus ad me: Ecce dedi verba mea in ore tuo. . . .
>
> (Jer. 1:4–9)

The word of the Lord came to me: "Before I formed you in the womb I knew you for my own; before you were born I consecrated you, I appointed you a prophet to the nations." "Ah! Lord God," I answered, "I do not know how to speak; I am only a child." But the Lord said, "Do not call yourself a child; for you shall go to whatever people I send you and say whatever I tell you to say. Fear none of them, for I am with you and will keep you safe." This was the very word of the Lord. Then the Lord stretched out his hand and touched my mouth, and said to me, "I put my words into your mouth. . . ."

The word of the Lord is grain, placed in a child's mouth; the child, who originally did not know how to speak, will now preach to the Gentiles. Change that last word of the previous sentence to *Jews,* and you have the situation in almost all of the analogues to the Prioress's Tale, where the Jews are converted. Even without this interesting Gentile / Jew inversion, which the Prioress obscures by killing off her own Jews, the connection is still startlingly strong: the Blessed Virgin will not forsake the little clergeon ("Be nat agast; I wol thee nat forsake" [VII, 669]) just as the Lord will be with the child Jeremiah.

In both the tale and the Bible the grain is, as Cooper suggests, spiritual truth "beyond the 'chaff' of words"—words that both the clergeon and Jeremiah cannot speak before what amounts to a mystical vision—the Lord touching Jeremiah's mouth, the Blessed Virgin speaking to the little boy. Pseudo-Dionysius develops the mystical idea that names simultaneously affirm and deny spiritual truths: only from the point of view of God and with his valorizing authority may we speak the spiritual names proceeding from him. As Cooper puts it about the Prioress's Tale, it "displays a concern for the function of language. . . . Here, the concern is with the inadequacy of earthly language to express the spiritual."[79] Thus the Prioress prays in the invocation to her tale,

> O mooder Mayde, O mayde Mooder free!
> O bussh unbrent, brennynge in Moyses sighte,
> That ravyshedest doun fro the Deitee.
>
> .  .  .  .  .  .  .  .  .  .  .  .  .
> Lady, thy bountee, thy magnificence,
> Thy vertu and thy grete humylitee
> Ther may no tonge expresse in no science.
>
> .  .  .  .  .  .  .  .  .  .  .  .  .
> My konnyng is so wayk, O blisful Queene,
> For to declare thy gret worthynesse
> That I ne may the weighte nat susteene;
> But as a child of twelf month oold, or lesse,

> That kan unnethes any word expresse,
> Right so fare I, and therfore I yow preye,
> Gydeth my song that I shal of yow seye.
>                    (VII, 467–69, 474–76, 481–87)

The Prioress's word *ravyshedest* is frequently used in mystic speech and is by nature Pseudo-Dionysian, divesting an essentially sexual word of meaning and affirming a spiritual meaning in its stead.[80] The *Cloud*-author, for instance, writes:

> þer was neuer ȝit pure creature in þis liif, ne neuer ȝit schal be, so hiȝe rauishid in contemplaccion & loue of þe Godheed, þat þer ne is euermore a hiȝe & a wonderful cloude of vnknowyng bitwix him & his God.[81]

The author of the anonymous Middle English *Revelation of Purgatory* initiates her vision with words similar to the Prioress's: "betwix ix and x [o'clock] I thoght I was rauyshed into purgatory."[82] Walter Hilton, in his *Scale of Perfection,* explains," . . . bi rauischinge of lufe, þe soule is oned for þe time and conformed to þe ymage of þe Trinite."[83] And Rolle,[84] in his famous lyric, "Love is lif,"[85] uses the same spatial relationships as the Prioress:

> Loue vs couereth and maketh in quert and lifteth to heuyn-rike;
> Loue rauyssheth Crist in to oure hert; I wot no lust hit lyke.
>                    (lines 15–16)

The Prioress's "Ther may no tonge expresse" is one of many, many replications and alterations of an old topos traceable back to Paul's definition of mystical vision in his First Letter to the Corinthians:

> Quod oculus non vidit, nec auris audivit, nec in cor hominis ascendit, quae praeparavit Deus iis qui diligunt illum. (2:9)

> The things that no eye has seen and no ear has heard, things beyond the mind of man, all that God has prepared for those who love him.

Paul himself is thinking about passages from Isaiah, Jeremiah, and the Apocalypse of Elijah; Chaucer uses the topos elsewhere in different contexts (see, for instance, II, 899; IV, 1341; and *Troilus* 3.1693). Perhaps the apotheosis of the topos is Bottom's version of it in *A Midsummer Night's Dream,* where he awakes, searches for his vanished ass's ears, and says, "The eye of man hath not heard, the ear of man hath not seen, man's hand is not able to taste, his tongue to conceive, nor his heart to report what my dream was" (4.1.208–11).

The point is not simply that Chaucer puts a well-worn cliché in the mouth of his Prioress, but that it was a staple of the mystics as well as of earlier literary authors. The list of repetitions of this topos among the mystics would indeed be a very long one, but for our purposes the examples of two Middle English mystics will suffice.[86] In his famous *Meditation on the Passion,* Richard Rolle writes:

> A, lady [i. e., St. Mary], þat sorewe may no tunge telle þat þou þere soffryd at þat ilke chawngynge. . . . Lord, þi mykyl mercy may non herte thenkyn.[87]

Mary is here addressed as well as her dying son: we are in the same spiritual environment as that inhabited by the Prioress. But more important is the centrality of the topos to Pseudo-Dionysian attitudes about language, for it is a disclaimer of the referentiality of language. In the original instance of the topos, Paul anticipates Pseudo-Dionysius, for he depicts the soul having arrived at the ultimate point of the neoplatonic return, where language is divested of meaning.

The connection between Pseudo-Dionysian language theory and the Corinthians topos is perhaps even clearer in another passage from Rolle. In his *Form of Living,* a treatise addressed to Margaret Kirkby, a nun of his acquaintance who has entered upon the life of a recluse, he writes:

> Ryghtwysnes es nother in Fastyng ne in eetyng: Bot þou ert ryghtwys If al [ilyke] be to þe Dispite and Loouyng, Poeuert and Rychesse, Hunger and nede als delites and dayntes. . . . For to draw vs þat we confourme our wile til goddis wile, þer er thre thyngs: . . . Þe thrid es: Þe woundirful ioy of þe kyngdome of heuene, þat es mare þan tung may telle or hert may thynke or eghe may se or eer may heer.[88]

We have here a Pseudo-Dionysian affirmation and denial of the valency of words like *righteousness, poverty, richness,* and *hunger,* combined with the full Neoplatonic passage from Paul.

The author of the anonymous *A Talking of the Love of God* is also fond of the topos: "þi worþ and þi worschupe ne may no tonge telle," he writes. Again, when he speaks of the Passion, we find, "But what tonge may tellen what herte may þenken for serwe or for rouþe, of þat hard boffetyng."[89] For the mystic, language is inadequate.

Chaucer's phrase "No science," words that end the same line that contains the Corinthians topos, is a literal translation of the word Pseudo-Dionysius coined and the *Cloud*-author brought to Chaucer's England—*unknowing*—and "My konnyng is so wayk" is a fair enough paraphrase. The Prioress, like Jeremiah and Pseudo-Dionysius before her, like her contemporary the *Cloud*-author, and like her own character the little clergeon, despairs over the capabilities of language. Her twin paradox that begins her prayer, "mooder mayde . . . bussh unbrent, brennynge" shows how much the Pseudo-Dionysian wedge between signifier and signified affects her.[90] A mother cannot be a maid, an unburned bush cannot burn, a dead child cannot sing—unless God invests these signifiers with referentiality. According to the anonymous Middle English translator of the enormously popular *Speculum Humanae Salvationis* (ME *The Mirour of Mans Saluacioune*), St. Joseph needs some encouragement on the first of these matters:

> And when þat Josep of hire thus hoege reueerent drede hadde,
> Gods aungel come hym to, to make his hert be sadde,
> Bidding he ne shuld noght dout his spouse for to take than,
> So grete of the Haly Gast, and neuer of erthly man.
> This concepcioune mirable of thilk swete virgyne ȝynge
> Was shewed to Moyses sometyme in a grene bushe brennyng.[91]

I will have cause to comment on the words *sad* and *dread* in connection with the Clerk's Tale.

Again one thinks of the anonymous *A Talking of the Love of God,* where the reader finds not only the Prioress's "ther may no tonge expresse" but also her paradox, "O mooder Mayde! of mayde Mooder":

> Þenk heer on þis wrecche Moder and Mayden, þat falleþ þe tofote in hope of þin helpe, cryinde reuþely after þi grace.[92]

Like the Prioress, the author of *A Talking* seeks aid from the mother-maid, and like the Prioress's mother in the tale, who weeps for her slain son, so does the mother-maid from the anonymous treatise:

> Ladi seinte Marie Moder & Mayden, muche was þe serwe set at þin herte, whon þou at þi sones deþ stoode him so neih![93]

In his last repetition of this paradoxical phrase, the author of *A Talking* reveals how Pseudo-Dionysian this paradox is in its simultaneous affirmation and denial of meaning to words:

> Maiden and Moder þou art: and his Mooder þou art, his hondwerk þou art his spouse and his douȝter.[94]

Each of these words normally has a semantic range that excludes the others. In mystic speech, where we accept words as part of a procession from God and then deny them in return, the signifiers float freely among the signifieds. There is even some indication that the Prioress's very words were associated with Pseudo-Dionysius. In the Middle English translation of St. Bridget's *Liber Celestis,* she recounts a vision she has of Saint Denis:

> Qwhen I was in praying, I saw how Saint Denyse spake vnto þe maide Mary and saide, "Whene [*sic,* emend "Welle"] of mercy, þou arte þat persone to whome is gyuen all mercy, and þou arte maide þe moder of Gode.[95]

Moreover, her identification with her own main character as she describes herself "as a child. / That kan unnethes any word expresse," is significant, given the tendency of tellers of *The Canterbury Tales* to sink into their own tales. As he sings songs of praise to the Virgin, so does she; as he labors to learn foreign languages at school, so had she (see I, 126); as he falls forever silent at the end of her tale, so does she.

# 5

## Good Women

When asked for a tale, the Man of Law responds with what amounts to a fourfold literary blunder:

> But nathelees, certeyn,
> I kan right now no thrifty tale seyn
> That Chaucer, though he kan but lewedly
> On metres and on rymyng craftily,
> Hath seyd hem in swich Englissh as he kan.
>
> (II, 45–49)

He follows with a long list of Chaucerian tales, all about good women, most from Chaucer's *Legend of Good Women*. The howlers are: (1) Chaucer, of course, as Eustache Deschampes maintained, was among the greatest of living poets; (2) Chaucer never wrote tales about several of the women listed—Dianire, Hermyon, Hero, Helen, Ladomya, and Penelope; (3) the previous existence of a story was never a reason for a medieval author not to retell it;[1] and (4) Chaucer wrote in more than one genre, his interests ranging far beyond the narrow confines of narratives about good women. Yet such narratives were nevertheless important to him, for not only does *The Legend of Good Women* concern itself with them, so do large stretches of *The Canterbury Tales*—so much so, in fact, that in his last and greatest work Chaucer still seems to be doing the penance appointed for him by the god Cupid through the mediation of the good Queen Alcestis.[2] *The Canterbury Tales* are, among many other things, a continuation of the fragmentary *Legend of Good Women*.

Nowhere, moreover, are Chaucer's Pseudo-Dionysian themes of control, silence, and fragmentation presented in a more metaphysical light than in his *Canterbury Tales* about good women. They partake in many ways of the kind of lives the women mystics led: they present women who are vulnerable, righteous, and long-suffering, women almost completely without control over their sur-

roundings in a worldly sense. They suffer silently and lead fragmented lives, yet they exert a spiritual control that ultimately
reveals a God who is in rigorous, absolute control of things.

## The Man of Law's Tale

Chaucer's Custance is in many ways the paradigm both the
women mystics and the Canterbury good women follow:[3] she floats
about the Mediterranean, Atlantic, and North Sea in a rudderless
boat,[4] utterly helpless, suffering terribly, yet through her God con-
verts England to Christianity. She is Everyperson;[5] her boat is
the Church.[6]

This almost paradoxical theme of control through its own lack
dominates the tale,[7] generating a Pseudo-Dionysian double vision.
When, for instance, the Syrian merchants spark the Sultan's love
for her early on in the tale, the narrator comments:

> Peraventure in thilke large book
> Which that men clepe the hevene ywriten was
> With sterres, whan that he his birthe took,
> That he for love sholde han his deeth, allas!
> For in the sterres, clerer than is glas,
> Is writen, God woot, whoso koude it rede,
> The deeth of every man, withouten drede.
>
> (II, 190–96)

The reader knows that the Sultan does not read that book, for his
attempt to control his nation, forcing his subjects to convert so he
can win the beautiful Custance as his wife, will not work: the stars
are inauspicious. The movement of the tale, of course, is away
from the impersonal stars as the invisible controllers of human
affairs and toward God, so the "God woot" here should be read as
not merely a filler. But both—the stars and God—are, if you will,
what I term "archcontrollers," that is, characters who usurp some
of the perogatives of authors, although neither, of course, strictly,
is a character within the tale.

The characters who are within the tale imitate the stars, God,
and the Miller's Nicholas by attempting to control things through
silence. The Sultan, for instance, makes his feeble attempts at controlling his nation through silence ("This Sowdan for his *privee*
counseil sente" [II, 204]); the beset Britons, who aid in the conversion of Hermengyld's husband, maintain their faith in secret

("somme . . . in hir privetee / Honoured Crist" [II, 548–49]); the
knight who murders Hermengyld does it "prively" (II, 594); and
Donegild steals the messenger's letters "pryvely" (II, 744).

Other characters react to situations with a silence[8] meant less
to control things than to express lack of control. When Custance
is framed for Hermengyld's murder, the narrator asks the rhetorical
question, "Allas, what myghte she seye?" (II, 608); the Saxons
who witness her miraculous exoneration stand "As mazed folk"
(II, 678); Alla seals the forged letter accusing Custance of being a
monster "pryvely wepynge" (II, 768); Custance embarks for the
second time in the rudderless boat admonishing her little baby to
keep silence ("Pees, litel sone, I wol do thee noon harm" [II, 836]);
"Ther is no tonge that it telle may" (II, 899—as we have seen, a
favorite phrase among the mystics) how Alla grieves for his lost
wife; and he finally greets his restored son with silence ("pryvely
he sighte" [II, 1035]), an act echoed by Custance herself, when
she first sees him ("And she, for sorwe, as doumb stant as a tree
[II, 1055]).

By the end of the tale, Custance learns to control things through
silence, refusing to tell the senator who takes her back to Rome
and adopts her who she is ("ne she nyl seye / Of hire estaat, althogh
she sholde deye" [II, 972–73]), and not revealing her identity to her
true father, the Emperor, for years ("She preyde hym eek he sholde
by no weye / Unto hir fader no word of hire seye" [II, 1084–85]).
This controlling silence may strike some readers as a bit odd, even
unnecessary, yet Custance's later voiced fears about being used
once more as a marriage prize to convert the pagans is doubtless
her well-justified reason: "Sende me namoore unto noon heth-
enesse" (II, 1112); she does not want to be controlled by another
anymore, even her father; in this she shares an attitude of women
mystics in the Middle Ages, who often wished to avoid parental
injunctions to marry.

Chaucer's source for the Man of Law's Tale is part of Nicholas
Trevet's Anglo-Norman *Chronicles;* his friend John Gower also
crafted a version of the same story for his *Confessio Amantis.*
Although he follows Trevet word for word in places,[9] there is compelling evidence that Chaucer wants his reader to think for comparative and contrastive purposes about Gower's version of the
tale instead,[10] for immediately before beginning his tale, the Man
of Law makes his famous reference to John Gower and two of the
other tales from the *Confessio Amantis:*

But certeinly no word ne writeth he [i. e., Chaucer]
Of thilke wikke ensample of Canacee . . .

. . . . . . . . . . . . . .
Or ellis of Tyro Appollonius . . .

(II, 77–78, 81)

There is perhaps a fifth aspect to the Man of Law's literary howler: in refusing to tell a tale Chaucer has already told, he elects to tell one that Gower has. In Gower, we have a different Constance. When, for instance, the senator finds her, Gower writes:

This lord hire axeth overmo
How sche believeth, and sche seith,
"I lieve and triste in Cristes feith,
Which deide upon the Rode tree."
"What is thi name?" tho quod he.
"Mi name is Coust," she him seide.[11]

Although she keeps mum about the rest of her circumstances, thus enabling her to live as incognito as the plot demands, this relatively loquacious Constance has little in common with Chaucer's.

But Chaucer's additions to his direct source, Trevet, are even more instructive than this minor quibble with Gower. There are, I suggest, several additions worthy of exploring at some length. First are the famous quotations from Pope Innocent III's devotional treatise *De Miseria Condicionis Humane*,[12] a work Chaucer, as we have seen, claims to have translated, even though his version has not survived (see *PLGW* G, 413–18).[13] There is some independent evidence that a Middle English translation of that work did exist. In the anonymous treatise *The Book of the Craft of Dying*, the author early on clarifies a point with a quotation from Innocent's work:

Forthermore, as Innocente þe pope in his þrid boke of þe wrecchidn-esse of mankynd seiþe: Euery men boþe good & euell, er his soule pas out of his body, he seith Crist put in þe crosse, the good man to his consolacion, the euell man to his confusion, to make hym aschamyd þat he hath lost þe frute of his redempcion.[14]

It is the custom of the author of this devotional treatise to quote from the original Latin before giving an English translation, yet here he does not—an almost unprecedented instance in that particular text. That he was working from a Middle English translation, perhaps Chaucer's, is thus likely, especially considering the similar title he and Chaucer give it; for Chaucer it is "Of the Wreched Engendrynge of Mankynde" (*PLGW* G, 414), not the more exact rendering of its Latin title, "Of the Misery of the Human Condition." The quotation, in other words, should perhaps be included in some further volume of the "Complete Works" of Chaucer to make them truly complete.

At four points along the way, Chaucer's narrator—not Trevet's or Gower's—interrupts the tale's action and comments in the dismal words of the early thirteenth-century pope. The passages, followed by Innocent's Latin and modern English translations, are as follows:

> O sodeyn wo, that evere art successour
> To worldly blisse, spreynd with bitternesse,
> The ende of the joye of oure worldly labour!
> We occupieth the fyn of oure gladnesse.
> Herke this conseil for thy sikernesse:
> Upon thy glade day have in thy mynde
> The unwar wo or harm that comth bihynde.
>
> (II, 421–27)

Semper mundare letitie tristicia repentina succedit. . . . Mundana quippe felicitas multis amaritudinibus est respeusa. . . . "extrema gaudii luctus occupat." . . . Salubre consilium: "In die bonorum ne immemor sis malorum."

Sudden woe always follows worldly joy. . . . Worldly happiness is indeed sprinkled with many bitternesses. . . . "mourning takes hold of the ends of joy." . . . Sound [literally, "saving"] counsel: "In the day of good things be not unmindful of evils."[15]

This is Innocent's chapter (Book I: Chapter 21), *De Inopinato Dolore,* "Of Unexpected Sorrow."

> O messager, fulfild of dronkenesse,
> Strong is thy breeth, thy lymes faltren ay,
> And thou biwreyest alle secreenesse.
> Thy mynde is lorn, thou janglest as a jay,
> Thy face is turned in a newe array.
> Ther dronkenesse regneth in any route,
> Ther is no conseil hyd, withouten doute.
>
> (II, 771–77)

Quid turpius ebrioso, cui fetor est in ore, tremor in corpore; qui promit stulta, prodit occutta; cui mens alienatur, facies transformatur? "Nullum enim secretum ubi regnet ebrietas."

What is more unsightly than a drunkard, in whose mouth is a stench, in whose body a trembling; who utters foolish things, betrays secrets; whose reason is taken away, whose face is transformed? "For there is no secret where drunkeness reigneth."[16]

Appropriately, this passage is from Innocent's chapter, *De Ebrietate*, "Of Drunkeness" (Book II: Chapter 19). Note how Chaucer directs Innocent's general comments to a specific character in the tale. Drunkeness was of course in the Middle Ages a form of the Deadly Sin of Gluttony. The next interpolation, from Innocent's chapter *De Luxuria* (Book II: Chapter 21), "Of Lust," shortly follows on the preceding one and is a part of the pope's treatment of the Seven Deadly Sins. We are again in Chaucer in the same devotional environment as the Parson's and Summoner's tales:

> O foule lust of luxurie, lo, thyn ende!
> Nat oonly that thou feyntest mannes mynde,
> But verraily thou wolt his body shende.
>
> (II, 925–27)

O extreme libidinis turpitudo, que non solum effeminat, set corpus enervat.

O extreme foulness of desire, which not only weakens, but debilitates the body.[17]

The last interpolation of Innocentian material is a composite of two passages from Innocent's chapter *De Brevi Leticia*, "Of Brief Joy" (Book I: Chapter 20), in reverse order. Here is Chaucer's version, followed by Innocent's in the original order:

> But litel while it lasteth, I yow heete,
> Joye of this world, for tyme wol nat abyde;
> Fro day to nyght it changeth as the tyde.
>
> Who lyved euere in swich delit o day
> That hym ne moeved outher conscience,
> Or ire, or talent, or som kynnes affray,
> Envye, or pride, or passion, or offence?
>
> (II, 1132–38)

Quis unquam vel unicam diem duxerit totam in sua delectacione iocundam, quem in aliqua parte diei reatus consciencie vel impetus ire vel motus concupiscencie non turbaverit? Quem livor invidie vel ardor avaricie vel tumor superbie non vexaverit? Quem aliqua iactura vel offensa vel passio non commoverit?. . . . A mane usque ad vesperam mutabitur tempus."

Who indeed has even spent one whole delightful day in his own pleasure, whom the guilt of conscience or an attack of anger or the agitation of concupiscence has not disturbed in some part of the day? Whom the spite of envy or the burning of avarice or the swelling of pride has not vexed? Whom some loss or offense or passion has not upset? . . . From the morning until the evening the time shall be changed."[18]

There is also a longer quotation from Innocent in the Man of Law's Prologue (II, 99–121). Critics have long recognized Innocent's presence in Chaucer's text and have explained it, usually, as allegorical coloring[19] or homiletic didacticism[20] or the Man of Law's pure gloom.[21] Sometimes critics note that the passages from Innocent function in the same way as passages from Boethius's *Consolation of Philosophy*—of course, another of Chaucer's translations—function in the Knight's Tale.[22]

The Innocentian material, I suggest, is of importance to the Man of Law's Tale mostly because it does *not* function in the same way as the Boethian material in the Knight's Tale. A Boethian passage from Gower's *Tale of Constance* is useful here in explaining what I mean:

> Now herke how thilke whel,
> Which evere torneth, wente aboute.
> The king Allee, whil he was oute,
> As thou tofore hast herd this cas,
> Deceived thurgh his Moder was.[23]

(1226–30)

Boethius's famous wheel of the goddess Fortune is the philosophical explanation of the sufferings Constance must face: as queen, she was on the wheel's top; as repudiated and exiled wife, on the bottom. The point is that Innocent's scheme is not so much that of a wheel but of a slide. Fortune's wheel is capable of bringing one up as much as sending one down, yet for Innocent, the miserable condition of humanity is that all joys lead to sorrow, all pleasures to pain, all health to corruption. A Boethian universe, in other words, allows a Duke Theseus to declare, "I rede that we make of

sorwes two / O parfit joye, lastynge everemo" (I, 3071–72)—and
then effect a marriage between a Palamon and an Emelye. An
Innocentian universe does not: no wheel can turn funereal sorrow
to nuptial joy, and an Innocentian rather than Boethian Knight's
Tale would stop short with the death of Arcite.

Chaucer's use of Innocent thus establishes a tension in the Man
of Law's Tale between narrative content and metaphysical commentary, establishing, perhaps, what Mikhail Bakhtin would term
dialogic polyphony.[24] For Custance, more than any other character
in Chaucer, embodies the Boethian metaphysic rejected by the
Innocentian interpolations in her tale. She rides the trace of the
missing wheel. A Roman Emperor's daughter, she is sent grieving
to sea to marry a heathen sultan. The Sultan weds her in great joy,
yet she survives the reactionary carnage to be sent again to sea
and probable death in a rudderless boat. She lands in Northumbria
at last safely and is honored by a nobleman and his wife only to
be falsely accused of the wife's death. She is vindicated before the
king, who quickly marries her, yet she is seemingly repudiated by
him and sent back again into the rudderless boat with the child
she has borne. She lands safely only to suffer attempted rape. She
arrives back in Rome and is finally united with both her husband
and her father and returns home to England as queen only to suffer
her husband's death after just one year of happiness. She is re-
united with her father at Rome only to suffer his death. And then
she dies, but not before seeing her son crowned emperor. Fortune's
wheel spins often and fast in the Man of Law's Tale, yet the Innocentian ideas that intrude on the tale deny such movement and do
not allow for joy and success after sorrow and failure.

Most of the Innocentian passages in Chaucer begin with the
vocative "O." One passage that intrudes on the narrative events is
a similar evocation, yet not from Innocent, although it shares with
the Innocentian material a tendency to undercut the text. Describing the evil Sultaness, the narrator writes:

> O Sathan, envious syn thilke day
> That thou were chaced from oure heritage,
> Wel knowestow to wommen the olde way!
> Thou madest Eva brynge us in servage;
> Thou wolt fordoon this Cristen mariage.
> Thyn instrument so, weylaway the while!
> Makestow of wommen, whan thou wolt bigile.

(II, 365–71)

In a tale praising a woman faithful to God and constant in sufferings, this antifeminist diatribe, which generalizes from the evil
mother-in-law to all women in the person of Eve, undermines the
tale's meaning. In a similar fashion, Custance's prayer to the Virgin, "In hym triste I, and in his mooder deere, / That is to me my
seyl and eek my steere" (II, 832–33), helps undercut a poem where
mothers are invariably evil and sails are attached only to rudderless boats.

Perhaps the most unsettling example of this sort of textual dis-
turbance is the narrator's repeated and insistent insertions into his
text of the reasons why Custance was able to sustain the sufferings
of being a political pawn and the rigors of rudderless navigation:

> Men myghten asken why she was nat slayn
> Eek at the feeste? who myghte hir body save?
> And I answere to that demande agayn,
> Who saved Danyel in the horrible cave
> Ther every wight save he, maister and knave,
> Was with the leon frete er he asterte?
> No wight but God that he bar in his herte.
>
> (II, 470–76)

> Where myghte this womman mete and drynke have
> Thre yeer and moore? how lasteth hire vitaille?
> Who fedde the Egipcien Marie in the cave,
> Or in desert? No wight but Crist, sanz faille.
> Fyve thousand folk it was as greet mervaille
> With loves fyve and fisshes two to feede.
> God sente his foyson at hir grete neede.
>
> (II, 498–504)

Note here in passing the reference to the saint's Life of Mary
of Egypt discussed in the last chapter: Chaucer picks up on the
importance of food for that story by alluding to it in his attempt
to explain his heroine's independence—one so similar to that of
the women saints described by Bynum[25]—from the normal gather-
ing and ingesting of earthly food. The last insertion of a narrator's
probing doubts of his own story is pertinent to Custance's struggle
with her would-be rapist:

> How may this wayke womman han this strengthe
> Hire to defende agayn this renegat?
> O Golias, unmesurable of lengthe,
> Hou myghte David make thee so maat,
> So yong and of armure so desolaat?

Hou dorste he looke upon thy dredful face?
Wel may men seen, it nas but Goddes grace.

Who yaf Judith corage or hardynesse
To sleen hym Olofernus in his tente,
And to deliveren out of wrecchednesse
The peple of God? I seye, for this entente,
That right as God spirit of vigour sente
To hem and saved hem out of meschance,
So sente he myght and vigour to Custance.

                                                    (II, 932–45)

Innocent, of course, vigorously states that no one may be delivered
out of "wrecchednesse." The Man of Law is, moreover, engaging
in a kind of dialogue with his reader in which he anticipates objec-
tions to his narrative, almost the way a sufferer might question the
goodness of a God who would let her suffer. The Man of Law is
so persistent in this that his words become almost a taunt: I am
telling you something far-fetched, and you must generate faith in
God to believe me. Or is it "faith in me to believe God"? The two
become blurred.

What we see here, in other words, is a narrator challenging his
own text, giving his reader the tools to dismantle it but denying
her the right to use those tools. This is an act of textual violence
unprecedented among writers of medieval Saints' Lives, where a
St. Andrew, say, rises suddenly whole from three days' torture to
convert the Mermedonians or a St. Katherine endures her wheel
without apparent discomfort—all without authorial question. Nar-
rators of Saints' Lives never question miracles, and thus mystics
like Margery Kempe feel free to pattern their lives after their ideology, expecting similar miracles as those found in their texts. Yet
the Man of Law does—and often—so much so, in fact, that by the
last of the passages quoted above, the acute reader is anticipating
him in his metaphysical and narrative doubts. The genre of the
Saint's life here comes apart because the narrator constantly im-
poses on it, if only to deny them, the expectations of realistic
narrative. Used to the conventions of Saints' Lives, we would pass
by Custance's miraculous sustenence without a second thought,
but the narrator trips us up, points out the impossibility of the
situation, and then tells us to ignore that impossibility, trusting in
God. It is almost as if the Man of Law had been reading Kierkeg-
aard's *Fear and Trembling,* and not a long list of Chaucer's works,
before he went to bed back at the Tabard Inn the night before.

The cumulative effect of the Innocentian passages, where no joy after sorrow is possible, the antifeminist and Marian passages, which run counter to what we know of women and mothers in the tale, and the narrative attacks on the miraculous elements of his genre, which generate the reader's skepticism, is to unsettle the reader profoundly, forcing her into a rudderless narrative boat. This mimesis not only makes us identify on an unusually intense level with the heroine, but it also connects an out-of-control narrator with a God who seems so much out of control that he allows his faithful daughter Custance to suffer repeated miseries and never receive the secure, happy ending she deserves.

The Constable's despairing words before sending the innocent Custance once more out to sea are, I suggest, as central to the tale's meaning as the image of the rudderless boat explicated so forcefully by Kolve:[26]

> O myghty God, if that it be thy wille,
> Sith thou art rightful juge, how may it be
> That thou wolt suffren innocentz to spille,
> And wikked folk regne in prosperitee?
> O goode Custance, allas, so wo is me
> That I moot be thy tormentour, or deye
> On shames deeth; ther is noon oother weye.
>
> (II, 813–19)

This is a classic statement of that most disturbing of metaphysical problems—the existence of pain in a world created by a good God. Pseudo-Dionysius reminds us of the doubleness in ascribing that word to the deity; the Man of Law does the same on a purely narrative level. Metaphorically, the Constable's are the words of a critic about to send his reader onto the choppy interpretive seas of a narrative out of control. The missing Chaucerian translation of Innocent's devotional treatise is, I suggest, of first importance for understanding the Man of Law's Tale.

Some further words should be said here about the connections between Constance and medieval women mystics, for her powerlessness that paradoxically bespeaks control, even political control, is the normal province of the female saint in the Middle Ages. Briefly put, the paradigm is a simple one: deprived of power in the male-dominated Church, women often gained that power through powerlessness—passive visions, serious illnesses, and self-inflicted starvation.[27] This paradigm, moreover, is Pseudo-Dionysian in its simultaneous affirmation and denial of the meaning residing in the word *power*. Two brief examples before we take up this same matter again in our treatment of the Franklin's Tale should here suffice—those of Hildegard of Bingen and Catherine of Siena.

For Hildegard I must break biographical convention in my treatment of this very unconventional woman by starting a list of pertinent details about her not with her birth, but with her prenatal experiences.[28] Speaking about her gift of vision, she writes:

> In prima formatione mea, cum deus in utero matris mee spiraculo vita suscitavit me, visionem istam infixit anime mee.

> In my first formation, when in my mother's womb God raised me up with the breath of life, he fixed this [gift of] vision in my soul.[29]

Her spiritual precocity, manifest shortly after her birth in 1098, coupled with the doubtless more compelling fact that she was the tenth child born to the Rhenish nobleman Hildebert and his wife, Mechtild, led her parents to dedicate her to God at age seven by giving her over to the double monastery of Disibodenberg, near the town of Bingen on the Rhine. She lived cloistered until her death in 1179. Hers was a turbulent life by monastic standards, marked by her ascending to the abbessy in 1136, her removal in 1148 of her convent of nuns, against Abbot Kuno's wishes, from Disibodenberg to nearby Rupertsberg, her increasing fame as her visions became known outside of her monastery—occasioning such twelfth-century luminaries as St. Bernard, Emperor Friedrich Barbarossa, and Pope Eugenius III to become her correspondents and often seek her advice as a seer—and her courageous and successful fight against an unfair interdict imposed on her convent in 1178, the year before her death.

Silence and powerlessness were her means of trying to control things in the male-dominated world in which she lived. She fell seriously ill, for instance, at most important junctures of her life—before she went on preaching-tours, before she separated her nuns from Abbot Kuno's monks. When that last event took place, she gained Kuno's very reluctant permission by falling into a paralytic fit. Kuno came to her bedside and tried to lift her but could not, since she was so inert. In a fit of remorse he repented of his resistance; she rose miraculously from her bed and led her nuns away.

Catherine of Siena was, of course, much closer in time to Chaucer. There is no evidence that he encountered her during his mission to Italy in 1378, but she was certainly there and at the height of her considerable fame. She was born the twenty-third or -fourth (she was a twin) of twenty-five children, resisted all attempts of

her parents to marry her off, associated herself with the Dominican
Order as a kind of tertiary, fed and healed the sick in her home
town of Siena during the plague of 1374, and lived a life of such
rigorous aceticism that she starved herself to death in 1380, at the
significant age of thirty-three.[30] Her life was complex. Her resistance to marriage is a subject I have already mentioned and shall
take up again when I discuss the Franklin's Tale. Her long mystical
treatise, *The Dialogue* (translated into Middle English as *The Orcherd of Syon*), has earned her a place as one of the official doctors
of the Catholic church, but it need not long detain us here. One
short passage can give us the sense of control through passivity
that links her to Chaucer's Custance. God, in "dialogue" with Catherine, speaks to her:

> Therfore a soule, whanne sche purposeþ to loue me, he schal purpose
> oonli & sympely to suffre peynes for þe glorye of my name in wha-
> teuere maner, and for whateuere cause, I haue ordeyned hym to suffre.
> For pacyence is not preuyd but in peynes. And as it is seid bifore:
> Pacyence is oonyd to charite. Þerfore manly and myȝtily bereþ
> sych laburs.[31]

These words accurately describe the painful labors for God endured in patience by both Constance and Catherine herself. Catherine fell into a comalike trance in 1370—a "mystical death," she
called it—as a first response to political tensions, tried in 1375 to
convince warring factions in Italy to turn their martial energies to
the Holy Land in a crusade, was chosen by the city of Florence in
1376 to go to Avignon as an ambassador to help win the lifting of
an interdict, and persuaded Gregory XI in 1377 to return the papacy from Avignon to Rome. For all these actions her authority
was the passivity of her self-starvation and mystical trances.

Like Hildegard and Catherine, Chaucer's Custance exerts political power, but it is a Pseudo-Dionysian "power," affirming valency
to that word by denying it simultaneously in the loss of control of
mystic speech.

## The Clerk's Tale

Patient Griselda is, of course, Custance buffeted about not by a
silent God but by a silent husband.[32] As the Clerk himself acknowl-
edges, his source is the Latin version of the tale of patient Griselda
prepared by Francis Petrarch from the Italian exemplum that con-

cludes Giovanni Boccaccio's *Decameron*.[33] More properly, it is the
Clerk's adaptation of not only Petrarch's but also of an anonomous
French version, for his reveals an occasional word-by-word translation from the French.[34] Able critical hands have worked over Chaucer's additions and alterations of his sources and reveal him in
control of his materials, developing his own thesis about Griselda
and her demanding husband, the Marquis Walter.[35]

Briefly, what Chaucer really does to his source is add things
designed to make Griselda more vulnerable than she is in them
(the grim sergeant, for instance, who snatches away her children
is not so grim elsewhere) and to heighten the religious connotations
inherent in the tale. Chaucer's Clerk, for instance, adds the word
*grucche* to the dispute between Walter and his subjects over the
necessity of his marriage:[36] "And forthermoore," says Walter, "this
shal ye swere, that ye / Agayn my choys shul neither grucche ne
stryve" (IV, 169–70). Walter thus demands absolute control—control to the point of silencing his subjects. The "oxes stalle" promi-
nent in the tale (IV, 207, 291, 398) is reminiscent of the Nativity.[37]
Chaucer's additions, in fact, establish a paradox. As Alfred L.
Kellogg puts it,

> Walter is a composite of all the supernatural forces to which medieval
> man felt himself exposed. He is Fortune, raising aloft and casting down;
> stripping and clothing. He is Satan, making of the vicissitudes of For-
> tune appropriate temptations. He is God, the master of both, proving
> his creature, but always with her, urging against the act which would
> sever the bond between them, revealing ultimately that the world pos-
> sesses no reality.[38]

The word *grucche* is worth considering further. It was a decidedly political word in late Middle English, as it is in this passage:
in the midfifteenth century Richard, duke of York, used it do describe the attitude of malcontents during Cade's Rebellion.[39] Yet
the Clerk redirects the meaning of the word toward the personal
when he has Walter apply it to Griselda:

> I seye this: be ye redy with good herte
> To al my lust, and that I frely may,
> As me best thynketh, do yow laughe or smerte,
> And nevere ye to grucche it, nyght ne day?
>
> (IV, 351–54)

We are very close to both the general thesis and the individual
vocabulary of the anonymous Middle English treatise, *The Twelve*

*Profits of Tribulation,* a translation of Petrus Blesensis's *Douode-
cim utilitates tribulationis,* which, as I have already discussed, was
likely the treatise left in his will by Chaucer's friend Lewis Clifford
to Clifford's son-in-law Philip de la Vache under the title of a *Book
of Tribulation.*[40] The soul suffering from tribulation should accept
it as God-given, intended for her ultimate spiritual well being:

> þof þai [i. e., tribulations] ben sumtyme heuysome, nereþoles þei are
> to susteyne for god gladly & with-outen grucchyng: vmwhile þof a mon
> be sette agaynes tribulacions with grucchingis, þen he lettis his help-
> ers, & helpus his enmyes.[41]

We are close here to Kellogg's concept of Walter as God. Similarly,
in the anonymous *A Talking of the Love of God,* the word shifts
from the suffering soul to the suffering God. Addressing Jesus in
his Passion, the author writes:

> For aȝeyn alle schomes & serwes þat men duden þe, neuer ne opnedest
> þou þi mouþ to grucchen aȝeyn.[42]

To *grucchen* is the opposite of "to be silent": silence becomes the
proper response to God-given suffering. Walter/God sends tribula-
tions to Griselda/the soul/Jesus. Roles mix and merge.

The ultimate tribulation is, of course, death; there one must of
all times and places most avoid grucching. As *The Book of the
Craft of Dying* puts it,

> Therfor a man þat wyll dey well, yt is nedful þat he gruche not in no
> maner of seknesse þat fallyth to hym be-fore his deth or in hys dyinge,
> be yt neuer so paynefull or greuouse, lone tyme or schort tyme dur-
> ynge; for as seynt Gregory witnessith in his Morallys: Iusta sunt [cun-
> cta] que patimur, et ido valde iniustum est si de iusta passione
> murmuremus: All þingis þat we suffren we suffyr ryghtfully, & þerfor
> we ben vnryȝtfull yf we grucch of þat we suffer ryȝtfully. Than euery
> man schuld be pacient, [for] as seynt Luke seith: In paciencia vestra
> possidebitis animas vestras: In youre pacyence ye schull possesse
> youre soules; for [as] be pacience mannys soule is trewly had and kept,
> so be vnpacience & murmuracion it is loste & dampned, wittnessyng
> seynt Gregory in his omely þat seith þus: Regnum celorum nullus mur-
> murans accipit, nullus qui accipit murmurare potest, Ther schal no man
> haue þe kyngdom of heuen þat grucchith & is inpacient, and ther may
> no man gruch þat hath it.[43]

*Grucchyng* and *patience* are thus opposites. The latter is of course
Griselda's epithet, one that has raised her out of the literary fold

of Boccaccio, Petrarch, and Chaucer and has made her a cliché. Patient Griselda is such because, according to the witness of Middle English devotional writers, she does not grucch.

Not only is the word *grucch* worth analysis with attention to Middle English mystical writing, so is Griselda's ox's stall. In her first appearance in the Clerk's Tale, this detail from the Nativity story figures in prominently:[44]

> Amonges thise povre folk ther dwelte a man
> Which that was holden povrest of hem alle;
> But hye God somtyme senden kan
> His grace into a litel oxes stalle;
> Janicula men of that throop hym calle.
> A doghter hadde he, fair ynogh to sighte,
> And Grisildis this yonge mayden highte.
>
> (IV, 204–10)

There is, of course, a Pseudo-Dionysian attitude here toward the word *poor—povre*. Like the poverty attending the Christ child and his mother, another "yonge mayden," this poverty signifies through the *via negativa* its opposite.

In the late- fifteenth-century *Tretyse of Loue,* a Middle English translation of an earlier French treatise that, in turn, is largely an expansion of some passages from the *Ancrene Riwle,* we have a Nativity scene very much evocative of Chaucer's Griselda:

Parauentur it was first, and the pure vyrgyne mary grete wyth chylde, and wente to seke sum place wher she myght reste hyr. She was so wery of the gret trauayle that she hath in walkynge moche of that day tell it was nye nyght, and wyst not whether to go, sauf at the ende of the town was ij hye walles of rokkes, and thys pytous wery vyrgyne entryd ther and founde an oxe and an asse teyed ther. . . . Now I pray yow, ryght dere sustyr, remembyr yow stedfastly whanne ye lye in your large softe bed . . . how she that was the quene of angellys and Empresse of all þe worlde, how hyr bed was streyght and harde and aryed wyth pore clothys. . . . [45]

The analogue with Griselda appears even closer as we progress through the Clerk's Tale. The Clerk comments of "this newe markysesse" that it did not seem as if

> she was born and fed in rudenesse,
> As in a cote or in an oxe-stalle,
> But norissed in an emperoures halle.
>
> (IV, 397–99)

This "Empress," later stripped and sent home, walks back to her ox's stall in a manner not unlike the Virgin of the *Tretyse of Loue* (IV, 894–900). The Empress walking in poverty is as much the central image of this tale as Constance's rudderless boat is for that of the Man of Law, and it is Pseudo-Dionysian in its very essence.

An analysis of two stanzas from the tale should indicate further the Clerk's methods. At the beginning of part 2, the Clerk explains why Walter decides to test his wife:

> Ther fil, as it bifalleth tymes mo,
> Whan that this child had souked but a throwe,
> This markys in his herte longeth so
> To tempte his wyf, hir sadnesse for to knowe,
> That he ne myghte out of his herte throwe
> This merveillous desir his wyf t'assaye;
> Nedelees, God wot, he thoghte hire for t'affraye.
>
> Hee hadde assayed hire ynogh bifore,
> And foond hire evere good; what neded it
> Hire for to tempte, and alwey moore and moore,
> Though som men preise it for a subtil wit?
> But as for me, I seye that yvele it sit
> To assaye a wyf whan that it is no nede,
> And putten hire in angwyssh and in drede.
>
> (IV, 449–62)

Much that is here is either altered from or added to the source, giving us the composite figure of Walter as God, as Satan, as Fortune. The English *tempte* is a word of theological importance lacking in Petrarch's participle *experiende,* simply, "trying, testing." A similar word lacking in theological content is the anonymous Old French *essaier,* "to try, to test"—exactly the meaning of the Latin.[46] Also absent from the sources is the idea that Walter has already tempted his wife enough.[47]

The persistent adjective, moreover, that the Clerk uses to describe Griselda, *sad*—here present in its nominal form, *sadnesse*— is not merely, as editors of Chaucer tell us, the Middle English word for "serious" or "constant;"[48] it is a specifically religious word, here missing in the Old French and changing significantly the direction of Petrarch's "fidem."[49] In Middle English prose devotional treatises, *sad* often defines a person's relationship to God: "constant" and "serious" are adequate translations only if run through the particularly religious filter of "devout." The author of *A Tretise of Ghostly Battle,* for instance, as part of the allegory of

the warrior's horse that I considered briefly in the section about
the Reeve's horse, advises the spiritual knight to sit "sadly" on the
saddle. This means "constantly" or "securely" on a literal level but
"devoutly" on the level of the allegory:

> The styropes of hys sadylle shalle be lownes and sadnes; lownes ayenst
> pryde, and sadnes ayenst worldly couetyse and flesshly lustis; so that
> thow be nat [to] sory for no wo, ne to glad for no wele ne welfare. Now
> syt sadly in thys sadylle and kepe well thy styroppys, that for no pryde
> off strengthe, off byrthe, off fayrnes, off kunnyng, or ryches, or any
> vertew that gode hath sent the other bodyly or gostly, thow be not cast
> owte off thy styroppes off lownes and sadnes.[50]

Significant is the list of "names" that the stirrups of lowness and
sadness deny: they are an exact description of Walter by nature,
potentially Griselda by his election.

*Contemplations of the Dread and Love of God,* roughly contemporary with *The Canterbury Tales,* moreover, uses *sad* repeatedly
in this manner:

> For many men & women there be that whyle they be in prosperyte /
> that is to say / whyle they be in welth & in rest gladly they wyll shewe
> loue to god suche as they can, But yf god sendeth hym ony dysease
> or ony maner of chastysynge anone her loue swageth & that is no
> sadde loue.[51]

The situation here is roughly equivalent to that in the Clerk's Tale,
with Walter in God's position and Griselda in the sad believer's.
God sends prosperity but also "disease" ( = distress) and chastising
and demands sadness in return. The "drede" (IV, 462) that Walter
inspires in Griselda also has its religious meaning. As the late-
fourteenth- or early fifteenth-century Middle English translation
of the visions the twelfth-century Benedictine nun Mechtild of
Hackeborn has it:

> Than to this maydens semynge oure lorde delfede in þe erth in lyknes
> of a gardynere. Þis maydene sayde þan to oure lorde: "Lorde, whate
> es þy delfynge instrumente?" Oure lorde sayde: "Itt is my drede."[52]

Or as the author of *Contemplations of the Dread and Love of
God* explains,

> Drede, as clerkes haue wryten before this tyme is in many maners. . . .
> The fyrst is drede of man or drede of the worlde. . . . The thyrde is

called a chasted [*sic*] drede or a frendely drede. The fyrst whiche is drede of man or of the worlde is / whan a man or woman dredeth more the punysshynge of the worlde as betynges the body or prysonynge than the punysshynge of the soule. Also whan a man dredeth more to lese his temporall goodes in this passynge worlde than to lese the blysse without ende. . . . / The thyrde drede . . . [is] whan he dredeth that god wyll go fro hym / as peraduenture he withdraweth his grace fro hym. Also when he dredeth to dysplese god for the grete loue & desyre þ[at] he hath for to please god / suche drede cometh of loue & that pleaseth moche god.[53]

Again, this is the same situation as that in the Clerk's Tale: Griselda's dread, which involves less fear for worldly goods than for Walter's displeasure, as he seemingly withdraws his grace from her, much pleases Walter at the tale's close.

Dread is a common theme among the Middle English mystics. In the allegorical *Abbey of the Holy Ghost,* for instance, the personification Dread is the porter of the abbey's gate,[54] while in the related piece, *The Charter of the Abbey of the Holy Ghost,* Christ goes about seeking the dispersed sisters of the despoiled abbey and finds Dread in the garden of Gethsemane.[55] This abbey is, of course, situated in "a place that es callede conscyence";[56] the quality "dread" should thus be part of every person's moral makeup. Yet there is no mention of Griselda's dread in either Petrarch or the anonymous French version of the tale.

These alterations of the source heighten Walter's power, elevating it almost to either a demonic or a divine level. But if he is in some sense a God, he is one that is out of control: "he ne myghte out of his herte throwe / This merveillous desir his wyf t'asseye" (IV, 453–54). In other words, he cannot control in himself his desire to control. We find this comment in neither Petrarch nor the French. Walter, as archcontroller, demands and gets his will without demur throughout the tale, yet he lacks control over himself: his continued temptations of Griselda are a compulsion.

His method of control is silence.[57] We have already seen how he silences any grucching from either his subjects or his wife. Almost all his doings have such an aura of silence about them. He processes to Janicula's cottage without his retinue knowing his destination or the identity of his bride (IV, 267 73). He silences his people after the announcement of his surprise choice:

> This is my wyf," quod he, "that standeth heere.
> Honoureth hire and loveth hire, I preye,
> Whoso me loveth; ther is namoore to seye."

(IV, 369–71)

His reason for apparently murdering his daughter is the silence he
desires from both his wife and his grucching subjects (who of
course are not grucching). He tells Griselda,

> But I desire, as I have doon bifore,
> To lyve my lyf with hem in reste and pees.
> . . . . . . . . . . . . .
> I moot doon with thy doghter for the beste,
> Nat as I wolde, but as my peple leste.
>
> (IV, 486–87, 489–90)

Griselda responds in kind: "she noght ameved / Neither in word,
or chiere, or contenaunce" (IV, 498–99), while Walter responds in
turn to her with a silence obscuring his motives: "Glad was this
markys of hire answeryng, / But yet he feyned as he were nat so"
(IV, 512–13). The sergeant he sends to abduct the daughter is in
this respect Walter's simulacrum:

> He [Walter] prively hath toold al his entente
> Unto a man, and to his wyf hym sente.
>
> A maner sergeant was this privee man.
> . . . . . . . . . . . . .
> Into the chambre he stalked hym ful stille.
>
> (IV, 517–19, 25)

The adjective describing Walter's explanation transposes into the
adjective describing his henchman, who presently borrows Walter's own words to silence Griselda: "ther is namoore to seye" (IV,
532). Griselda embraces this way of socializing within the Clerk's
Tale and stays as mum as silly John in his tub: "And as a lamb she
sitteth meke and stille / And leet this sergeant doon his wille"
(IV, 538–39). The biblical allusion, absent in both Petrarch and
the French, is to Isaiah 53:7, a verse universally understood as a
prophesy of Christ before Pilate:

> Oblatus est quia ipse voluit,
> Et non aperuit os suum;
> Sicut ovis ad occisionem ducetur,
> Et quasi agnus coram tondente se obmutescet,
> Et non aperiet os suum.

> Harshly dealt with, he bore it humbly,
> he never opened his mouth,
> like a lamb that is led to the slaughter-house
> like a sheep that is dumb before its shearers
> never opening its mouth.

Even more significant than the allusion,[58] however, is the rhyme linking a word of silence with a word of control: "stille" / "wille." One could prolong the discussion of silence among Walter, the sergeant, and Griselda, where each imitates the other[59] (see IV, 545, 573, 580, 582, 601, and 606), but the point remains the same: the means of control and the response to it are alike silence and the result the fragmentation of the ducal family.

If Walter seeks to control with silence, the Clerk seeks to control with words. The whole point, in fact, of the Clerk's Prologue is the establishing of a dichotomy between silence and rhetoric:

> "Sire Clerk of Oxenford," oure Hooste sayde,
> "Ye ryde as coy and stille as dooth a mayde
> Were newe spoused, sittynge at bord;
> This day ne herde I of youre tonge a word."
>
> (IV, 1–4)

Out of the silence between Fragments III and IV come the words of the Host about silence. Here the connection between the Clerk and his heroine—both still, silent young brides—is evident. Out of his own silence comes the Clerk, who paradoxically submits to and rebels against Harry Bailly's control with words. The Host addresses him:

> "Telle us som murie thyng of aventures.
> Youre termes, youre colours, and youre figures,
> Keepe hem in stoor til so be that ye endite
> Heigh style, as whan that men to kynges write.
> Speketh so pleyn at this tyme, we yow preye,
> That we may understonde what ye seye."
> This worthy clerk benignely answerde:
> "Hooste," quod he, "I am under youre yerde;
> Ye han of us as now the governance."
>
> (IV, 15–23)

Almost immediately the Clerk, in the guise of compliance, grucches against the archcontroller, and commences a tale full of the very rhetorical furniture the Host inveighs against. He announces the source of his tale:

Fraunceys Petrak, the lauriat poete,
Highte this clerk, whos rethorike sweete
Enlumyned al Ytaille of poetrie.

. . . . . . . . . . .

But forth to tellen of this worthy man
That taughte me this tale, as I bigan,
I seye that first with heigh stile he enditeth.

(IV, 31–33, 39–41)

What follows is not the merry tale the Host requires. To emphasize this, the Clerk, near the end, repeats his words: "therfore Petrak writeth / This storie, which with heigh stile he enditeth" (IV, 1147–48). Where Griselda submits to her arch-controller with silence, the Clerk resists his with the high style of rhetoric.[60]

If the Clerk chooses the opposite means as his character Griselda, he and his character Walter are in some ways alike. Walter is a hunter; the Clerk takes pains to emphasize that he is as well: "But shortly forth this matere for to chace" (IV, 341) and its almost exact repetition, "And shortly forth this tale for to chace" (IV, 393), both connect the act of narration with Walter's premarital favorite pastime, for to "chace" of course is Old French Englished for the verb to "hunt." As Walter refuses to submit his will to that of his people in choosing a noble wife, the Clerk refuses to submit to Harry Bailly's will in choosing a merry tale. Walter answers with low-born Griselda, the Clerk with Francis Petrarch's high-born rhetoric. Like many of the tellers of tales, the Clerk too sinks into his tale.

## The Second Nun's Tale

Like the other tellers explicated in this chapter the Second Nun tells a tale with the hallmarks of the Good Woman genre: rhyme royal treatment of a victim whose fragmented life bespeaks utter control through the lack of it. Saint Cecelia's dossier contains a fragmented marriage, a fragmented life ended through a curiously fragmented execution, the passive death of a martyr, and her dominance of those about her based on that passivity, the last of course the hallmark of the medieval woman mystic.

At first she exerts control, like Custance, through silence:

The nyght cam, and to bedde moste she gon
With hir housbonde, as ofte is the manere,
And pryvely to hym she seyde anon,

> "O sweete and wel biloved spouse deere,
> Ther is a conseil, and ye wolde it heere,
> Which that right fayn I wolde unto yow seye,
> So that ye swere ye shal it nat biwreye."
>
> (VIII, 141–47)

We can almost imagine Nicholas uttering these words. The secretive time of night has come; she speaks to him "pryvely" and enjoins him not to tell her counsel to anyone else. She is, moreover, passive, enduring the marriage bed as she will later endure execution. In fact, the movement of this stanza is a microcosm of the movement of the tale as a whole. She is passive, controlled at the beginning, with some unnamed force—her parents? Valerian? God? Fate? custom?—making her do something ("to bedde moste she gon"). Then she passes through silence finally to exert control with words. And the control that she exerts with her words is Pseudo-Dionysian, for she simultaneously negates and affirms the referentiality of names. "Sweet and wel biloved," names usually used in an earthly context[61] shift to their heavenly meaning—that is, sweet and well beloved to God, and "spouse" takes on a spiritual meaning possibly reminiscent of that in the Song of Songs. The Pseudo-Dionysian shift here is what fragments Cecelia's marriage, for of course the counsel is to lead a celibate life together.

The fragmentation of the marriage infects the main characters' lives. For instance, Cecelia's major reason to remain chaste is prophetic of later events in the Tale. There is an angel, she tells Valerian, who will defend her against his sexual advances:

> And if that he may feelen, out of drede,
> That ye me touche, or love in vileynye,
> He right anon wol sle yow with the dede,
> And in youre yowthe thus ye shullen dye.
>
> (VIII, 155–58)

(I have already discussed Margery Kempe's imitation of this type of marriage, with her overt threats against John Kempe's life.) The logic of the Second Nun's Tale, moreover, is in danger here as well. If the main argument to submit to a celibate marriage and convert to Christianity is to avoid being cut down in his youth, then Valerian gets sorely duped: he is cut down in his youth regardless— *because* he has led a celibate marriage and converted to Christianity. The fragmentation of his marriage is the cause of the fragmentation of his life, as it is of his wife, Cecelia, and his brother, Tiberius, whom the couple later convert.

Almost everything in the Second Nun's Tale seems fragmentary. Characters who seem important either disappear, leaving only a trace—the angel so solicitous of Cecelia's virginity, the old man who expounds doctrine to the postulant Valerian (VIII, 210–17)— or avoid taking much part in the denoument—Pope Urban who is almost culpably offstage while the best sheep in his flock are being slaughtered, as he is not in the *Legenda Aurea,* the source for the tale.[62]

The most curious of these narrative fragmentations, though, is Cecelia's execution. After being boiled in a hot bath—miraculously, with little effect—she must be beheaded:

> Thre strokes in the nekke he smoot hire tho,
> The tormentour, but for no maner chaunce
> He myghte noght smyte al hir nekke atwo;
> And for ther was that tyme an ordinaunce
> That no man sholde doon man swich penaunce
> The ferthe strook to smyten, softe or soore,
> This tormentour ne dorste do namoore.
>
> (VIII, 526–32)

Instead of finishing his job and severing her head from the body, the executioner leaves it, presumably only half cut off—a fragmentation fragmented. But more importantly, this opens up narrative vistas that soon become clouded, for she has now by law escaped further punishment and—if she recover—is free to continue living her devout life. But she does not. She dies three days later, after giving instructions for the building of a church on the site of her house.

The fragmentations besetting individual characters in the tale affect the narrator's control over her materials. By this I mean that there are large gaps left out entirely. The narrator devotes much time and space to three narrative episodes—the conversion of Valerian, the conversion of Tiberius, and the judicial encounter between Cecelia and the prefect Almachius. We have long speeches, many details, adequate motivation. But an episode seemingly deserving of much attention is only barely summarized—the martyrdom of two of the three main characters, Valerian and Tiberius:

> But whan they weren to the place broght
> To tellen shortly the conclusioun,
> They nolde encense ne sacrifise right noght,
> But on hir knees they setten hem adoun

With humble herte and sad devocioun,
And losten bothe hir hevedes in the place.
Hir soules wenten to the Kyng of grace.

(VIII, 393–98)

Note the language drawn from not only devotional prose but also
the Clerk's Tale: "with . . . sad devocioun." When we compare
these martyrdoms to that of Cecelia, we see the quick movement
of what is otherwise a slowly developing plot. It is difficult to avoid
the impression that something important has been cut out here.
The voices of the main characters, especially Cecelia's, are silent.

Cecelia, though, is the least silent of Chaucer's good women
in *The Canterbury Tales*. She is the one who most controls her
circumstances through language. We have already seen that she
initially must speak "prively" to Valerian about the delibidinizing
of their marriage. She does use words, though, but she is not yet
the aggressive logocentrix she becomes by the end of the tale.[63]
She gets off, in other words, to a slow verbal start. At first she
even needs Pope Urban to speak for her. After flagging Valerian's
epithalamic ardor with the threat of angelic violence, she significantly sends him away to another rather than use her own words
to convert him:

"If that yow list, the angel shul ye see,
So that ye trowe on Crist and yow baptize.
Gooth forth to Via Apia," quod shee,
"That fro this toun ne stant but miles three,
And to the povre folkes that ther dwelle,
Sey hem right thus, as that I shal yow telle.

"Telle hem that I, Cecile, yow to hem sente
To shewen yow the goode Urban the olde,
For secree nedes and for good entente.
And whan that ye Seint Urban han biholde,
Telle hym the wordes whiche I to yow tolde."

(VIII, 170–80)

Secrecy still clings to Cecelia's words, but she is becoming more
aggressive with them, giving them away to Valerian, instructing
him about what he should say. But Urban and the mysterious old
man are the ones who announce the Word of God to Valerian,
not Cecelia.

But later—with Urban offstage, doubtless in his secret hiding
place—Cecelia becomes the evangelist, outspeaking her judge Al-

machius by an impressive margin.[64] One section of the debate between the two is worth quoting not only as an example of the
relative verbal quantity of the two but also as a further example of
Cecelia's Pseudo-Dionysian attitudes about language. Almachius
speaks to her:

> "Unsely wrecche,
> Ne woostow nat how fer my myght may strecche?
>
> "Han noght oure myghty princes to me yiven,
> Ye, bothe power and auctoritee
> To maken folk to dyen or to lyven?
> Why spekestow so proudly thanne to me?"
> "I speke noght but stedfastly," quod she;
> "Nat proudly, for I seye, as for my syde,
> We haten deedly thilke vice of pryde.
>
> "And if thou drede nat a sooth to heere,
> Thanne wol I shewe al openly, by right,
> That thou hast maad a ful gret lesyng heere.
> Thou seyst thy princes han thee yeven myght
> Bothe for to sleen and for to quyken a wight;
> Thou, that ne mayst but oonly lyf bireve,
> Thou hast noon oother power ne no leeve.
>
> "But thou mayst seyn thy princes han thee maked
> Ministre of deeth; for if thou speke of mo,
> Thou lyest, for thy power is ful naked."
>
> (VIII, 468–86)

Now Cecelia's language is no longer secret, given to others, or
directing others to secret places; it is public ("Thanne wol I shewe
al openly") and aggressive, wrenching Almachius's words from
what he thinks are their fixed referents and, through Pseudo-
Dionysian doubling, investing them with different a meaning, one
that signifies on a spiritual rather than earthly level. His "proudly"
becomes her "stedfastly"; his "power"—an arrogation of control—
becomes her "power . . . ful naked"—a divesting of that control. Cecelia throws a wedge between Almachius's signifier and
signified.[65]
   We are reminded of the injunction in *The Cloud of Unknowing:*

> & þus me þinkeþ þat it nediþ greetly to haue moche warnes in vnders-
> tonding of wordes þat ben spokyn to goostly entent, so þat þou con-
> ceyue hem not bodily, bot goostly.[66]

St. Cecelia enjoins such great care upon Almachius to interpret her spiritual words correctly; this spiritual redirection of the valency of words, Pseudo-Dionysian in its origin, is one of the strongest characteristics of mystic speech. The author of Chaucer's friend Lewis Clifford's book, *The Twelve Profits of Tribulation*, for instance, compares earthly and spiritual love:

> And if perauenture þou playne þe þat þis glading taries ouer-mykel, as playnen þese loouers: here answeris Cassiodor, sayand þat þo selue swiftnesse semes slownesse to þo hert þat is desyrande & louande.[67]

Or Julian of Norwich can write near the beginning of her *Revelations* of "þe precious amendes that he [Jesus] hath made for mans synne, turnyng all our blame in to endlesse worshippe."[68] God's lover St. Cecelia experiences the valency of words differently than Almachius, for she wrenches them into new meanings.

But we should not overlook the emergence of this open and aggressive language from a privy place, for it originates in Urban's *hid divinitee,* as we find out from Tiberius, who is initially suspicious of seeking the outlaw Pope in his hideout. He speaks to his brother Valerian:

> "Ne menestow nat Urban," quod he tho,
> "That is so ofte dampned to be deed,
> And woneth in halkes alwey to and fro,
> And dar nat ones putte forth his heed?
> Men sholde hym brennen in a fyr so reed
> If he were founde, or that men myghte hym spye,
> And we also, to bere hym compaignye;
>
> "And whil we seken thilke divinitee
> That is yhid in hevene pryvely,
> Algate ybrend in this world shul we be!"
>
> (VIII, 309–18)

We see Urban from two perspectives: pastor of a Christian flock and an outlaw condemned to death. More important, though, is the provocative phrase "Divinitee / That is yhid . . . pryvely"—a possible direct reference to Pseudo-Dionysius's treatise *Mystical Theology,* translated by the *Cloud*-author as *Deonise Hid Diunite.* The Latin source for this phrase in the *Legenda Aurea* is *diuinitatem latentem,*[69] literally "secret divinity," close enough to "hid divinity" to allow here for coincidence. But the coincidence is a striking one, nevertheless, given Cecelia's immediate Pseudo-Dionysian double perspective on Tiberius's names:

> To whom Cecile answerde boldely,
> "Men myghten dreden wel and skilfully
> This lyf to lese, myn owene deere brother,
> If this were lyvynge oonly and noon oother.
>
> "But ther is bettre lif in oother place."
>
> (VIII, 319–23)

She divests Tiberius's word *life* of its meaning, simultaneously affirming and denying its validity, finally redefining it from God's perspective. To use Pseudo-Dionysian shorthand, *life* becomes *superlife,* something so far above life that the word in Neoplatonic return loses its referent. The gap between signifier and signified here is moreover mimetically accompanied by a gap between stanzas, as the old meaning is denied in the last line of one stanza before the new meaning is affirmed in the first line of the next.

# 6
## Other Women

### The Merchant's Tale

From a certain perspective, the Merchant's Tale is about language. When the narrator comments on January's lovely paraphrase of the Song of Songs with the brutal and blunt "Swiche olde lewed wordes used he" (IV, 2149), he, as Douglas A. Berger writes, "places special stress on speech itself, calls attention to words as words in order to demonstrate the disjunction between them and reality."[1] From another perspective, the Merchant's Tale is about perspective. As an old critical controversy made clear, from the point of view of the tale itself, it is a comic fabliau not too different from the Miller's Tale,[2] yet from the point of view of the framework, that is, the Merchant's laconic invective against his own young wife, the tale is a bitter, grim comment on marriage, indeed on life itself.[3] As has been adequately shown, the controversy is reconcilable, either by assuming that Chaucer and the Merchant share the same voice,[4] carefully delineating irony (Chaucer's) from sarcasm (the Merchant's),[5] or separating the seriousness of the tale from the Merchant and his problems.[6] I suggest that another way to mediate between the funny and repulsive aspects of the Merchant's Tale is to realize that language is spoken in context: a tale about an adulterous woman in the mouth of a man not cuckolded (like, we assume, the Miller) can produce a woman if not exactly good at least attractive, yet in the mouth of one with marital woes, it will create a woman distinctly bad. One need not perhaps suggest here that this doubling is at least analogously Pseudo-Dionysian. Yet from the three major perspectives of the tale—January's, May's, and the Merchant's own—language means different things and, significantly, alters in different ways.

For January, speech originally is a way of controlling a world that is slipping rapidly out of his control. He is an aging lecher who needs help from aphrodisiacs (see IV, 1807–12) and will soon be blind. He seeks marriage as a way of continuing his sexual exploits in a manner approved by Church and society:

> And sixty yeer a wyflees man was hee,
> And folwed ay his bodily delyt
> On wommen. . . .
>
> . . . . . . .
> . . . but swich a greet corage
> Hadde this knyght to been a wedded man
> That day and nyght he dooth al that he kan
> T'espien where he myghte wedded be,
> Preyinge oure Lord to graunten him that he
> Mighte ones knowe of thilke blisful lyf
> That is bitwixe an housbonde and his wyf,
> And for to lyve under that hooly boond
> With which that first God man and womman bond.
>
> (IV, 1248–50, 1254–62)

His daily and nightly attempts at marriage are entirely verbal, consisting of speeches to himself or to others about the wisdom of his decision. The long (129 lines) paraphrase, spiced by an occasional direct quotation, of his self-addressed profeminist argument, however undercut by ironic references to such treacherous women as Eve and Rebecca (IV, 1263–1392), is followed by a long speech to his friends (IV, 1400–1468).

His relationship to May, once she is procured, is likewise mainly verbal: at the wedding feast he speaks to her for the first time:

> . . . Allas! O tendre creature,
> Now wolde God ye myghte wel endure
> Al my corage, it is so sharp and keene!
> I am agast ye shul it nat susteene.
> But God forbede that I dide al my myght!
> Now wolde God that it were woxen nyght,
> And that the nyght wolde lasten everemo.
> I wolde that al this peple were ago.
>
> (IV, 1757–64)

Note that the first word he speaks to her is a significant "alas." His overconfidence in his sexual vigor (or his aphrodisiacs) is undercut by the helpless subjunctive cast of his verbiage—would that it were night, would that we were alone. When those two necessities are realized and the two are abed, what follows is not sharp *corage* scarcely sustained (the only "sharp" aspect of his physical vigor will be the bristles of his beard), but an even longer speech, beginning with the same helpless word, a word of power-lessness, of impotence:

> . . . Allas! I moot trespace
> To yow, my spouse, and yow greetly offende
> Er tyme come that I wil doun descende.
>
> (IV, 1828–30)

It begins like this and goes on for another ten lines before ending up in bad medieval theology and a metaphor as muddled as his subsequent sexual performance:

> A man may do no synne with his wyf,
> Ne hurte hymselven with his owen knyf,
> For we han leve to pleye us by the lawe.
>
> (IV, 1839–41)

As more than one critic has pointed out, the Parson, writing his devotional treatise, later gets both the theology and the proverb straight:[7]

And for that many man weneth that he may nat synne for no likerousn-esse that he dooth with his wyf, certes, that opinion is fals. God woot, a man may sleen hymself with his owene knyf, and maken hymselve dronken of his owene tonne. (X, 858)

Significant also is the evolution of rhyme: the earlier "lyf" / "wyf" (IV, 1259–60) becomes, given the subsequent marital doings, the prophetic "wyf" / "knyf," a rhyme reconfirmed in the first speech January utters upon entering his garden: "Levere ich hadde to dyen on a knyf / Than thee offende, trewe deere wyf!" (IV, 2163–64). In this chiasm, the third term threatens the first, through the media-tion of the second.

January's verbiage continues unabated until almost the end. It is unnecessary to quote or summarize all his speeches to his wife (IV, 1855–56, 1899–1901, 1920–28, 2138–48, 2160–84, 2338–40, 2346–47); what is important is that May does not speak to him at all until line 2188, from which point the amount of words they trade is fairly even. For most of their married life, in other words, January does all the talking. He never, it seems, shuts up.

But the sounds coming from his mouth do at one point change drastically. After gaining his sight only to see May in the midst of her compromising and rather acrobatic activities with Damian in the pear tree, his speech does not subside into silence but into loud and inarticulate noise:

> Up to the tree he caste his eyen two,
> And saugh that Damyan his wyf had dressed
> In swich manere it may nat been expressed,
> But if I wolde speke uncurteisly;
> And up he yaf a roryng and a cry,
> As dooth the mooder whan the child shal dye:
> "Out! Help! Allas! Harrow!" he gan to crye,
> "O stronge lady stoore, what dostow?"
>
> (IV, 2360–67)

The bellows meet their match in the inarticulate words of the last line, where "stronge" is uttered instead of an intended "straunge" and "stoore" wrenched out of its normal lexical context. Words, Pseudo-Dionysian or not, lose meaning. January's verbal movement, in other words, is from constant speeches to an incoherent roar—all at loud volume. Where sound first meant control, it now signifies chaos.

Before I analyze May's opposite verbal movement, it would be well to investigate the Merchant's, for in some ways he shares the same verbal turf with his character January. He is among the most intrusive of Chaucer's tellers, often referring to himself as a teller within the tale (see, for instance, IV, 2350–51 and 2363); he is more than matched in this by the Knight and the Squire, who constantly control—or try to—their material with authorial intrusions explaining omissions in their texts, but none of the other tellers of fabliaux intrudes as much as the Merchant. His paraphrase of January's rationalizing, moreover, is as much his irony as his character's self-deception: he can dominate all his characters with his verbiage, submerging their words in his own (as he does in the long opening speech about the joys of marriage) as much as January dominates May.

What is even more important, I feel, is the flabby, wordy, euphemistic nature of much of what he has to say. When May disposes her love letter in a place as offensive to our olfactory nerves as to our expectations of courtly love, for instance, he describes it as "Ther as ye woot that every wight moot neede" (IV, 1951)—a marvelous if cumbersome circumlocution.[8] If this were not enough, his euphemisms accelerate to the point where they barely communicate at all, as in his description of January's reason for his turning love making into an outdoor sport:

> In somer seson, thider [i.e., into his walled garden] wolde he go,
> And May his wyf, and no wight but they two;
> And thynges whiche that were nat doon abedde,
> He in the gardyn parfourned hem and spedde.
>
> (IV, 2049–52)

The comedy, of course, is that the enclosed garden is a staple of mystical literature, where it is commonly a metaphor for the Blessed Virgin, as it is in *The Mirour of Mans Saluacioune:*

> Forsoth, Marye, thow ert gardin of alle swettenesse,
> And well of sawles witt, euer flowyng in fulnesse.[9]

What are these things that January does in his garden? We do not know, for he euphemizes; we are, I think, grateful for it.

Such euphemisms strain language to the breaking point, fitting the Pseudo-Dionysian wedge between signified and signifier. The break actually comes at the climax of the tale:

> He [January] stoupeth doun, and on his bak she stood,
> And caughte hire by a twiste, and up she gooth—
> Ladyes, I prey yow that ye be nat wrooth;
> I kan nat glose, I am a rude man—
> And sudeynly anon this Damyan
> Gan pullen up the smok, and in he throng.
>
> (IV, 2348–53)

As January moves from words to an inarticulate roar, the Merchant moves from wordy euphemism to the bluntest of words.[10] But the point is that the Merchant really can "glose": he has been doing it all along, and within nine lines he is doing it again, glossing the verb *thringen* with another euphemistic gem: "Damyan his wyf had dressed / In swich manere it may nat been expressed, / But if I wolde speke uncurteisly" (IV, 2361–63). We hear a faint yet devastating echo of Pseudo-Dionysius, who defined for the Middle Ages the limits of the inexpressible.

The Merchant here shares some attitudes about language with the most Pseudo-Dionysian of the Middle English mystics, the *Cloud*-author. In his *Book of Privy Counselling,* he writes:

> trewly I tell þee þat ʒif a soule, þat is þus ocupied [i.e., in contempla-
> tion], had tonge & langage to sey as it feliþ, þan alle þe clerkes of
> Cristendome schuld wondre on þat wisdam. ʒe! & in comparison of

it, al here grete clergie schuld seme apeerte foly. & þerfore no wondre þof I kan not telle þee þe worþines of þis werk wiþ my boystouse beestly tonge. & God forbede þat it scholde be so defoulid in it-self for to be streynid vnder þe steringes of a fleschly tonge![11]

The clergy are the ones who, to use the Merchant's word, *glose;* language fails them, the *Cloud*-author, and the Merchant. The *Cloud*-author's beastly and fleshly tongue that cannot express spiritual things has its antitype in that of the Merchant, who laments his lack of refined language to express the beastly and the fleshly. Chaucer's comedy is all the more apparent when placed in the context of mystic speech.

If the verbal movements of January and the Merchant run in certain ways parallel, May's does not. She emerges from long and deep silence into a speech that qualifies her as an archcontroller. That emergence is, moreover, what signals the increasing moral degeneracy noted by so many critics[12] and qualifying her as one of Chaucer's "bad" women.

Her initial silence is more than merely verbal: we never know anything about her, except that she is "fresh." Her looks, her age, her dress—things important for other young women in *The Canterbury Tales* like, for instance, Emelye and Alisoun—are missing.[13] The one meager description is not of her at all—only January's thought about an ideal bride not yet specifically May, and it does not come until about four hundred lines of the tale have elapsed:

> He purtreyed in his herte and in his thoght
> Hir fresshe beautee and hir age tendre,
> Hir myddel smal, hire armes longe and sklendre,
> Hir wise governaunce, hir gentillesse,
> Hir womanly berynge, and her sadnesse.
>
> (IV, 1600–1604)[14]

In the ambiguous trace this silence creates (that is, does May conform to these qualities?), we may, if we are so inclined, idealize her—not only in beauty but with sadness—the devotion and constancy we have seen in prose devotional treatises and have associated with good women like Patient Griselda. The Pseudo-Dionysian doubling, of course, is here: these lines simultaneously do and do not describe May. Her reaction to January's similarly chaotic attempts at lovemaking is similar: "The bryde was broght abedde as stille as stoon" (IV, 1818).[15] After January's nuptial performance, the narrator wryly comments:

> But God woot what that May thoughte in her herte,
> Whan she hym saugh up sittynge in his sherte,
> In his nyght-cappe, and with his nekke lene;
> She preyseth nat his pleyyng worth a bene.
>
> (IV, 1851–54)

The last line is significantly ambiguous: in the trace it leaves, we get the impression that she had complained about his lovemaking, denigrating it as worthless, but what the narrator has said is, simply, that she was silent.

Her silence continues well into their marriage and well into her maneuverings with Damian. The would-be lovers pass letters to each other—silent communication, at times described adverbially with words like "prively" (IV, 1879) and "secrely" (IV, 2006). How she disposes of her letter from Damian is remarkable not only for its dismantling of the expectations of courtly love, not only for the Merchant's euphemism, but also for her silence:

> She feyned hire as that she moste gon
> Ther as ye woot that every wight moot neede;
> And whan she of this bille hath taken heede,
> She rente it al to cloutes atte laste,
> And in the pryvee softely it caste.
>
> (IV, 1950–55)

Before she ever speaks we are prepared for the lies that will tumble out of her mouth. Here she first feigns and then, to borrow parlance from more recent times and more political contexts, shreds the incriminating document. Words silent because written are, in a compelling symbol, fragmented and then sent "softely"[16]—a glorious word of many connotations, including "silently"—into a "pryvee," a noun constructed from Chaucer's favorite adjective and adverb describing silent nouns and silent verbs.

All these actions transpire without a word from May's mouth. The Merchant, indeed, eases us into her speaking slowly, softly, gradually. Her first words comprise a thought that never gets uttered aloud (IV, 1982–85), her second, however, is uttered:

> She taketh hym by the hand and hard hym twiste
> So secrely that no wight of it wiste,
> And bad hym been al hool . . .
>
> (IV, 2005–7)

"Hym" refers to the love-stricken Damian, and the speech is a secret one—so secret that the narrator reports it in indirect discourse. The forceful gesture that accompanies it, moreover, seems to engulf the literal words, twisting them toward their secret meaning.

With line 2185, her first words to January, occurring significantly once she enters his garden, she has found her true voice:

> "I have," quod she, "a soule for to kepe
> As wel as ye, and also myn honour,
> And of my wyfhod thilke tendre flour,
> Which that I have assured in youre hond,
> Whan that the preest to yow my body bond;
> Wherfor I wole answere in this manere,
> By the leve of yow, my lord so deere:
> I prey to God that nevere dawe the day
> That I ne sterve, as foule as womman may,
> If evere I do unto my kyn that shame,
> Or elles I empeyre so my name,
> That I be fals; and if I do that lak,
> Do strepe me and put me in a sak,
> And in the nexte ryver do me drenche.
> I am a gentil womman and no wenche.
> Why speke ye thus? But men been evere untrewe,
> And wommen have repreve of yow ay newe.
> Ye han noon oother contenance, I leeve,
> But speke to us of untrust and repreeve."
>
> (IV, 2188–2206)

The loquaciousness of this is startling in one who has been so silent and privy. In fact, May here sounds like a simulacrum of the Wife of Bath, a character never accused of being taciturn. The point is not only that, like the Wife, she begins to speak for all wives, thus generalizing herself ("If evere I do unto my kyn that shame"), but also that all she says is a lie—all the while she is gesturing to Damian with her finger that he should climb the pear tree (IV, 2209).

The Pluto/Proserpina interlude pits on a supernatural level the verbosity January has not yet lost with the verbosity May has just found. Proserpina, doubtless picking up May's tendency to generalize herself, swears to give clever answer when discovered in adultery not just to her but to all women:

> Now by my moodres sires soule I swere
> That I shal yeven hire suffisant answere,
> And alle wommen after . . .
>
> (IV, 2265–67)

Her tenacious lie about restoring her husband's sight by (euphemistically) struggling with a man in a tree (IV, 2368–75) thus frees all women found in similar circumstances from guilty silence. She has mastered the situation through a supernatural gift of words, making her for all her sect, as the Clerk might put it, the arch-controller, the paradigm for all similarly beset women silently groping for words. But they are words dangerously cut off from the truth.

## The Franklin's Tale

The Franklin's Dorigen and the Merchant's May are of course in many ways similar: both are married to knights whose squires love them unlawfully, yet May ends up, via an unsavory privy, in a tree in a garden, swyved by the churl, while Dorigen emerges from her garden doubtless rejoicing in virtue well preserved. In one sense she is the ideal of wifely faithfulness defined in *The Legend of Good Women* and exemplified in *The Canterbury Tales* by Patient Griselda, Sad Constance, and St. Cecelia. I affirm this, but the burden of this section is to return to Dorigen and see her in a different light, one informed by the lives of the women mystics.

Her evident virtue is an important component in the interpretation that claims the Franklin's Tale as Chaucer's own solution to the question about the nature of marriage proposed by the Wife of Bath and debated by the Clerk and the Merchant. Kittredge first proposed this interpretation in 1912;[17] it became the standard one. Like most standard interpretations, it has certainly been challenged, yet it still gathers its proponents.[18] Those arguing that the marriage between Arveragus and Dorigen is an ideal one usually privilege the admittedly sound, even modern agreement between the two:

> And for to lede the moore in blisse hir lyves,
> Of his free wyl he swoor hire as a knyght
> That nevere in al his lyf he, day ne nyght,
> Ne sholde upon hym take no maistrie
> Agayn hir wyl, ne kithe hir jalousie,
> But hire obeye, and folwe hir wyl in al,
> As any lovere to his lady shal,
> Save that the name of soveraynetee,
> That wolde he have for shame of his degree.
>      She thanked hym, and with ful greet humblesse
> She seyde, "Sire, sith of youre gentillesse

Ye profre me to have so large a reyne,
Ne wolde nevere God bitwixe us tweyne,
As in my gilt, were outher werre or strif.
Sire, I wol be youre humble trewe wyf—
Have heer my trouthe—til that myn herte breste."
Thus been they bothe in quiete and in reste.

(V, 744–60)

Here it is as if the Loathly Lady refuses to ask her new husband for submission, Walter gives up his control, and January and May seek each other's well-being above their own. It is a marriage defined, in fact, by the Pauline texts about marriage so rudely manhandled by the Wife of Bath. The generosity each of the male characters exhibits as the tale winds down of course supports the ideal nature of this marriage: everyone in the Franklin's sunny world respects truth,[19] is worthy of trust.

Dissensions from this compelling interpretation take two paths. The first, charted by Robertson,[20] is an ironizing one: the Franklin is a bourgeois Epicurean whose own moral limitations circumscribe his text. The second, argued by Huppé,[21] Gaylord,[22] and others,[23] maintains that the characters in the tale do not act so well as it seems:[24] Arveragus has no right to break the sacrament of his marriage and command his wife to commit adultery in obedience to a lesser vow of maintaining "truth"[25] to Aurelius,[26] Aurelius has only made the rocks appear to go away ("It *semed* that alle the rokkes were aweye" [V, 1296, my emphasis]), the clerk has produced a mere illusion.

Dorigen, who is in no position to give away anything in the tale, does not escape the notice of the revisionary critics, usually being depicted as somehow silly and fussy.[27] The passage most often quoted to support her less than exemplary behavior is the long list of exempla she provides as reasons for suicide rather than immorality (V, 1367–1456)—Phidon's daughters, the fifty maidens of Lacadamonia, Stymphalides, Hasdrubal's wife, Lucrece, and the rest. The point is that these exempla, as the list gets longer, have less and less relevance to Dorigen's own situation, almost as if she has forgotten the reason for giving them; of course, she in the end also forgets to act in accordance with them, never attempting suicide.[28] She is, according to this interpretation, a "somewhat hysterical and even occasionally silly woman."[29] There have been some recent reactions to this interpretation of Dorigen, maintaining that she is the tale's moral center[30] or that she exhibits the Christian virtue of patience.[31]

Since I feel that humans by nature mix the good and the bad, the silly and the steadfast, I have no trouble through the means of a kind of *via positiva* to accept simultaneously both propositions about Dorigen. What a study of medieval women mystics has to offer, though, supports those who would decenter her from any kind of moral center, either the tale's or *The Canterbury Tales'* as a whole. The passage that strikes me as important is the following: While earlier Arveragus is away questing,

> [s]he moorneth, waketh, wayleth, fasteth, pleyneth;
> Desir of his presence hire so destreyneth
> That al this wyde world she sette at noght.
> Hire freendes, which that knewe hir hevy thoght,
> Conforten hire in al that ever they may.
> They prechen hire, they telle hire nyght and day
> That causelees she sleeth hirself, allas!

(V, 819–25)

Until the publication of Caroline Walker Bynum's *Holy Feast and Holy Fast: The Religious Significance of Food to Medieval Women*,[32] the meaning of this statement was unclear. Medieval women, largely denied a controlling role in medieval society, sometimes combined severe sleep deprivation and lamentation with self-starvation sometimes to the point of death to gain control of social circumstances—all activities that Dorigen adopts to deal with her separation. Their place in their families as children forced to do housework, their role in the marriage market, and their biological function as childbearers and nurturers circumscribed women's lives, made them powerless. Some women learned to control these things, even to the point of gaining ecclesiastical and political power through extreme physical behavior—importantly casting this behavior in a religious or mystical mold. Through behavior we would today classify as mentally aberrant (i.e, anorectic, bulemic), many women became saints—archcontrollers in life and especially in death, usually against the private and public censure of ecclesiastical officials ("They *prechen* hir . . . / That causelees she sleeth hirself, allas!" [my emphasis]).

The point about Dorigen is that she attempts this controlling activity but does so in a context that would divorce her actions from their religious meaning: she wakes, wails, and fasts not to escape an earthly husband in favor of a heavenly but to protest against her earthly husband's absence. Then, worse, she gives it up, doubtless generating an unfavorable comparison with the holy anorectics: "By proces . . . hir grete sorwe gan aswage" (V, 829–

35). She is soon in the company of her friends in a springtime garden, watching Aurelius dance (V, 901–30).

It is well here to place Dorigen's behavior in its historical context. One of the best examples of behavior analogous to Dorigen's is that of the Italian mystic Catherine of Siena,[33] an exact contemporary of Chaucer. She gained, as we have earlier seen, considerable fame in her short lifetime (dying in 1380 at the age of thirty-three), largely through her asceticism, acts of charity, and political maneuverings. She was influential in bringing the papacy back to Rome from Avignon, and was at the height of her fame in 1378, the year of Chaucer's trip to Milan.

Catherine had an unfortunately close example of an earthly marriage gone wrong. An older sister's husband was profligate, and the sister, Bonaventura, refused to eat until he reformed. Shortly after the two were reconciled, Bonaventura, doubtless weakened by her self-starvation, died in childbirth. Catherine herself was proposed as her brother-in-law's new bride, but she refused him and all others, cutting off her hair, attempting to scald herself with boiling water to disfigure herself, and, above all, refusing to eat. Her reputation for sanctity grew as her asceticism became more extreme. She finally gave up eating altogether and died of starvation. Like Dorigen, she fasted, but, unlike that of Chaucer's character, her fast was not to regain a husband but to avoid one and thus gain mystical union with God: it was she whose mystical marriage ceremony with Jesus set the pattern for women mystics of later generations, including Margery Kempe.

Catherine of Siena was exceptional only in her fame and political influence, not in her asceticism and attitude toward an earthly husband; the pattern is repeated many times. Lutgard of Aywières, a Flemish mystic from the early thirteenth century, for instance, like Dorigen, repeatedly fasted as a means of disfiguring herself to avoid prospective husbands, one of whom attempted to rape her.[34] A slightly different story may be told of Mary of Oignies, the beguine from the Low Countries whose life spanned the twelfth and thirteenth centuries and whom I mentioned earlier because Kempe had her Life read to her. She married against her will and began to fast and, like Dorigen and Margery Kempe, she shed tears ("She moorneth . . . wayleth . . . pleyneth") to regain control of her life; like the Second Nun's St. Cecelia, she forced her husband to submit to a chaste marriage.[35] Lidwina of Schiedam (early fifteenth century), when faced with marriage, took to her sickbed, and, like Dorigen, resisted sleep ("She . . . waketh"). The civic authorities of Schiedam even investigated her case, and affirmed her marvelous ability to stay awake.[36] Chaucer's younger contemporary Jane Mary of Maillé fasted and, again like the Second Nun's St. Cecelia on her wedding night, convinced her husband to consent to a chaste marriage.[37] This list of women saints may be lengthened considerably.

Such extreme behavior certainly led to religious ecstasy and, for some, fame, but most often it met stern opposition from family, clergy, and even civic authorities. The fifteenth-century saint Columba of Rieti, for instance, faced stern pressure from her family to marry and take over the traditional roles expected of women in the Middle Ages—housework and nurturing children.[38] She fasted, cut off her hair, and had Eucharistic visions. To test her, some local nuns—who should, one might think, have known better—tried to force-feed her, "suspecting," as Bynum writes, "that she starved herself because of unrequited love."[39] This is very close to Dorigen here:

> They prechen hire, they telle hire nyght and day
> That causelees she sleeth hirself, allas!

The story of the twelfth-century Englishwoman Christina of Markyate is particularly instructive in this context.[40] She wished to enter a convent, but her parents, the clergy about her, and even the "justiciar of the whole of England" (probably William Rufus's chief minister, Ranulf Flambard) united to resist her calling. She too was married against her will, but, unable to persuade her husband to engage in a chaste marriage, she escaped and went into hiding. Several hermits helped her, until finally she was enclosed in a tiny cubicle attached to the cell of an old hermit named Roger, where she endured severe fasting and kept vigils. She finally took vows and was attached as a female recluse to the monastery of St. Albans; her fame grew, and she became a counselor to the higher clergy and even the barons involved in the political turmoil of King Stephen's reign.

Christina's paradigm, one as we have seen so often repeated in the succeeding centuries, is instructive for what it tells us of Dorigen. Through extreme behavior that is essentially passive—that is, refusing to eat, refusing to sleep, mourning and wailing without the ability to control oneself—the woman mystic was able to gain a power and authority that the male-dominated society and Church denied her. The right to choose or refuse a husband and the right to take a position of leadership within the Church simply were not often enough in a woman's hands in the Middle Ages. Sometimes the passivity resulted even in political power, as in the cases of

Catherine of Siena and Christina of Markyate. As Bynum says, "To put it very simply, . . . the extreme asceticism and literalism of women's spirituality were not, at the deepest level, masochism or dualism but, rather, efforts to gain power and give meaning."[41]

We know that Dorigen's marriage is based on a power negotiation that addresses some of these concerns of the women mystics. The Franklin tells us of her that

> . . . pryvely she fil of his [Arveragus's] accord
> To take hym for his housbonde and hir lord,
> Of swich lordshipe as men han over hir wyves.
> And for to lede the moore in blisse hir lyves,
> Of his free wyl he swoor hire as a knyght
> That nevere in al his lyf he, day ne nyght,
> Ne sholde upon hym take no maistrie
> Agayn hir wyl, ne kithe hire jalousie,
> But hire obeye, and folwe hir wyl in al,
> As any lovere to his lady shal,
> Save that the name of sovereynetee,
> That wolde he have for shame of his degree.
>       She thanked hym, and with ful greet humblesse
> She seyde, "Sire, sith of youre gentillesse
> Ye profre me to have so large a reyne,
> Ne wolde nevere God bitwixe us tweyne,
> As in my gilt, were outher werre or stryf.
> Sire, I wol be youre humble trewe wyf—
> Have heer my trouthe—til that myn herte breste."
>
> (V, 741–60)

One significant aspect of this very significant passage is that Dorigen need not, because of Arveragus's willing submission, go through the extremities of behavior the female mystics often had to endure in order to avoid or negotiate their marriages. The irony is that this behavior comes later, and for the opposite motive— regaining a husband rather than avoiding or controlling one. And God is missing from the picture entirely.

As she later shows in her long appeal to written authorities in her unsuccessful attempt to persuade herself that suicide is her best course of action to deal with the dilemma in which her unwanted lover has trapped her (V, 1367–1456), Dorigen is a woman influenced by texts. The lives of the women mystics whom we have been considering exhibit the strongest interrelation between "text" and "life." As we have seen, a woman saint's life, usually through the medium of a male confessor or amanuensis (unnamed priests for Margery Kempe, Raymond of Capua for Catherine of Siena, etc.), is negotiated into a "Saint's Life—an individual exam-

ple of a literary genre. Then these Saints' Lives as texts provide
role models for their readers in negotiating the choices of their own
lives. St. Cecelia as text—perhaps even in Chaucer's own version
of it—with its emphasis on a chaste marriage, thus influenced people like Margery Kempe, Jane Mary of Maillé, and the others who
tried and sometimes succeeded in convincing their husbands to
give up the pleasures of the marriage bed. But Dorigen's relationship to lives and Saints' Lives—a reality and text thoroughly inter-
related—is to fragment them, divorce motive from paradigmatic
situation. She mourns, wakes, wails, fasts, and complains for reasons lives and Saints' Lives do not valorize, ignoring those they do.

I suggest that Dorigen is thus in sharp contrast with the three
major male characters in the Franklin's Tale, each of whom is in a
contest with the others to relinquish—not gain—control. Arveragus gives over his wife to Aurelius; Aurelius gives her back; the
clerk refuses his remuneration. Dorigen is the only one who wants
control, but her attempts at it fail.

Chaucer has the Franklin end his tale with the famous
*demaunde:*

> Which was the mooste fre, as thynketh yow?
> Now telleth me, er that ye ferther wende.
> I kan namoore; my tale is at an ende.

(V, 1622–24)

Boccaccio first posed the question in an analogue, perhaps source,
in the *Decameron;* significantly the tale's fictional auditors there
debate openly the answer, with the accolades going to the husband.[42] *The Canterbury Tales,* however, fragment at this point with
neither debate, answer, nor link to the next tale. The Franklin has
interrupted and thus fragmented the Squire's Tale; almost no one
realizes that his is a fragment as well—one self-imposed. The effect
of this fragmentation is twofold: first, it forces the reader to sink
into the Franklin's Tale and try to answer the question, as more
than one critic has done;[43] second, it sounds suspiciously as if
someone (the Franklin? Chaucer?) has lost authorial control by
running out of words just when the trace of meaning is within
reach.

### The Shipman's Tale

Unlike Dorigen, the unnamed wife of the Shipman's Tale requires no critical dexterity to qualify her as one of Chaucer's "bad"

women.[44] Her exchange of sexual favors for money through the currency of language[45] makes her in one sense even worse than that other unnamed wife whose entrance fragments the Cook's Tale: at least the earlier wife "swyved for hir sustenance" (I, 4422), not merely for some clothing. Language is, however, more than just a currency for exchanging sex and money in the tale; it is a means characters use of controlling others. But it is, as others have pointed out,[46] a curious, doubled, and, I would add, Pseudo-Dionysian language—one with odd silences attending it.

As C. David Benson points out, the plot of the Shipman's Tale, unlike those of the other fabliaux of *The Canterbury Tales,* moves more by speech than by action.[47] Characters, in other words, spend more time speaking than doing things, and much of their speech is devoted to swearing oaths to each other.[48] The Middle English rule written for Franciscan Tertiaries reminds us, though, that oaths are to be avoided by those who have taken religious vows: "They muste also absteyne fro Solempne othes withoute nede require it."[49]

The first of these proscribed oathes in the Shipman's Tale is one of blood relationship:

> The monk hym [the merchant] claymeth as for cosynage,
> And he agayn; he seith nat ones nay,
> But was glad therof as fowel of day,
> For to his herte it was a greet plesaunce.
> Thus been they knyt with eterne alliaunce,
> And ech of hem gan oother for t'assure
> Of bretherhede whil that hir lyf may dure.
>
> > (VII, 36–42)

Curious here is the negative casting of the merchant's indirect speech ("he seith nat ones nay"), and more curious the divesting of meaning that subsequent betrayals in the tale mandate for some words: *cosynage* escalates to *bretherhede* only to pejorate silently to its homonym *cozenage* (i.e., *trickery*) by the end.[50] *Eterne, alliaunce, assure* completely loose meaning.

The second oath is of secrecy:

> ". . . therfore telleth me [the monk]
> Al youre anoy, for it shal been secree.
> For on my portehors I make an ooth
> That nevere in my lyf, for lief ne looth,
> Ne shal I of no conseil yow biwreye."
> "The same agayn to yow," quod she, "I seye.

By God and by this portehors I swere,
Though men me wolde al into pieces tere,
Ne shal I nevere, for to goon to helle,
Biwreye a word of thyng that ye me telle,
Nat for no cosynage ne alliance,
But verraily, for love and affiance."
Thus been they sworn, and heerupon they kiste,
And ech of hem tolde oother what hem liste.

(VII, 130–42)

A *portehors* is a breviary. The wife reduces God to words ("By
God and by this portehors"), a reduction of the one Pseudo-
Dionysius names as unnameable to silent words written on a page.
*Conseil* is divested of meaning as its meaning shifts silently to
"sexual favors." And *cosynage,* affirmed in the first oath, is here
denied, accompanied by a resounding silence about that oath on
the monk's part. The wife moreover seems rather obsessive here,
for the circumstances of the moment do not warrant her extreme
language about being torn to pieces and going to hell—words that
amount to an allusion to Ovid's treatment of the Orpheus/Euridice
myth yet one that undercuts the meaning of that myth: Orpheus is
the one who is torn to pieces, not his wife, and the motive is
fidelity, not infidelity. Why make this allusion and why cast the
consequences of betraying this confidence in so violent and eschatological terms? The wife is silent about her motives.

The third oath is one of love:

"Nay," quod this monk, "by God and seint Martyn,
He is na moore cosyn unto me
Than is this leef that hangeth on the tree!
I clepe hym so, by Seint Denys of Fraunce,
To have the moore cause of aqueyntaunce
Of yow, which I have loved specially
Aboven alle wommen, sikerly.
This swere I yow on my professioun."

(VII, 148–55)

The monk here consciously divests a word of meaning in his disa-
vowal of the relationship signified by *cosyn.* The monk calls attention to the fact that *cosyn* is a mere name he applies to the
merchant—a signifier with a Pseudo-Dionysian gap between it and
its signified ("I clepe hym so"). His *leef* recalls for us his words
*lyf* and *lief* in his previous oath—a playfulness of sound that also
undercuts his meaning: life and that which is beloved sinking into

a mere leaf whose worthlessness the monk points out. When he swears his love on his "profession," we moreover cannot escape the irony, for a monk's profession involves other oaths about which he and the narrator behind him are significantly silent, including one of chastity. Subsequent oaths, in other words, erase meanings of earlier ones in the Shipman's Tale.

The fourth and last oath involves money:

> "Daun John, I seye, lene me thise hundred frankes.
> Pardee, I wol nat faille yow my thankes,
> If that yow list to doon that I yow praye.
> For at a certeyn day I wol yow paye,
> And doon to yow what plesance and servise
> That I may doon, right as yow list devise.
> And but I do, God take on me vengeance
> As foul as evere hadde Genylon of France."
>     This gentil monk answerde in this manere:
> "Now trewely, myn owene lady deere,
> I have," quod he, "on yow so greet a routhe
> That I yow swere, and plighte yow my trouthe,
> That whan youre housbonde is to Flaundres fare,
> I wol delyvere yow out of this care;
> For I wol brynge yow an hundred frankes."
> And with that word he caughte hire by the flankes,
> And hire embraceth harde, and kiste hire ofte.
> "Gooth now youre wey," quod he, "al stille and softe."
>                                         (VII, 187–204)

The wife here is the one who is divesting words of meaning. Her *thankes* become successively money ("I wol yow paye"), *plesance,* and *service*—all euphemisms. It is interesting to note that she still inhabits a world of violence, for Ganilon too met his death by being torn apart. Sex may mean money to her, but there is also a faint trace of masochism about it. The monk's significant transformation of *franks* to *flanks* at the point where his words stop and his actions begin has not escaped sharp critics.[51] His emphasis on silence ("al still and softe") is perhaps the ultimate readjustment of meaning. Language so shifting, so unstable as the type in this tale, finally fails to signify.

The other references to silence in the Shipman's Tale support this idea, for they create an environment where such nonsignifying language may flourish. The first encounter between the monk and wife, for instance, is in a silent garden: "This goode wyf cam walkynge pryvely / Into the gardyn, there he [the monk Daun John] walketh softe" (IV, 92–93).[52] Subsequent events divest the wife of this favorite of Pseudo-Dionysian names, "good." She later expresses a chaste desire not to betray her marital "privetee" (VII, 164)—which of course she does. The merchant reinvests this seemingly sexual word with mercantile meaning somewhat later when he says,

> We [i.e., we merchants] may wel make chiere and good visage,
> And dryve forth the world as it may be,
> And kepen oure estaat in pryvetee.
>
> (VII, 230–32)

Daun John picks up this silence when he approaches the merchant for the loan—taking him aside and speaking to him "prively" (VII, 256) and requesting that the loan "be secree" (VII, 277). The merchant agrees, handing over the franks to him "prively" (VII, 294). Even the narrator catches the infection of this secrecy and silence, making a transition from words about the monk to words about the merchant with the clause "namoore of hym I seye" (VII, 324).

The oddest silence, though, attending the tale is that of the fourth character. As the wife walks out into the silent garden to meet Daun John she has a female child with her:[53]

> A mayde child cam in hire compaignye,
> Which as hir list she may governe and gye,
> For yet under the yerde was the mayde.
>
> (VII, 95–97)

The narrator is silent about this child, presumably daughter to the merchant and his wife. Why is she there? Why does the wife conduct the long commercial seduction in her presence? Perhaps she is so much under the wife's control that the wife need not fear disclosure of the privy doings. Or perhaps the girl is too young to understand the shifty language that comes to her ears. But that language culminates in hard and frequent kisses—signifiers that even a fairly young child might understand and find worthy of recounting to her father or to the head of the household. The girl says no words in the tale, and the narrator is silent about her. She is the merest trace, a ghost, a silence.

The reader may justify her presense/absence perhaps because the narrator relates to his readers the same way characters relate to each other in the tale. C. David Benson puts the matter well when he says,

Throughout, the reader is shown how difficult it is to know what to believe. Are the monk and merchant really cousins? Has the monk always loved the wife or does he just say he has to gain an advantage? Does the wife have genuine complaints against her husband or is she only pretending to have? How much does the merchant know or guess about his wife's infidelity? The gap between reality and appearance . . . is here a key to deeper questions that lie beneath the tale's surface attractiveness.[54]

I would add that these questions indicate silences on the narrator's part by which he seeks to control us the way the characters in his tale seek to control each other. Perhaps this collusion with, this sinking into the language of his own tale is best indicated by his comments on the final linguistic exchange. Confronted by the necessity to repay the hundred franks to her husband, the wife, doubtless benefiting by the readiness of language granted by Proserpina to May and all her sect, says, "I am youre wyf; score it upon my taille, / And I shal paye as soone as ever I may" (VII, 416–17). Almost everyone who explicates the tale[55] notes the pun here, as the wife reinvests the commercial *tally* with the meaning of her own *tail*. It is the narrator himself, not one of his characters, who does the final reinvestment of meaning in his tale by providing the pun with a third valency: "Thus endeth my tale, and God us sende / Taillynge ynough unto oure lyves ende" (VII, 433–34). *Tale*, despite its slight Middle English difference in pronunciation from the other two words, is sometimes suggested as the pun's third meaning.[56] *Tail* and *tally* connect sex and money; *tale* adds the medium of exchange—language.

It is my contention that the method of this language exchange—as with the rest of *The Canterbury Tales*—is Pseudo-Dionysian. But it is in the Shipman's Tale more than the others that we can discern that anonymous Syrian monk's direct presence—for in this tale Chaucer mentions him by name. I have already quoted the passage in its context—the tale's third oath, that of love. In it, as we have seen, the monk denies the name *cosyn* to the merchant:

> He is na moore cosyn unto me
> Than is this leef that hangeth on the tree!
> I clepe hym so, by Seint Denys of Fraunce.
>
> (VII, 149–51)

Pseudo-Dionysius was not, as he is to modern scholars, someone who appropriated the name of a biblical character to give his works nearly canonical authority. He was simply Denis—a saint who, with the usual conflation of similar names, not only encountered the apostle Paul on the Acropolos and wrote important mystical treatises but evangelized France, thus becoming that nation's patron saint. In his patronizing role he had both a locality near Paris and Abbot Suger's famous proto-Gothic abbey named after him. It is of course possible to take the monk's words as merely an interjection here—like, say, the Prioress's "Saint Loy!" or John the carpenter's "Saint Frideswide!" or, indeed, the merchant-husband's own "Saint Yve!" (VII, 227) or the monk's "Seint Martyn!" (VII, 148). But the context, if nothing else, is highly suggestive, with the monk simultaneously affirming and denying a name in a manner not unlike that prescribed in Pseudo-Dionysius's *Divine Names* itself.

When we add to this the insistence the Shipman places on "Seint-Denys" as the locale for the language transactions of his tale, we must conclude that for some reason Chaucer wants this name resounding in our ears:

> A marchant whilom dwelled at Seint-Denys
>
> (VII, 1)

> That he sholde come to Seint-Denys to pleye
>
> (VII, 59)

> And unto Seint-Denys he comth anon
>
> (VII, 67)

> To Seint-Denys ycomen is daun John.
>
> (VII, 308)

> To Seint-Denys he gan for to repaire
>
> (VII, 326)

The Miller is not so insistent on Oxford, the Reeve on Cambridge, the Cook on London, or the Merchant on Lumbardy as the Shipman is on Saint-Denis. The locale is indeed important as "the capital city of a foreign country, instead of a provincial English university town,"[57] but this insistence on the master of the unnaming peculiar to mystical speech is striking in a tale that so persist-

ently affirms and denies meanings to words, casts so constantly
the Pseudo-Dionysian gap between signifier and signified.

## The Manciple's Tale

A god is certainly one who controls. With the exception of brief
appearances here and there in *The Canterbury Tales*—notably the
Olympians in the Knight's and Pluto and Proserpina in the Merchant's tales—the classical gods stay out of the way. In the Manciple's Tale, however, Phoebus Apollo is the main character who
must control his unnamed wife, who is named Coronis in Ovid.
And a very bad one she is, indeed. Where May and Dorigen had
the social sense to conduct their illicit affairs with members of
their own class if somewhat lower in rank, squires serving their
knightly husbands, and where the wife in the Shipman's Tale
chooses a rather well-off member of the first estate, the outrider
monk Daun John, Phoebus's wife, as the narrator remarks, chooses
"A man of litel reputacioun, / Nat worth to Phebus in compar-
isoun" (IX, 199–200).

All we hear about Phoebus at the beginning of the tale bespeaks control:

> He was the mooste lusty bachiler
> In al this world, and eek the beste archer.
> He slow Phitoun, the serpent.
>
> (IX, 107–9)

His martial accomplishments are matched by musical, for he is
adept on not just one but all instruments:

> Pleyen he koude on every mystralcie,
> And syngen, that it was a melodie
> To heeren of his cleere voys the soun.
>
> (IX, 113–15)

He is also comely:

> Therto he was the semelieste man
> That is or was sith that the world bigan.
> What nedeth it his fetures to discryve?
> For in this world was noon so faire on-lyve.
> He was therwith fulfild of gentillesse,
> Of honour, and of parfit worthynesse.
>
> (IX, 119–24)

The language of this last passage in fact is so grand that it puts us in mind of language describing Christ in the Apocalypse. "That is or was, sith that the world bigan," like the similar line in the Invocation to book 1 of *The House of Fame,* "That is and was and ever shal," (HF, 82) is likely an evocation of Apocalypse 4:8b, "qui erat, et qui est, et qui venturus est."[58] And the list of divine virtues is similar to several in the Apocalypse, most notably that in 5:13, "benedictio, et honor, et gloria, et potestas in saecula saeculorum."[59] Phoebus is, in other words, an archcontroller of an altogether higher order than others like Harry Bailly, Duke Theseus, Handy Nicholas, or Prudence. An actual diety, indeed the classical god of poetry, of speech itself, he may claim by right what the others must usurp—almost authorial control over the tale he inhabits.

The narrator emphasizes how the other two main characters of the tale are so controlled by Phoebus that they actually belong to him:

> Now hadde this Phebus in his hous a crowe
> Whiche in a cage he fostred many a day.
>
> (IX, 130–31)

> Now hadde this Phebus in his hous a wyf
> Which that he lovede moore than his lyf.
>
> (IX, 139–40)

The verbal similarities in the first lines force us to equate the concepts in the second: love equals a cage. The narrator supports this four lines later, making this implied comparison direct: "Jalous he was, and wolde have kept hire fayn" (IX, 144). Yet, as we know from other jealous husbands like John the carpenter and January, such control always fails.

Phoebus's loss of control is actually a complex process. It involves what James Dean calls a "demythologizing"[60] (perhaps more accurately a euhemerizing): a recasting of a god in a seemingly human environment—house, wife, a pet bird—whose character by the end of the tale is "ignoble and petty, at base all too human."[61] It involves also what William Askins describes as the historicizing of the god Phoebus in his excesses, cruelty, fondness for music, and good looks into Chaucer's contemporary, Gaston "Phoebus," count of Foix, Froissart's seemingly favorite nobleman.[62] Mostly, however, it involves the fragmentation of everything about him.

Not only do the Crow's words informing him of his wife's adultery break his household, leading to the wife's murder and his own exile and disfigurement, they also start Phoebus onto a tantrum of fragmentation:

> This Phebus gan aweyward for to wryen,
> And thoughte his sorweful herte brast atwo.
> His bowe he bente, and sette therinne a flo,
> And in his ire his wyf thanne hath he slayn.
> This is th'effect; ther is namoore to sayn;
> For sorwe of which he brak his mynstralcie,
> Bothe harpe, and lute, and gyterne, and sautrie;
> And eek he brak his arwes and his bowe.
>
> (IX, 262–69)

Hearts break, musical instruments break, bow and arrows break. Harp, lute, gittern, and psaltery—all stringed instruments and thus in the physics of their construction related to a bow—are not, like the bow, the symbol of the violence his broken heart has just caused. They are the symbols of his art, of poetry. This powerful image of the god of poetry, like a maddened, cuckolded Prospero, destroying the accoutrements of his art, is so powerful that the narrator himself momentarily loses his own art, lapsing into silence—"ther is namoore to sayn."

The Manciple's Tale of course is a beast fable, and its moral is one of silence: "Kepe wel thy tonge and thenk upon the crowe" (IX, 362). The tale and its prologue exist alone as Fragment IX of *The Canterbury Tales*—a narrative sequence that emerges out of silence to present a moral about silence before subsiding into silence. Critics have not been silent about this point, however, for almost all either call attention to the long speech the Manciple claims as his mother's which concludes the tale with a torrent of words advising silence (IX, 309–62)[63] or—especially recently—relate the call to silence to the incipient end to the tale-telling on the Canterbury Pilgrimage:[64] the Manciple's is the last tale of all save the Parson's, which, of course, is no tale at all. The contrast between the Manciple's silence and the upcoming Parson's devotional treatise has also caught the attention of perceptive critics.[65]

I wish to suggest that the Manciple's silence is even deeper than what has yet been explicated. It is, in fact, a kind of narrative fragmentation. The ultimate source of the tale is Ovid's story of Phoebus, his unfaithful wife Coronis, his crow, and the birth of his son, the great physician Aesculapius (*Metamorphoses* II, 531ff.). The *Ovide Moraliseé* (II, 2130ff.), Machaut's *Le Livre du Voir Dit* (7773 ff.), and Gower's *Confessio Amantis* (III, 768ff.) are either sources or analogues.[66] Ovid and the *Ovide Moraliseé* established the myth for Chaucer and his contemporaries, while Machaut, Gower, and Chaucer's Manciple demythologized it by omitting its point—the birth of Aesculapius—thus turning it into a beast's fable. Whether or not Chaucer got the idea from Machaut or Gower is irrelevant to the effect his Manciple's Tale has on the reader: the point is missing. In Ovid, after Phoebus kills Coronis, he rescues his son, Aesculapius, from the body of his dead pregnant wife. When we reach the point in the Manciple's Tale where this narration should be, what we have instead is the prolix speech of the Manciple's mother about silence—both a paradox *and* a performatory utterance, for it generates the narrative silence that demotes this myth into a fable, shifting our attention to the color of the crow's feathers and the loss of its singing voice from the birth of the archetypal physician.

This fragmenting of Ovid's narrative indicates, perhaps, a curious connection between the Manciple and the Physician. The Physician, of course, has told a very legal story about a good woman in which the evil judge Apius maneuvers in court to procure the innocent Virginia. There is no evidence of his profession in his tale. The Manciple, a scout or butler to those practicing law at one of the Inns of Court, would have been a more appropriate teller.[67]

More important, there is one rather long passage worthy of comment for its Pseudo-Dionysian content. The narrator, having called the "man of litel reputacioun" the wife's "lemman,"[68] comments:

> Hir lemman? Certes, this is a knavyssh speche!
> Foryeveth it me, and that I yow biseche.
>     The wise Plato seith, as ye may rede,
> The word moot nede accorde with the dede.
> If men shal telle proprely a thyng,
> The word moot cosyn be to the werkyng.
> I am a boystous man, right thus seye I.
>
> (IX, 205–11)

What follows are another twenty-six lines of explaining that the only difference between a "wyf" and a "wenche" or a "capitayn" and a "theef" is one of social degree. Immediately after this excursus, the Manciple resumes his tale by, surprisingly, affirming the word he has just denied: "Whan Phebus wyf had sent for hir lemman, / Anon they wroghten al hire lust volage" (IX, 238–39). We should, of course, here recall the Merchant, who is likewise given to prurient speech and excuses it by appealing to the rough edges of his nature, momentarily quailing before the word *throng,*: "Ladyes, I prey yow that ye be nat wrooth; / I kan nat glose, I am a rude man" (IV, 2350–51).

A curious parallel in the use of this word *lemman* can be found in the anonymous *A Talking of the Love of God,* a text of some importance, as we have seen, for this analysis of the Prioress's and Miller's tales. Halfway through his semipoetical meditation, the author startles the reader with an almost blasphemous comparison:

> Bote moni for richesse lemmon cheoseþ; ffor eueriwher mai men wiþ catel loue chepen. Bot is þer eny Ricchore þen þou my leue lyf my lemmon, þat richeliche regnest in heuen & in eorþe?[69]

The rich may buy the services of a "lemmon;" God is the richest and is thus the author's lemmon. The enthymeme is faulty, but the logic here is not the Aristotelian one so beloved of the schools but that of mystic speech, where the word's meaning is simultaneously affirmed and denied. For the rest of the treatise, the author addresses Christ with this word, *lemmon.*

More striking, though, is the direct quotation in the Manciple's passage of words I have already explicated—those of Chaucer himself in the General Prologue:

> Whoso shal telle a tale after a man,
> He moot reherce as ny as evere he kan
> Everich a word, if it be in his charge,
> Al speke he never so rudeliche and large.
> . . . . . . . . . . . . . .
> Eek Plato seith, whoso that kan hym rede,
> The wordes moote be cosyn to the dede.
> (I, 731–34, 41–42)

Here is the same concern with the gap between signifier and signified. The Manciple, Chaucer, and Pseudo-Dionysius alike are equally concerned about the problems of naming things.

That Chaucer's words come at the very beginning of *The Canterbury Tales* and the Manciple's near the end—if we accept the order of the Ellesmere Manuscript reflected in Robinson's, Fisher's,[70] and Benson's standard editions—adds some weight to the argument that the Manciple's tale contributes to the process of closure of the work as a whole,[71] what one perceptive critic calls its "dismantling."[72] Such a view of course privileges the Ellesmere order. But the Manciple's Prologue and Tale exist as a separate fragment without links to what precedes and follows it. All the emphasis on silence in the Tale admittedly sounds like closure—or more properly preclosure, given the mass of the Parson's Tale that blocks its access to the Retraction. Yet the themes of control and fragmentation it shares with all the other tales and the moral of silence it shares with the Nun's Priest's Tale (see VII, 3422–35)—which by no stretch of critical or scribal ingenuity stands near the end of the work as a whole—all argue otherwise. Instead of a Chaucer who plans, intends closure with the dismantling theme of silence introduced by the Manciple near the end, it seems we have a Chaucer who, wherever we poke at him, reveals silence. *The Canterbury Tales* tends not toward closure only at the end but toward fragmentation throughout—tale by tale, almost line by line. It is better to speak, I think, of Chaucer's tendency than of his intentions.[73]

# 7

## Chaucer Himself

Most admit that Chaucer the Pilgrim contributes two tales to the storytelling of the Canterbury Pilgrimage. One can, I suppose, argue that he is the only one of the pilgrims to produce the contractual number of four that Harry Bailly demands at the beginning—if we include the General Prologue and the Retraction. If that suggestion is too far-fetched, we at least are left with the fact that there are four sections of *The Canterbury Tales* that come from Chaucer's "own" voice. I suggest that the movement of three of these pieces charts the movement of Chaucer's whole career and that the relationship of *Sir Thopas, The Tale of Melibee,* and the Retraction to the prose genre of devotional treatises is essential for understanding that career.

### Sir Thopas

The only poet less adept than the Squire is,[1] of course, Chaucer himself. Not only in *The Canterbury Tales* but throughout his works Chaucer parodies himself: he is the obtuse dreamer who does not understand the Black Knight's chess allegory in *The Book of the Duchess* (BD, 742–48); he is the overweight burden whom the eagle might drop in *The House of Fame* (HF, 573–74), who gets dazed at his books (HF, 658), and who has never had the least reward from the God of Love (HF, 628); he is the dim witted hesitater who is not intelligent enough to know which way to go at the garden's gate in *The Parliament of Fowls* so that Africanus, doubtless in exasperation, must shove him in (PF, 145–54). In *The Canterbury Tales,* the Man of Law remarks alike on his feeble skills and prodigious output (II, 45–56)—a bad combination. In the Prologue to *Sir Thopas* the Host and Chaucer exchange remarks even more parodic:

> . . . oure Hooste japen tho bigan,
> And thanne at erst he looked upon me,
> And seyde thus: "What man artow?" quod he;
> "Thou lookest as thou woldest fynde an hare,
> For evere upon the ground I se thee stare.
>
> "Approche neer, and looke up murily.
> Now war yow, sires, and lat this man have place!
> He in the waast is shape as wel as I;
> This were a popet in an arm t'enbrace
> For any womman, smal and fair of face.
> He semeth elvyssh by his contenaunce,
> For unto no wight dooth he daliaunce.
>
> "Sey now somwhat, syn oother folk han sayd;
> Telle us a tale of myrthe, and that anon."
> "Hooste," quod I, "ne beth nat yvele apayd,
> For oother tale certes kan I noon,
> But of a rym I lerned longe agoon."
>
> (VII, 693–709)

We have here the same corpulent Chaucer who spread himself over the pages of *The House of Fame,* the same literary incompetent who tries hard with little success that the Man of Law had mentioned earlier in *The Canterbury Tales.* But unlike the Man of Law's Chaucer, this one does not write too much, knowing instead only one meager rhyme. And this Chaucer, silent and unknown, it seems, to the Host, is certainly not the garrulous pilgrim who gets to know everyone in the General Prologue:[2]

> And shortly, whan the sonne was to reste,
> So hadde I spoken with hem everichon
> That I was of hir felaweshipe anon.
>
> (I, 30–32)

Evidently part of the parody is its inconsistency.

That Chaucer lives in the same realm of poetic ineptitude as the Squire is of course the point of the tale. It is, I would suggest, not exactly the complementary point that *Sir Thopas* is a parody of the sort of Middle English romances recorded in the Auchinleck Manuscript.[3] Self-parody, in other words, is more interesting here than literary parody,[4] though both run in tandem. The parodic elements have been well explicated by critics;[5] re- and further consideration of them assures us that the self-parody is of a poet losing what little control he has over both material and audience, heading inexorably toward fragmentation and silence.

Squiresque blunders compete with prosodic gaffs. The Squire had a fairly good grasp of meter and is faithful to his chosen rhymed couplet. Where he fails is in exerting narrative control over his materials. So does Chaucer. Sir Thopas hales from Flanders (VII, 719), a bourgeois region not noted for chivalry; like a burgher, he prefers the socially inferior bow and arrow to lance and spear (VII, 739) and goshawk to peregrine or merlin (VII, 738). His looks are more appropriate for a heroine than hero:

> Sire Thopas wax a doghty swayn;
> Whit was his face as payndemayn,
> His lippes rede as rose;
> His rode is lyk scarlet in grayn,
> And I yow telle in good certayn,
> He hadde a semely nose.
>
> (VII, 724–29)

This epicene deportment should, on further consideration, not give us pause, for one of the heroes Chaucer likens Sir Thopas to is Lebeaux (VII, 899), a knight who spends a large portion of his own romance impersonating a woman.[6] Sir Thopas likes to hear the birds sing, but the sparrowhawk (VII, 767), first of the melodious birds listed, of course, emits squawks, not song. He goes about his errantry without armor, realizing it only when a fight is imminent, so he must put off the appropriate pugilism till the morrow (VII, 8190–20). His adversary, a giant whose name, Sir Olifaunt, would have reminded a medieval person, perhaps, more of the musical instrument named after Roland's horn than the animal, is unchivalrously resistant to such a postponement, and chases after him with a slingshot, thus inverting the literary allusion to David and Goliath (VII, 827–32). After this abortive encounter, Chaucer remarks of his hero:

> His myrie men comanded he
> To make hym bothe game and glee,
> For nedes most he fighte
> With a geaunt with hevedes three.
>
> (VII, 839–42)

The last, a detail most would consider significant enough to mention right away, is here shuffled back a full five stanzas after the giant has shown up.

If such literal details give Chaucer difficulties, so do the metaphorical. Sir Thopas finally armed, we find as part of his equip-
ment's description a metaphor: "His brydel as the sonne shoon, /
Or as the moone light" (VII, 879–80). Which? The two are different
in color, intensity, and literary connotation; Chaucer cannot decide. Farther on, he attempts a metaphor even more disastrous:

> But sir Thopas, he bereth the flour
> Of roial chivlary!
> His goode steede al he bistrood,
> And forth upon his wey he glood
> As sparcle out of the bronde;
> Upon his creest he bar a tour,
> And therinne stiked a lilie flour—
> God shilde his cors fro shonde!
>
> (VII, 901–9)

"Bears the flower" was an outworn metaphor in the Middle Ages,
applied indiscriminately to ladies throughout romances and lyrics.
Occasionally in Middle English works of devotion it refers to the
Virgin, as it does in the anonymous poem entitled by its editor,
"Hymn to Jesus Christ and the Virgin": "Bethynke þe, Lady, euer
and ay, / Þat of women þou beris þe flour."[7] This phrase and its
close variant "bears the bell" mean, roughly, "wins the prize." That
it was a cliché is perhaps excusable; that it was applied to women
and not knights-errant is not; that it has the bad taste to step over
the bounds of metaphor and attach itself to Sir Thopas's crest as
a literal flower is worse.

Chaucer is, moreover, a metrical and stanzaic bumbler of such
stature that even the Squire fades in comparison. As Owen points
out, *forest* in line 754 "not only throws its stress to the second
syllable but lengthens its vowel to rhyme with *best*."[8] Even without
this sort of metrical wrenching, other lines simply do not scan, for
instance, line 785:

> Whăt eýleth thĭs lóve ăt me

There are only seven syllables here, not the required eight; a stress
is lost between "eyleth" and "this." Likewise, in line 837, an un-
stress is missing before the first word:

> Prĭkyng óveř hĭll ănd dale

Had the Renaissance and Restoration readers, who complained
about Dan Chaucer's rough and rude numbers, concentrated on

*Sir Thopas* rather than on the lines where the pronunciation of a
final *-e* usually straightens things out, they would have had a case.

The shifts in stanza structure also are inept. The first change
comes between stanzas thirteen and fourteen:

> O Seinte Marie, benedicite!
> What eyleth this love at me
> To bynde me so soore?
> Me dremed al this nyght, pardee,
> An elf-queene shal my lemman be
> And slepe under my goore.
>
> An elf-queene wol I love, ywis,
> For in this world no womman is
> Worthy to be my make
> In towne;
> Alle other wommen I forsake,
> And to an elf-queene I me take
> By dale and eek by downe!
>
> (VII, 784–96)

One-stress bob-lines are of course found in Middle English romances, most notably in *Sir Gawain and the Green Knight,* but
the sudden insertion of them into an otherwise stable stanza structure is unsettling. As Owen remarks, "The weight of more than
eighty absolutely regular lines throws its emphasis on what seems
at first to be a run-on."[9] Critics have occasionally commented on
the extension of the seven-line rhyme royale stanzas from the preceding Prioress's Tale into the Prologue to *Sir Thopas,*[10] suggesting
a contrast between the two tales that works to *Sir Thopas*'s disadvantage. One perhaps also gets the impression that Chaucer, halfway through his first tale, realizes that he is not faring well in
comparison with what has gone before and desperately lengthens
his stanzas to equal those of the Prioress. But with the next stanza,
Chaucer again lengthens his form, this time to ten lines:

> Into his sadel he clamb anon,
> And priketh over stile and stoon
> An elf-queene for t'espye,
> Til he so longe hath riden and goon
> That he foond, in a pryve woon,
> The contree of Fairye
> So wilde;
> For in that contree was ther noon
> That to him durste ride or goon,
> Neither wyf ne childe.
>
> (VII, 797–806)

The first six lines of this new form are, actually, Chaucer's original stanza. The bob-line follows, perhaps indication that he remembers that he has just begun employing it. He is, in other words, momentarily torn between two differing stanzas and so produces a hybrid.

The bob-lines generate some marvelously anticlimatic effects along the way, as in Sir Olifaunt's grim threat,

> Anon I sle thy steede
> With mace.
>
> (VII, 812–13)

But after four stanzas, Chaucer drops them, doubtless remembering to be consistent with his original form. The effect is chaotic.[11] Yet after nine more stanzas he forgets his form again:

> His jambeaux were of quyrboilly,
> His swerdes shethe of yvory,
> His helm of latoun bright;
> His sadel was of rewel boon,
> His brydel as the sonne shoon,
> Or as the moone light.
>
> His spere was of fyn ciprees,
> That bodeth werre, and nothyng pees,
> The heed ful sharpe ygrounde;
> His steede was al dappull gray,
> It gooth an ambil in the way
> Ful softely and rounde
> In londe.
> Loo lordes myne, heere is a fit!
> If ye wol any more of it,
> To telle it wol I fonde.
>
> (VII, 875–90)

*Londe* barely rhymes with *rounde* and *grounde,* but it does warrant *fonde* in the last line. Rhyme, in other words, becomes as shifty as meter or stanzaic form. But, more importantly, the original six-line stanza again gives way to a ten-line, before falling back to the original six-line as the last fit begins.

This lack of control—both of form and of matter—is signaled by Chaucer's increasingly emphatic attempts to keep his audience's attention. The first lines comprise a fairly normal minstrel's call to attention, not only characteristic of almost all Middle English romances but of other originally oral genres, for instance, the Old English epic, as in *Beowulf.* Chaucer begins:

> Listeth, lordes, in good entent,
> And I wol telle verrayment
> Of myrthe and of solas.
>
> (VII, 712–14)

After eighteen stanzas, he must repeat his call for attention: "Yet listeth, lordes, to my tale" (VII, 833). This second call to attention, rarer in Middle English romances than the first, is nonetheless common enough.[12] Yet at the end of the ninth stanza that follows, Chaucer gives a third call for attention, one unprecedented in length and aggression:

> Loo, lordes myne, heere is a fit!
> If ye wol any more of it,
> To telle it wol I fonde.
>
> Now holde youre mouth, *par charitee* . . .
>
> (VII, 888–91)

*Fit* may of course be a pun working to Chaucer's disadvantage— both a canto and a fitful performance. This desperate and abusive call for attention is in effect a call for silence: the pilgrims have doubtless become restless at so poor a performance. Each, we may suppose, is looking about for someone to take a hint from the Franklin's earlier interruption of the Squire and put an end to this fitful and chaotic babble. What follows are four and a half more inept stanzas before the Host matches Chaucer's desperate abuse with his own: "Namoore of this, for Goddes dignitee. . . . thy drasty rymyng is nat worth a toord!" (VII, 919, 930).

When Chaucer, out of poetic control, is silenced by the Host, fragmenting his Tale, we are faced with an interpretive crux of Pseudo-Dionysian proportions:

> "Namoore of this, for Goddes dignitee,"
> Quod oure Hooste, "for thou makest me
> So wery of thy verray lewednesse
> That, also wisly God my soule blesse,
> Myne eres aken of thy drasty speche.
> Now swich a rym the devel I biteche!
> This may wel be rym dogerel," quod he.
> "Why so?" quod I, "why wiltow lette me

Moore of my tale than another man,
Syn that it is the beste rym I kan?"

(VII, 919–28)

Chaucer, of course, has given us many rhymes by this point in *The
Canterbury Tales;* only his persona, whom I have insisted upon
calling "Chaucer" above but without the quotation marks, is the
inept hack. To put it another way, *Sir Thopas* is a logical conundrum, a paradox, for in presenting his persona totally out of artistic
control, Chaucer is exerting artistic control of the highest order.
As Derek Pearsall puts it, "*Thopas* is unfinished, a structural imperfection which contributes to its artistic perfection."[13] In
Pseudo-Dionysian terms, just as names both describe God and fail
utterly in their description—simultaneously—so also do adjectives
like *perfect, imperfect, finished,* and *unfinished* apply and yet fail
to apply to Chaucer's text.

An example of an insightful critical explication of his text will
serve to clarify this point. Helen Cooper, fully realizing the paradox of *Sir Thopas,* writes that it "has to be read on two entirely
different levels," that it is "two completely different poems from
exactly the same text."[14] In explicating Chaucer's persona's poetic
difficulties, she notes that the three calls for attention fall with
mathematical regularity in the text, dividing it into three sections:
"The first section runs for eighteen stanzas, the second for nine,
and there are four and a half in the third before the Host interrupts:
whether or not the precise halving is intentional, it does show the
narrative structure getting into deep trouble."[15] Certainly this is
true, a major insight into the structure of the tale. But *simultaneously* it is false, showing a poet in utter control, halving away at
his parodic text until there is nothing left, placing structural and
structuring markers to signify to his readers his virtuoso tricks of
self-dismantling.

Yet, one step further, the reader cannot rest with an interpretation that presents, in Donaldsonian terms, a Chaucer-Poet who
parodies his own creation, Chaucer the Pilgrim, because the persona who is a poetic bumbler of hyper-Squirean proportions has
at least one disturbing fact in common with the poet who has created him: the tendency to break off before completing a work. Just
as Chaucer has fragmented so many poems that have gone before
and, presumably, will come after *Sir Thopas,* he cannot finish this
one either. That is why I have insisted on calling the persona simply
Chaucer in most of the above discussion: the two in this crucial
way are identical. Perhaps the fragmentation is self-parodic of

Chaucer's earlier difficulties in completing his own texts; perhaps also it is prophetic of the future fragmentation of *The Canterbury Tales* as a whole.

## The Tale of Melibee

Chaucer does not stay silent for long. Unlike that of the Squire or for that matter the Cook or, later in *The Canterbury Tales,* the Monk, the fragmentation of his tale does not lead to the teller's total silence. He responds rather wordily to the Host's constricting demand for a piece of prose:

> "Gladly," quod I, "by Goddes sweete pyne!
> I wol yow telle a litel thyng in prose
> That oghte liken yow, as I suppose.
> . . . . . . . . . . . .
> Therfore, lordynges alle, I yow biseche,
> If that yow thynke I varie as in my speche,
> As thus, though that I telle somwhat moore
> Of proverbes than ye han herd bifoore
> Comprehended in this litel tretys heere,
> To enforce with th'effect of my mateere;
> And though I nat the same wordes seye
> As ye han herd, yet to yow alle I preye
> Blameth me nat; for, as in my sentence,
> Shul ye nowher fynden difference
> Fro the sentence of this tretys lyte
> After the which this murye tale I write.
> And therfore herkneth what that I shal seye,
> And lat me tellen al my tale, I preye."
>
> (VII, 936–38, 953–66)

The redundancy of this excerpt, with its repetition of "sentence" (see also VII, 946), its frequent signposting, almost as if it were a freshman composition ("I wol yow telle," "After the which this murye tale I write," "lat me tellen"), and above all the triple reference to the treatise's littleness[16] indicate that Chaucer is still parodying himself. The repetitiveness that critics have found in *Melibee,* in other words, is a characteristic of the headlink as well; it is, in effect, Chaucer's self-parodic refusal to be silent.

The tale itself, however, is not Chaucer's own but is instead the least original of *The Canterbury Tales,* an almost exact, word-for-word translation of Renaud de Louens's French abridgment of Albert of Brescia's thirteenth-century Latin moral treatise, the *Liber consolationis et consilii*.[17] As such it is entirely consonant with Chaucer's self-parody as an author who knows only one rhyme: when that one is silenced, he obliges with a prose work almost entirely someone else's. There are, of course, a few changes, the most notable perhaps the omission of a passage criticizing youthful kings[18]—evidence useful in dating Chaucer's translation originally to the late 1370s and indicative to some of political reasons for its production, the pacifism it espouses being applicable to the French wars.[19] Regardless of its possible political meaning, it represents the type of writing that Chaucer privileges in his Retraction and that was tremendously popular in late-fourteenth-century England, the prose treatise of religious devotion. As I have already mentioned, it too, like the Parson's Tale, entered the vast sea of anonymous prose works of devotion.[20]

The central problem of *Melibee* is the extent to which it may be called Chaucer's own. Besides the excision of the passage possibly offensive to the young Richard II[21] and a couple of others of seemingly no importance, Chaucer adds two sentences (VII, 1824–25 and VII, 1884–86), also of little importance, and gives a significant name to Melibee's injured daughter—Sophie. Thus he strengthens the moral allegory already present in the name of his wife, Prudence, by turning the daughter into an abstraction for Wisdom.[22] Chaucer's text is in this sense his own, for his interpretation is significantly different.[23] Whereas in Albert and Renaud, Prudence urges Melibee to withstand vengeance, in Chaucer she must urge someone whose wisdom is impaired. Having said that, we are left with a vast and monumental little treatise where all the specific details a Chaucerian critic is fond of explicating are unsettlingly not Chaucer's but Albert's, filtered through Renaud.

To put it briefly, Melibee is out of control of himself because of the injuries to Prudence and Sophie:

> Whan Melibeus retourned was into his hous, and saugh al this meschief, he, lyk a mad man rentynge his clothes, gan to wepe and crie. (VII, 973)

Prudence, in a torrent of words, admonishes him to be silent:

> And Piers Alphonce seith, "If thou hast myght to doon a thyng of which thou most repente, it is bettre 'nay' than 'ye.' / This is to seyn, that thee is bettre holde thy tonge stille than for to speke. (VII, 1218–19)

Prudence's gloss is of course a misinterpretation suggesting silence where the text she is glossing recommends simple words. Melibee submits to her control, learns from her words not only to be silent but to forgive. Prudence then arranges a meeting with his enemies "in privee place" (VII, 1721), controls them with her words, and effects the reconciliation. She, in other words, is an archcontroller, a character who comes close to usurping the role of her author by arranging things within her story so that the proper ending may take place.

Without its placement within *The Canterbury Tales,* the originally independent Melibee would lack these interpretive signs. Its placement also indicates, I suggest, the solution to a critical problem. Briefly put, critics argue over whether *Melibee* is serious or a joke. The opposing arguments are as follows: For those who would take the treatise seriously,[24] the important interpretive clues are its style, the popularity of devotional treatises in Chaucer's England, the exacting labors Chaucer spent on translating it, and the political importance of its pacifist message. Those who ironize the tale[25] emphasize its wordiness, its connections with the obviously self-parodying Sir Thopas, and its dramatic placement within the links.

The two seemingly irreconcilable positions are paradoxically reconciled with the realization that whatever comedy is there is a comedy of placement. Taken by itself, as an exceptionally literal translation of a popular medieval devotional treatise, it is one of Chaucer's three or four serious attempts at the type of spiritual prose he valorizes in his Retraction. As such it is a fairly successful treatise; divorced from Chaucer's name, it did find a place secure enough in the genre of anonymous Middle English translations of Continental texts, like, say, St. Catherine of Siena's *Orcherd of Syon*[26] or *Barlaam and Josephat.*[27] Taken in its context, with its undercutting connections with other *Canterbury Tales* and with its coupling with its partner, *Sir Thopas,* it is an elaborate joke—one that shares with *Sir Thopas* a doubling of perspective. As *Sir Thopas* simultaneously is and is not bad writing, so *Melibee* both is and is not serious devotion. Chaucer, in short, simultaneously affirms and denies its serious purpose.

In this simultaneous affirmation and denial *Melibee* is Pseudo-Dionysian, as analysis of a specific passage should make clear. Speaking about the thorny theological problem of why a good God would allow pain and evil, Prudence says:

Now, sire, if men wolde axe me why that God suffred men to do yow
this vileynye, certes, I kan nat wel answere, as for no soothfastnesse. /
For th'apostle seith that "the sciences and the juggementz of oure Lord
God almyghty been ful depe; / ther may no man comprehende ne
serchen hem suffisantly."/ Nathelees, by certeyne presumpciouns and
conjectynges, I holde and bileeve / that God, which that is ful of justice
and of rightwisnesse, hath suffred this bityde by juste cause resonable.
(VII, 1405–9)

The issue here is the very one that caused Pseudo-Dionysius to
write *The Divine Names.* God may be termed good from one perspective, yet that name is meaningless from another. So also might
*Melibee* have the names "serious," "comic," "devotional," and
"parodic" from one perspective yet not from another. In himself,
God cannot be signified by human language; in itself *Melibee* cannot be interpreted by human criticism.

There remains one thing of importance to be said about Chaucer's two tales. They are, as C. David Benson points out, opposites
that set the limits for the rest of *The Canterbury Tales;* between
their styles we may locate the styles of all the other tellers.[28] But
they are even more than that. They set the limits for Chaucer's
whole career and indicate, at least partially, his reaction to fragmentation. As such they point forward to Chaucer's Retraction.

Melibee, at the very end of Chaucer's little treatise, forgives
his enemies:

"Wherfore I receyve yow to my grace / and foryeve yow outrely alle
the offenses, injuries, and wronges that ye have doon agayn me and
myne, / to this effect and to this ende, that God of his endelees mercy /
wole at the tyme of oure diynge foryeven us oure giltes that we han
trespassed to hym in this wrecched world. / For doutelees, if we be
sory and repentant of the synnes and giltes which we han trespassed
in the sighte of oure Lord God, / he is so free and so merciable / that
he wole foryeven us oure giltes / and bryngen us to the blisse that
nevere hath ende." Amen. (VII, 1881–8)

At the end of Chaucer's long collection of stories, he writes,

Wherfore I biseke yow mekely, for the mercy of God, that ye preye for
me that Crist have mercy on me and foryeve me my giltes; / and namely
of my translacions and enditynges of worldly vanitees. . . . But of the
translacion of Boece de Consolacione, and othere bookes of legendes
of seintes, and omelies, and moralitee, and devocioun, / that thanke I
oure Lord Jhesu Crist and his blisful Mooder . . . / bisekynge hem that
they from hennes forth unto my lyves ende sende me grace to biwayle

my giltes and to studie to the salvacioun of my soule. (X, 1084–85, 1088–90)

Not only are the situations similar between the two texts, but we hear much of the same language. There is moreover an analogous connection between the two: Chaucer's writing of worldly vanities is analogous to the sins of Melibee's enemies, and his writing of this book of morality and devotion is analogous to their penance. In other words, in the movement from *Sir Thopas* to *Melibee* is Chaucer's whole career in microcosm: the composition of worldly vanity that is fragmented leading into the controlling act of writing devotional prose as penance. The God of Love might once have imposed upon him the writing of legends of good women; his self-inflicted penance seems all the harder.

## The Retraction

It is, of course, disturbing to have the type of closure that the Retraction seems to offer—a dismantling of one of the monuments of English literature by its own author:[29] "and foryeve me my giltes; / and namely of . . . the tales of Caunterbury, thilke that sownen into synne." (X, 1084–86). And there are many unanswerable questions attending the critical explication of it: To borrow Donaldson's famous classification, is it Chaucer the man, the poet, or the pilgrim who is speaking? Has this Retraction been planned from the beginning of the work, or has a sudden fit of religious conscience, occasioned by something, perhaps the near approach of death itself, caused it? Is it ironical or not? I intend to answer none of these questions, passing over them, as Chaucer himself did, in silence.

I have, though, three brief observations. First, most understandably connect the Retraction to the Parson's Tale that immediately precedes it.[30] As the Parson closes off the tale-telling within sight of Canterbury yet redirects the pilgrimage toward the heavenly Jerusalem by calling for repentance of the Seven Deadly Sins, so Chaucer responds with his own penance. Such a response is consonant with Chaucer's mystical environment. As the anonymous author of the *Tretyse of Loue* puts it:

A god, what shall we wretchys do whanne we shall yelde acomptis befor þe face of Ihesu cryste, þat put hym yn the place to yelde so streyte acoumpt for vs as ys befor rehersyd?[31]

That writing poetry is not one of the Deadly Sins is perhaps a trivial objection to this doubtless correct interpretation. Yet if we follow the logic of the interpretation, it does, I suggest, tend to dismantle. According to medieval theology, as everyone knows, forgiveness of sins involves contrition, oracular confession, and penance. That Chaucer's words of retraction signify some sort of contrition is obvious. If they represent an oracular confession—as they seem to do, with their orderly listing of specific sins—then their auditor takes on the role of the priest—that is, the reader, not the Parson, since there is no textual evidence that the framework of *The Canterbury Tales* is still in place and the Parson is hearing Chaucer's confession. Yet the reader of Chaucer's poetry is the one, presumably, whom he will lead into sin because of it. Is it up to us to assign—as, say, Cupid does in the Prologue to the *Legend of Good Women*—some sort of penance to the contrite poet kneeling before us? We might counsel him to write only devout spiritual treatises from now on till the end of his life and link them together in a work entitled *Legends of Devout People*.

Second, retractions like this were quite common in the Middle Ages.[32] Ovid ends his *Art of Love* with a section usually titled "Remedium Amoris," the "Remedy for Love," and so Andreas Capellanus ends his *Art of Honest Loving* with his own "Remedium Amoris." John Gower ends his *Confessio Amantis* with Amans—now rather uncomfortably named "John Gower"—being expelled by Venus from her service because he is too old: Gower's own characters gather around him, stricken prostrate, and walk away from him in remorse, leaving him with a set of prayer beads, alone. Lancelot and Guenevere, in Malory and his sources and analogues, enter houses of religion after Arthur is slain. Malory even, like Chaucer, asks prayers for his soul. Chaucer himself ends his *Troilus* with a famous passage (V, 1807–55) denying the values the long poem has been affirming, leading Paul G. Ruggiers to comment, ". . . the palinode of *Troilus* and the Retraction of the *Canterbury Tales* share . . . the paradox of simultaneous affirmation and rejection"[33]—language evocative, I would add, of Pseudo-Dionysian theology and medieval language theory. As I mentioned at the beginning of this book, Ruggiers sees this simultaneous affirmation and negation as "informing principles" of *The Canterbury Tales* as a whole.[34] The conventionality of this all, in other words, generates closure.

Third, the closure is that of loss of control leading to fragmentation and silence. The author, the archcontroller, who has, godlike, called *The Canterbury Tales* into being, can no longer write. Words fail him. He speaks of "the defaute of myn unkonnynge" (X, 1082), quoting, of course, the term invented by Pseudo-Dionysius and Englished by the *Cloud*-author as "unknowing." He wishes he could "have seyd bettre" (X, 1082). He forgets a large portion of his *oeuvre* when he wishes to retract individual works—"and many another book, if they were in my remembrance" (X, 1087). And he needs the help of Christ, the Virgin, and all the saints (X, 1088) to bewail his sins.

The close connections between Chaucer's Retraction and the works of the *Cloud*-author need some further explication. At the very beginning of *The Cloud of Unknowing,* we find words that call to mind the very end of *The Canterbury Tales.* The *Cloud*-author begins his Prologue thus:

> I charge þee & I beseche þee, wiþ as moche power & vertewe as þe bonde of charite is sufficient to suffre, what-so-euer þou be þat þis book schalt haue in possession . . . þat in as moche as in þee is by wille & auisement, neiþer þou rede it, ne write it, ne speke it, ne ʒit suffre it be red, wretyn, or spokyn of any or to any, bot ʒif it be of soche one or to soche one þat haþ . . . in a trewe will & by an hole entent, purposed him to be a parfit folower of Criste.[35]

We hear here the same concern Chaucer has about the power of a text to affect life. But where Chaucer fears the wrong texts will find their way into the hands of his readers—*Troilus* or the *House of Fame* instead of "Boece de Consolacione, and othere bookes of legendes of seintes, and omelies, and moralitee, and devocioun" (X, 1088)—the *Cloud*-author fears his text will find its way into the hands of the wrong readers.

The *Cloud*-author continues:

> & ouer þis, I charge þee & I beseche þee bi þe autorite of charite, þat ʒif any soche schal rede it, write it, or speke it . . . to take hem tyme to rede it, speke it, write it, or here it, al ouer.[36]

Where Chaucer, in other words, prefers fragmentation, retracting only those *Canterbury Tales* "that sownen into synne" (X, 1085) and keeping those that savor of devotion, the *Cloud*-author prefers to keep his text whole. It is the audience that fragments:

> Fleshely ianglers opyn preisers & blamers of hem-self or of any oþer tiþing tellers, rouners & tutilers of tales, & alle maner of pinchers: kept I neuer þat þei sawe þis book. For myn entent was neuer to write soch þing unto hem.[37]

The list uncomfortably fits the pilgrims of the General Prologue, and the words "myn entent(e)" are shared between the two texts (see X, 1082). Both authors attempt the role of archcontroller, this time not as characters usurping the prerogatives of the author but as authors usurping the prerogatives of their readers, imposing one monolithic interpretation upon them[38] and even in the case of the *Cloud*-author excluding most of them.

In what may be his last work, the *Book of Privy Counselling,* the *Cloud*-author writes what is, like Chaucer's Retraction, in effect a résumé:

> For þis same werk, ȝif it be verrely conceyuid, is þat reuerent affeccion & þe frute departid from þe tre þat I speke of in þi lityl pistle of preier. Þis is þe cloude of vnknowyng; þis is þat priue loue put in purete of spirit; þis is þe Arke of þe Testament. Þis is Denis deuinite, his wisdom & his drewry his liȝty derknes & his vnknowyn kunnynges. Þis is it þat settiþ þee in silence as wele fro þouȝtes as fro wordes. Þis makiþ þi preier ful schorte. In þis þou arte lernid to forsake þe woreld & to dispise it.[39]

Like Chaucer, the *Cloud*-author lists his works, suggesting that despising the world is the proper response to it. Here we also see an attention to silence and fragmentation not unlike Chaucer's: words fail, become shortened.

This is, as is Chaucer's Retraction, a sad picture of an inert writer who can no longer control his words. But in the world of the mystics, of course, failure is paradoxically success, particularly failure of language. As the *Cloud*-author writes:

> For haue a man neuer so moche goostly vnderstondyng in knowyng of alle maad goostly þinges, ȝit may he neuer be þe werk of his vnderstondyng com to þe knowyng of an vnmaad goostly þing, þe which is nouȝt bot God. *Bot by þe failyng it may* [my emphasis]; for whi þat þing þat it failiþ in is noþing elles bot only God. & þherfore it was þat Seynte Denis seyde: "Þe most goodly knowyng of God is þat, þe whiche is knowyn bi vnknowyng."[40]

Whether Chaucer took comfort in this ultimately mystical idea, Pseudo-Dionysian in its affirmation and denial of the word *failing,* is beyond our own knowing, for his Retraction, his long poem, his life perhaps all fragment at this point, leaving us debilitated, staring at an empty page.

## Silence

If we imagine a NeoPlatonic, Pseudo-Dionysian allegory operative near the end of the *Canterbury Tales,* when the Parson redirects the pilgrimage toward "Jerusalem celestial" (X, 51) rather than the earthly Canterbury now drawing in sight, we can posit this: the pilgrimage, as the Knight's character Egeus would have it, is the pilgrimage of life ("This world nys but a thurghfare ful of wo, / And we been pilgrymes, passynge to and fro." [I, 2847–48]), in which we are *returning* towards God, from whom we have originally emanated. As we near the beatific vision, our words fail, fragment, and we become silent. The Parson himself claims trouble in marshaling words into poetry ("I kan nat geeste 'rum, ram, ruf,' by lettre" [X, 43]); Chaucer himself can no longer remember things ("and many another book, if they were in my remembrance" [X, 1086]), noticing that words proceed from God ("of whom procedeth al wit and al goodness" [X, 1081]), preferring now in his *return* words of *unknowing* ("they arrette it to the defaute of myn unknnynge and nat to my wyl, that wolde ful fayn have seyd bettre if I hadde had konnynge" [X, 1082]). In this allegory I am creating, the fragmentation of the *Canterbury Tales* is wholly understandable not as artistic failure or the depredations of death itself, but the fitting—even the only possible—conclusion to this poem. Yet an argument against this allegory is that from the pilgrims' point of view the journey is not so much a *return* as a *procession* outward—or in Pseudo-Dionysian terms, the appropriate place for language to gain rather than lose valency. The counterargument, of course, is that it is simultaneously both.

As the composer John Cage writes in his *Silence: Lectures and Writing,* "I am here                  and there is nothing to say     . . . .          What we re-quire

is silence                         ;                                but what silence requires                          is                                that I go
on talking          . . . .                                               But now
                    there are silences                              and the
words                           make                                      help
make                        the silences                              ."[41] The

spacing is Cage's, the ideas, his, Pseudo-Dionysius's, and Chaucer's. They are also the ideas of the great Japanese Zen painters who leave more out of their pictures than they put in. I argue that in Chaucer's very fragmentation the greatness of his poem lies, for what is not said—almost like Derrida's *trace*—is always attending what is said, always haunting it, simultaneously affirming and denying it.

I think we are too fond of creating in our minds a Chaucer totally in control—the archpoet who from the noisy chaos of fourteenth century life produces his great masterpiece. He is that, and I affirm it with all my strength. But haunting that privileged image are the traces of two other Chaucers, and these two are the great fragmenters. One is like Nicholas in the Miller's Tale, who has gotten us so very far but cannot complete the whole—for Nicholas the tale he is in, for Chaucer the original plan for *The Canterbury Tales*. The other is like Symkyn, Aleyn, and John in the Reeve's Tale, who create tricks and stratagems but then give them up and fall asleep at the wrong moment. This Chaucer sporadically gives things up along the way, thus fragmenting on a smaller scale the individual tales within *The Canterbury Tales* as a whole.

Long ago, E. Talbot Donaldson suggested that there are three Chaucers—the Man, the Poet, and the Pilgrim.[42] I suggest that Chaucer the Poet in turn fragments into three. We have well explicated the first and should continue to do so, but we have scarcely begun the exciting critical task of explicating the other two.[43] And to them we owe much. Imagine a fully completed *Canterbury Tales*—120 tales long with the supper at the Tabard to cap things off, the Knight graciously accepting the prize like an Oscar. How infinitely better is the broken pilgrimage, stopped—as we are at this moment in our own lives—part of the way somewhere.[44] In Chaucer's fragmentation and failure and silence paradoxically is his genius.

# Notes

## Chapter 1. Introduction

1. See, for instance, Jerome J. McGann, *A Critique of Modern Textual Criticism* (Chicago: University of Chicago Press, 1983); Stanley E. Fish, *Is There a Text in This Class? The Authority of Interpretive Communities* (Cambridge: Harvard University Press, 1980); and Betsy Bowden, *Chaucer Aloud: The Varieties of Textual Interpretation* (Philadelphia: University of Pennsylvania Press, 1987).

2. See, for instance, D. W. Robertson, Jr., and Bernard F. Huppé, *Fruyt and Chaf: Studies in Chaucer's Allegories* (Princeton: Princeton University Press, 1963); B. G. Koonce, *Chaucer and the Tradition of Fame: Symbolism in "The House of Fame"* (Princeton: Princeton University Press, 1966); and, as a recent defense of exegetical criticism, John V. Fleming, *Classical Imitation and Interpretation in Chaucer's "Troilus"* (Lincoln: University of Nebraska Press, 1990).

3. See, for instance, Bowden, *Chaucer Aloud;* Fish, *Text;* and Stanley E. Fish, *The Living Temple: George Herbert and Catechizing* (Berkeley: University of California Press, 1978).

4. See Stephen Greenblatt, ed., *The Power of Forms in the English Renaissance* (Norman, Okla.: Pilgrim Books, 1982), pp. 3–6; see also Stephen Greenblatt, *Renaissance Self-Fashioning from More to Shakespeare* (Chicago: University of Chicago Press, 1980); Stephen Greenblatt, *Marvelous Possessions: The Wonder of the New World* (Chicago: University of Chicago Press, 1991); Jonathan Goldberg, "The Politics of Renaissance Literature: A Review Essay," *ELH* 49 (1982): 514–42; and Jean E. Howard, "The New Historicism in Renaissance Studies," *English Literary Renaissance* 16 (1986): 13–43.

5. Linda Georgianna, "Love So Dearly Bought: The Terms of Redemption in *The Canterbury Tales*," *Studies in the Age of Chaucer* 12 (1990): 86–87, argues for the influence of popular religion on Chaucer's *Canterbury Tales,* especially the commercial aspects of it.

6. A similar argument has recently been made by Susan Crane, "Medieval Romance and Feminine Difference in *The Knight's Tale,*" *Studies in the Age of Chaucer* 12 (1990): 48, about the influence of the romance genre on Chaucer independent of his direct knowledge of individual texts.

7. Paul G. Ruggiers, *The Art of "The Canterbury Tales"* (Madison: University of Wisconsin Press, 1965), p. 41.

8. Ibid., p. 3.

9. The edition of Chaucer's works I use is Larry Benson, ed., *The Riverside Chaucer* (Boston: Houghton, Mifflin, 1987). Roman numerals refer to Fragment numbers within *The Centerbury Tales,* arabic numerals to line numbers.

10. Ruggiers, p. 192.

11. I prefer the roughly synonymous "denial" in this book to Ruggiers's "rejection" in accord with language in use among critics of mysticism.

12. The term *intertextual* has become a staple of literary theorists over the last two decades. I use it in a general sense to indicate cultural resources—especially texts—available to Chaucer but not necessarily *directly* influencing him. The influence of the intertext is on the society, which in turn influences an author. For modern and differing definitions of the intertext, see, for instance, Julia Kristeva, *Desire in Language,* ed. Leon S. Roudiez, trans. Thomas Gora, Alice Jardine, and Leon S. Roudiez (New York: Columbia University Press, 1980), pp. 36–63; Roland Barthes *S/Z* (Paris: Seuil, 1970), p. 6; Roland Barthes, *The Pleasure of the Text,* trans. Richard Miller (New York: Hill and Wang, 1975); Harold Bloom, *Poetry and Repression* (New Haven: Yale University Press, 1976), pp. 2–3; Harold Bloom, *A Map of Misreading* (New York: Oxford University Press, 1975), p. 32; Harold Bloom, *The Anxiety of Influence: A Theory of Poetry* (New York: Oxford University Press, 1973); compare Jonathan Culler, *The Pursuit of Signs* (Ithaca: Cornell University Press, 1981), pp. 107–10. For specialized treatments of the intertext, see T. S. Eliot, "Tradition and the Individual Talent," in T. S. Eliot, *Selected Essays,* pp. 3–11 (New York: Harcourt, Brace and World, 1964), p. 5 (although he and some of the others that follow do not use that term); Alan Nadel, "Translating the Past: Literary Allusion as Covert Criticism," *Georgia Review* 36 (1982): 639–51; Richard Poirier, *The Performing Self: Composition and Decomposition in the Language of Contemporary Life* (New York: Oxford University Press, 1971), p. 27; Paul A. Bové, *Deconstructive Poetics: Heidegger and Modern American Poetry* (New York: Columbia University Press, 1980); Joseph N. Riddel, *The Inverted Bell* (Baton Rouge: Louisiana State University Press, 1974); and Michel Foucault, *The Archeology of Knowledge,* trans. A. M. Sheridan (New York: Harper and Row, 1972). For specific studies of the intertext relating to Chaucer, see Leonard Michael Koff, *Chaucer and the Art of Storytelling* (Berkeley: University of California Press, 1988), pp. 102–3; and Susan Schibanoff, "The New Reader and Female Textuality in Two Early Commentaries on Chaucer," *Studies in the Age of Chaucer* 10 (1988): 71–108. For studies that in general seek to relate Chaucer to the concerns of modern literary theory, see Judith Ferster, *Chaucer on Interpretation* (Cambridge: Cambridge University Press, 1985); Jesse M. Gellrich, *The Idea of the Book in the Middle Ages: Language Theory, Mythology, and Fiction* (Ithaca: Cornell University Press, 1985); Robert M. Jordan, *Chaucer's Poetics and the Modern Reader* (Berkeley: University of California Press, 1987); H. Marshall Leicester, Jr., *The Disenchanted Self: Representing the Subject in "The Canterbury Tales"* (Berkeley: University of California Press, 1990); Dolores Warwick Frese, *An Ars Legendi for Chaucer's "Canterbury Tales": Re-constructive Reading* (Gainesville: University of Florida Press, 1991); and Elaine Tuttle Hansen, *Chaucer and the Fictions of Gender* (Berkeley: University of California Press, 1992), pp. 23–25.

13. For an explication of Chaucer and the exegetical critics who prefer allegorical interpretations, see Lee Patterson, *Negotiating the Past: The Historical Understanding of Medieval Literature* (Madison: University of Wisconsin Press, 1987), pp. 3–39.

14. For an analysis of authorial control and fragmentation in the Merchant's Tale, see Robert R. Edwards, "Narration and Doctrine in the Merchant's Tale," *Speculum* 66 (1991): 366; for fragmentation in that same tale, see Robert M. Jordan, "The Non-Dramatic Disunity of the *Merchant's Tale,*" *PMLA* 78 (1963): 293–99.

15. Laura Kendrick in *Chaucerian Play: Comedy and Control in "The Canter-*

*bury Tales"* (Berkeley: University of California Press, 1988) argues for an interpretation of Chaucerian comedy as a means of psychological control over oneself.

16. The "trace" is a term particularly associated with Jacques Derrida. For this and related concepts, see his *Of Grammatology,* trans. Gayatri Chakravorty Spivak (Baltimore: Johns Hopkins University Press, 1976); and *Writing and Difference,* trans. Alan Bass (Chicago: University of Chicago Press, 1978). For the influence of the mystics Pseudo-Dionysius and Meister Eckhart on his thinking, see his *Psyché: Inventions de l'autre* (Paris: Galilée, 1987), pp. 535–95. Compare Vincent B. Leitch, *Deconstructive Criticism: An Advanced Introduction* (New York: Columbia University Press, 1983), p. 28. For a debate concerning the use of Derrida's theories in explicating Chaucer, see Peggy A. Knapp, "Deconstructing *The Canterbury Tales:* Pro" and Traugott Lawler, "Deconstructing *The Canterbury Tales:* Con," in *Studies in the Age of Chaucer, Proceedings* no. 2 (1987): 73–81 and 83–91. Both are reprinted in Malcolm Andrew, ed., *Critical Essays on Chaucer's "Canterbury Tales"* (Toronto: University of Toronto Press, 1991).

17. For an incisive comment about Chaucer's "doubleness of language" not specifically related to mystical theology, see John M. Ganim, *Chaucerian Theatricality* (Princeton: Princeton University Press, 1990), p. 131.

18. See Stephen Greenblatt, *Shakespearean Negotiations: The Circulation of Social Energy in Renaissance England* (Berkeley: University of California Press, 1988).

19. Derek Pearsall, *The Canterbury Tales* (London: George Allen and Unwin, 1985), p. 38. John H. Fisher, *The Importance of Chaucer* (Carbondale and Edwardsville: Southern Illinois University Press, 1992), p. 142, reminds us that "there are very few manuscripts of any secular literature in English dating from before 1400," citing A. S. G. Edwards and Derek Pearsall, eds., *Book Production and Publishing in Britain, 1375–1475* (Cambridge: Cambridge University Press, 1989), pp. 257–78.

20. See Paul Strohm, *Social Chaucer* (Cambridge: Harvard University Press, 1989), pp. 28–29, 44; and Lee Patterson, *Chaucer and the Subject of History* (Madison: University of Wisconsin Press, 1991), pp. 38–39. Paul A. Olson, *"The Canterbury Tales" and the Good Society* (Princeton: Princeton University Press, 1986), pp. 7–8, reminds us that Clifford was a member of the crusading Order of the Passion.

21. For the debate over Chaucerian authorship of *The Equatorie of the Planetis,* see Sigmund Eisner, "Chaucer as Technical Writer," *Chaucer Review* 19 (1985): 179–201; Pamela Robinson, "Geoffrey Chaucer and the *Equatorie of the Planetis:* The State of the Problem," *Chaucer Review* 26 (1991), 17–30; A. S. G. Edwards and Linne R. Mooney, "Is the *Equatorie of the Planets* a Chaucer Holograph?" *Chaucer Review* 26 (1991): 31–42; and Jeanne E. Krochalis, "Postscript: The *Equatorie of the Planetis* as a Translator's Manuscript," *Chaucer Review* 26 (1991): 43–47.

22. See Siegfried Wenzel, ed., *Summa Virtutum de Remediis Anime* (Athens: University of Georgia Press, 1984).

23. See Marta Powell Harley, *A Revelation of Purgatory by an Unknown, Fifteenth-Century Woman Visionary* (Lewiston, N.Y.: Edwin Mellen Press, 1985), p. 41. See also John M. Manly and Edith Rickert, *The Text of "The Canterbury Tales,"* 8 vols. (Chicago: University of Chicago Press, 1940), 1:345.

24. See Robert E. Lewis, ed., *Lotario dei Segni: De Miseria Condicionis Humane* (Athens: University of Georgia Press, 1978).

25. Quotations from Chaucer's works other than *The Canterbury Tales* are

referenced by abbreviations, followed by line number. "F" and "G" refer to the two versions of the Prologue to the *Legend of Good Women*.

26. See Pearsall, *Canterbury Tales*, pp. 257–58.

27. See Michael B. Ewbank, "Diverse Orderings of Dionysius's *Triplex Via* by St. Thomas Aquinas," *Mediaeval Studies* 52 (1990): 82–109.

28. Bernard McGinn, ed., with Frank Tobin and Elvira Borgstadt, *Meister Eckhart: Teacher and Preacher* (New York: Paulist Press, 1986), p. 16.

29. Charlotte D'Evelyn, ed., *Meditations on the Life and Passion of Christ*, EETS 158 (London: Oxford University Press, 1921).

30. For a discussion of the authorship of the Pseudo-Dionysian oeuvre, see Ronald F. Hathaway, *Hierarchy and the Definition of Order in the Letters of Pseudo-Dionysius* (The Hague: Martinus Nijhoff, 1969), pp. 31–35. Liturgical references date him as a late-fifth-, early sixth-century Syrian; see Josef Stiglmayr, "Die Lehre von den Sakramenten und der Kirche nach Ps.-Dionysius," *Zeitschrift für Katolische Theologie* 22 (1898): 246–303; Josef Stiglmayr, "Eine syrische Liturgie als Vorlage des Pseudo-Areopagiten," *Zeitschrift für Katolische Theologie* 33 (1909): 383–85; E. Boularand, "L'Eucharistie d'après le pseudo-Denys l'Areopagite," *Bulletin de Littérature Ecclesiastique* 58 (1957): 193–217, and 59 (1958): 129–69; and Paul Rorem, *Biblical and Liturgical Symbols within the Pseudo-Dionysian Synthesis* (Toronto: Pontifical Institute of Mediaeval Studies, 1984), p. 27.

31. Pseudo-Dionysius, of course, could have been a woman, but I follow the male pronouns in referring to her/him, since the identity s/he chose was male— i.e., Dionysius the Areopagite.

32. There are actually three separate "Denises" who, conflated, became St. Denis for the later Middle Ages. The first was Paul's Athenian disciple, the second the St. Denis who preached the Gospel in Paris, thus becoming the patron saint of France, the third the Syrian theologian. The first two were conflated at least since the early ninth century (see Raymond J. Loenertz, "La legénde parisenne de s. Denys l'aréopagite: son genèse et son premier té moin," *Analecta Bollandiana* 69 [1951]: 217–37), the third since his writings became widely distributed, given his pseudonymous appropriation of the Areopagite's name.

33. For Pseudo-Dionysius's wordplay, see Rorem, *Biblical and Liturgical Symbols*, pp. 15, 71.

34. Translations from Pseudo-Dionysius are taken from Colm Luibheid, trans., *Pseudo-Dionysius: The Complete Works* (New York: Paulist Press, 1987). This quotation is from p. 49.

35. The *Cloud*-author probably picked up the term from Pseudo-Dionysius's *Mystical Theology*, which he translated, rather than *The Divine Names;* see Rorem, *Biblical and Liturgical Symbols*, pp. 140–41. Pseudo-Dionysius likely did not himself get the term from St. Augustine, who in *De Trinitate* 8.2.3 speaks of the "learned ignorance [docta ignorantia] of God: the connections between the Latin West and the Syrian East were too tenuous in the early sixth century. See Jeffrey F. Hamburger, ed., *The Rothschild Canticles: Art and Mysticism in Flanders and the Rhineland, Circa 1300* (New Haven: Yale University Press, 1990), p. 122.

36. Luibheid, *Pseudo-Dionysius*, p. 53.

37. Ibid., pp. 55–56.

38. See, for instance, Bede Griffithes, *Return to the Center* (Springfield, Ill.: Templegate, 1976); and Liubheid, *Pseudo-Dionysius*, p. 32.

39. Luibheid, *Pseudo-Dionysius*, p. 58.

40. Ibid., p. 130.

41. Ibid., p. 190.

42. Ibid., p. 135.

43. The quotation comes from folio 101v. See Hamburger, *The Rothschild Canticles,* pp. 121, 207. The Latin reads, "Optime et pulcerrime loquitur quide deo tacet."

44. Luibheid, *Pseudo-Dionysius,* p. 89.

45. Ibid., p. 74.

46. Ibid., p. 107.

47. See Paul de Man, *Allegories of Reading* (New Haven: Yale University Press, 1979), pp. 8–9.

48. Luibheid, *Pseudo-Dionysius,* p. 222.

49. Ibid., p. 150.

50. See Rorem, *Biblical and Liturgical Symbols,* pp. 58–66.

51. For the role of Pseudo-Dionysian symbols in medieval sign theory, see Gerhart B. Ladner, "Medieval and Modern Understanding of Symbolism: A Comparison," *Speculum* 54 (1979): 223–54. Ladner emphasizes the affirmative aspect of Pseudo-Dionysian thought.

52. Rorem, *Biblical and Liturgical Symbols,* p. 90.

53. See Wolfgang Riehle, *The Middle English Mystics,* trans. Bernard Standring (London: Routledge and Kegan Paul, 1981), p. 1.

54. Russell A. Peck, "Chaucer and the Nominalist Questions," *Speculum* 53 (1978): 759–60; and Paul B. Taylor, "Chaucer's *Cosyn to the Dede,*" *Speculum* 57 (1982): 315–27 seek to relate this passage to concerns among the nominalist philosophers like Ockham and Holcot. See also David C. Steinmetz, "Late Medieval Nominalism and the *Clerk's Tale,*" *Chaucer Review* 12 (1977): 38–54. Pseudo-Dionysius, I suggest, is an even closer analogue, yet the nominalists' idea that, in Taylor's words, "particulars precede the idea of a universal and that words are without real referents" (318), is concordant with Pseudo-Dionysian thought. For Chaucer's use of Holcott specifically as a source for the dream theory of the Nun's Priest's Tale, see Robert Pratt, "Some Latin Sources of the Nonnes Preest on Dreams," *Speculum* 52 (1977): 538–70.

55. See Phyllis Hodgson, ed., *Deonise Hid Diunite and Other Treatises on Contemplative Prayer,* EETS 231 (London: Oxford University Press, 1955), pp. 6–7.

56. Ibid., pp. 71–72.

57. For the influence of scholastic philosophy on Chaucer, particularly in the Knight's Tale, see Lois Roney, *Chaucer's Knight's Tale and Theories of Scholastic Psychology* (Tampa: University of South Florida Press, 1990); and Rodney Delasanta, "Chaucer and Strode," *Chaucer Review* 26 (1991): 205–18.

58. F. N. Robinson, *Works,* p. 668.

59. The chronicler is Ralph of Diceto, the work his *Images of History* (1201). See Elizabeth Hallam, trans., *The Plantagenet Chronicles* (New York: Weidenfeld and Nicholson, 1986), p. 118. See also Frank Barlow, *Thomas Becket* (Berkeley: University of California Press, 1986), p. 179. Becket might have been familiar with Pseudo-Dionysius's writings (as opposed to merely his role of patron of France) through Richard of St. Victor (see below), a translator and adapter of Pseudo-Dionysius's ideas, who in turn the *Cloud*-author translated into Middle English. Richard knew Becket and was one of the theologians called in to settle the dispute between Becket and Henry II. See Barlow, *Thomas Becket,* pp. 152, 182. John of Salisbury, Becket's friend, biographer, and sometime member of his

household, commissioned a translation of the entire body of Pseudo-Dionysius's works from John Sarracenus. See G. Théry, "Documents concernant Jean Sarrazin," *Archives d'Histoire Doctrinale et Littéraire* 18 (1951): 181–96.

60. Forthcoming in William F. Pollard and Robert Koenig, eds. *the English Mystics* (Gainesville: University of Florida Press, 1996).

61. See Jean-Pierre Poly and Eric Bournazel, *The Feudal Transformation, 900–1200,* trans. Caroline Higgitt (New York: Holmes and Meier, 1991), pp. 186, 209–10.

62. For the influence of Pseudo-Dionysian ideas on Abbot Suger, see Conrad Rudolph, *Artistic Change at St-Denis: Abbot Suger's Program and the Early Twelfth-Century Controversy over Art* (Princeton: Princeton University Press, 1990); and Grover A. Zinn, "Suger, Theology, and the Pseudo-Dionysian Tradition," in Paula Lieber Gerson, ed., *Abbot Suger and Saint-Denis: A Symposium,* (New York: Metropolitan Museum of Art, 1986) pp. 33–40.

63. David Knowles, *The English Mystical Tradition* (New York: Harper, 1961), chaps. 4 and 8.

64. For a selective list of important criticism on the theology of Maximus Confessor, see D. J. Geanakoplos, "Some Aspects of the Influence of the Byzantine Maximus the Confessor on the Theology of East and West," *Church History* 38 (1969): 150–63; P. Miquel, "*Peira:* Contribution a l'étude du vocabulaire de l'expérience religieuse dans l'oeuvre de s. Maxime le Confesseur," *Studia Patristica* 7 (1966): 355–61; E. Montmasson, "La doctrine de l'apatheia d'après s. Maxime," *Echos d'Orient* 14 (1911): 36–41; P. Sherwood, "Explanation and Use of Scripture in St. Maximus as Manifested in the Questiones ad Thalassium," *Orientalia Christiana Perodica* 24 (1958): 202–7; P. Sherwood, "Survey of Recent Work on Maximus the Confessor," *Traditio* 20 (1964): 428–37; A. K. Squire, "The Idea of the Soul as Virgin and Mother in Maximus the Confessor," *Studia Patristica* 8 (1966): 456–61; and George C. Berthold, "Did Maximus the Confessor Know Augustine?" *Studia Patristica* 17 (1982): 14–17.

65. See Jaroslav Pelikan, "Introduction," in George C. Berthold, trans., *Maximus Confessor: Selected Writings* (New York: Paulist Press, 1985), pp. 6–7.

66. Maximus, *Ambigua* 5 (PG 91:1057), trans. Jaroslav Pelikan, in Berthold, *Maximus Confessor, p. 9.*

67. For a translation of Symeon the New Theologian's important works, see C. J. deCatanzau, trans., *Symeon the New Theologian: The Discourses* (New York: Paulist Press, 1980).

68. For a selective list of explications of Gregory Palamas, see John Meyendorf, *A Study of Gregory Palamas* 2d ed. (London: Faith Press, 1974); R. E. Sinkewicz, "A New Interpretation for the First Episode in the Controversy between Barlaam the Calabrian and Gregory Palamas," *Journal of Theological Studies* 31 (1980): 489–500; John Meyendorff, *St. Gregory Palamas and Orthodox Spirituality* (Crestwood, N.Y.: St. Vladimir's Seminary Press, 1974); A. de Halleux, "Palamisme et tradition," *Irénikon* 4 (1975): 479–93; and John Meyendorff and Nicholas Grendle, eds. and trans., *Gregory Palamas: The Triads* (New York: Paulist Press, 1983).

69. For a selective list of criticism about Richard of St. Victor, see F. Andres, "Die Stufen der Contemplatio in Bonaventures *Itinerarium mentis ad Deum* und in *Benjamin major* des Richards von St. Viktor," *Franziskanische Studien* 8 (1921): 189–200; Caroline Walker Bynum, "The Spirituality of Regular Canons in the Twelfth Century: A New Approach," *Medievalia et Humanistica* 4 (1973): 3–24; Jean Châtillon, "Les trois modes de la contemplation selon Richard de Saint-Victor," *Bulletin de Littérature Ecclésiastique* 41 (1940): 3–26; Grover A.

Zinn, "Personification Allegory and Visions of Light in Richard of St. Victor's Teaching on Contemplation," *University of Toronto Quarterly* 46 (1977): 190–214; and Grover A. Zinn, trans., *Richard of St. Victor: "The Twelve Patriarchs," "The Mystical Ark," "Book Three of the Trinity"* (New York: Paulist Press, 1971).

70. Hodgson, *Deonise Hid Diuinite,* pp. 11–46.

71. For a selective list of explications of Albertus, see F. J. Kovach and R. W. Shahan, eds., *Albert the Great: Commemorative Essays* (Norman: University of Oklahoma Press, 1980); James A. Weisheipl, ed., *Albertus Magnus and the Sciences: Commemorative Essays* (Toronto: Pontifical Institute of Mediaeval Studies, 1980); and Thomas M. Schwertner, *St. Albert the Great* (New York: Bruce Publishing Company, 1932).

72. For a translation of Albertus's commentary, see Simon Tugwell, O.P., ed. and trans., *Albert and Thomas: Selected Writings* (New York: Paulist Press, 1988), pp. 131–98.

73. For a selective list of explications of Thomas Aquinas, see Leo Elders, *The Philosophical Theology of St. Thomas Aquinas* (Leiden: E. J. Brill, 1990); Christopher Hughes, *On a Complex Theory of a Simple God: An Investigation in Aquinas' Philosophical Theology* (Ithaca: Cornell University Press, 1989); David B. Burrell, *Knowing the Unknowable God: Ibn-Sina, Maimonides, Aquinas* (Notre Dame, Ind.: University of Notre Dame Press, 1986); David B. Burrell, "Naming the Names of God: Muslims, Jews, Christians," *Theology Today* 47 (April 1990): 22–29; Robert M. Burns, "The Divine Simplicity in St. Thomas," *Religious Studies* 25 (1989): 271–93; and Fr. M. C. D'Arcy, trans., *Selected Writings of St. Thomas Aquinas* (New York: Dutton, 1950).

74. See Ewbank, "Diverse Orderings."

75. See Herbert McCabe, O.P., ed. and trans., *St. Thomas Aquinas: "Summa Theologiae,"* vol. 3, *Knowing and Naming God* (New York: McGraw-Hill, 1963), pp. 46–97.

76. For a selective list of explications of Bonaventure, see Etienne Gilson, *La Philosophie de Saint Bonaventure* (Paris: J. Vrin, 1953); Mary Rachael Dady, *The Theory of Knowledge of Saint Bonaventure* (Washington, D.C.: Catholic University of America Press, 1939); and Ewert H. Cousins, "Mysticism and the Spiritual Journey," *Studies in Formative Spirituality* 5 (February 1984): 11–20.

77. See Ewert H. Cousins, trans., *Bonaventure: "The Soul's Journey into God", "The Tree of Life", "The Life of St. Francis"* (New York: Paulist Press, 1978), p. 60.

78. For the best recent treatment of Eckhart's life and thought, see Frank Tobin, *Meister Eckhart: Thought and Language* (Philadelphia: University of Pennsylvania Press, 1986). For the influence of Pseudo-Dionysius, see esp. pp. 39–40, 70–71. For a selective list of criticism about Meister Eckhart, see C. F. Kelly, *Meister Eckhart on Knowledge* (New Haven: Yale University Press, 1977); Reiner Schürmann, *Meister Eckhart: Mystic and Philosopher* (Bloomington: Indiana University Press, 1987); John Caputo, "Fundamental Themes in Meister Eckhart's Mysticism," *The Thomist* 42 (1978): 197–225; John Caputo, "The Nothingness of the Intellect in Meister Eckhart's 'Parisian Questions,'" *The Thomist* 39 (1975): 85–115; Donald Ducklow, "Hermeneutics and Meister Eckhart," *Philosophy Today* 28 (1984): 36–43; Karl G. Kertz, "Meister Eckhart's Teaching on the Birth of the Divine Word in the Soul," *Traditio* 15 (1959): 327–63; Richard Kieckefer, "Meister Eckhart's Conception of Union with God," *Harvard Theological Review* 71 (1978): 203–25; Bernard McGinn, "The God beyond God: Theology and Mysticism in the Thought of Meister Eckhart," *Journal of Religion* 61

(1981): 1–19; Josef Quint, "Die Sprache Meister Eckharts als Ausdruck seiner Mystichen Geisteswelt," *Deutsche Vierteljahresschrift* 6 (1927): 671–701; and Edmund Colledge, O.S.A., and Bernard McGinn, trans., *Meister Eckhart: The Essential Sermons, Commentaries, Treatises, and Defense* (New York: Paulist Press, 1981).

79. See Colledge and McGinn, *Meister Eckhart,* p. 280.

80. For a representative selection of explications of Suso, see Richard Kieckhefer, *Unquiet Souls: Fourteenth-Century Saints and their Religious Milieu* (Chicago: University of Chicago Press, 1984); K. Gröber, *Der Mystiker Heinrich Seuse* (Freiburg: Herder, 1941); Jeffrey Hamburger, "The Use of Images in the Pastoral Care of Nuns: The Case of Heinrich Suso and the Dominicans," *Art Bulletin* 71 (1989): 20–46; and Uta Joeressen, *Die Terminologie der Innerlichkeit in den deutschen Werken Heinrich Seuses* (Frankfurt am Main: Peter Lang, 1983). See also Frank Tobin, trans., *Henry Suso: The Exemplar with Two German Sermons* (New York: Paulist Press, 1989).

81. For a selective list of explications of Tauler, see Louise Gnädinger, "Der minnende Bernhardus, seine Reflexe in den Predigten J. Taulers," *Cîteaux* 31 (1980): 387–409; and Steven E. Ozment, *Homo Spiritualis: A Comparative Study of the Anthropology of Johannes Tauler, Jean Gerson and Martin Luther (1509–16) in the Context of Their Theological Thought* (Leiden: E. J. Brill, 1969).

82. See James A. Wiseman, O.S.B., trans., *John Ruusbroec: The Spiritual Espousals and Other Works* (New York: Paulist Press, 1985), p. 25.

83. For a selective list of explications of Ruusbroec, see Albert Ampe, "La théologie mystique de l'ascension de l'âme selon le bienheureux Jean de Ruusbroec," *Revue d'Ascetique et de Mystique* 36 (1960): 188–201, 303–22; Alfredus Auger, *De Doctrina et Meritis Joannis van Ruysbroeck* (Louvain: J. van Linthout, 1892); Louis Dupré, *The Common Life: The Origins of Trinitarian Mysticism and Its Development by Jan Ruusbroec* (New York: Crossroad, 1984); Paul Mommaers, *The Land Within: The Process of Possessing and Being Possessed by God according to the Mystic Jan van Ruysbroeck,* trans. David N. Smith (Chicago: Franciscan Herald Press, 1975); Kent Emery, Jr., "The Carthusians, Intermediaries for the Teaching of John Ruysbroeck during the Period of Early Reform and the Counter-Reformation," *Analecta Cartusiana* 43 (1979): 100–129; and James A Wiseman, O.S.B., "The Birth of the Son in the Soul in the Mystical Theology of Jan van Ruusbroec," *Studia Mystica* 14, nos. 2–3 (Summer-Fall 1991): 30–44.

84. For a selective list of explications of Rolle, see John A. Alford, "Biblical *Imitatio* in the Writings of Richard Rolle," *ELH* 40 (1973): 1–23; Hope Emily Allen, *Writings Ascribed to Richard Rolle, Hermit of Hampole, and Materials for His Biography* (New York: Heath, 1927); Margaret Jennings, "Richard Rolle and the Three Degrees of Love," *Downside Review* 93 (1975): 193–200; Antonie Olmes, "Sprache und Stil der englischen Mystik des Mittelalters, unter besonderer Berücksichtigung des Richard Rolle von Hampole," *Studien zur Englischen Philologie* 76 (1933): 1–100; Mary Madigan, *The Passio Domini Theme in the Works of Richard Rolle: His Personal Contribution in Its Religious, Cultural, and Literary Context* (Salzburg: Institut für Englistik und Amerikanistik, 1978); Rita Copeland, "Richard Rolle and the Rhetorical Theory of the Levels of Style," pp. 55–80 in Marion Glasscoe, ed., *The Medieval Mystical Tradition in England* (Cambridge: D. S. Brewer, 1984); Rosamund Allen, "'Singuler Lufe': Richard Rolle and the Grammar of Spiritual Ascent," pp. 28–54 in Glasscoe, *Mystical Tradition;* Ann W. Astell, *The Song of Songs in the Middle Ages* (Ithaca: Cornell University Press, 1990), pp. 105–18; Robert Boenig, "The God-as-Mother Theme

in Richard Rolle's Biblical Commentaries," *Mystics Quarterly* 10 (1984): 171–74; and Patricia P. Fite, "To 'Sytt and Syng of Luf Langyng': The Feminine Dynamic of Richard Rolle's Mysticism," *Studia Mystica* 14, nos. 2–3 (Summer-Fall 1991): 13–29.

85. Riehle, *Mystics,* p. 77, points out that his Latin treatise *Melos Amoris* contains a list of divine names that surpasses even that of Pseudo-Dionysius.

86. For a lengthy explication of these three themes that valorizes *canor,* or "song," see Nicholas Watson, *Richard Rolle and the Invention of Authority* (Cambridge: Cambridge University Press, 1991).

87. See Carl Horstman, ed., *Yorkshire Writers: Richard Rolle of Hampole and His Followers,* 2 vols. (London: Swan Sonnenschein, 1985, 1896), vol. 1, pp. 50–51. Hereafter these volumes will be referred to as Horstman 1 and Horstman 2.

88. Horstman 1:10–11.

89. See, for instance, V. A. Kolve, *Chaucer and the Imagery of Narrative* (Stanford, Calif.: Stanford University Press, 1984), p. 91.

90. For a selective list of explications of the *Cloud*-author, see John Burrow, "Fantasy and Language in *The Cloud of Unknowing,*" *Essays in Criticism* 27 (1977): 283–98; J. P. H. Clark, "Sources and Theology in *The Cloud of Unknowing,*" *Downside Review* 98 (1980): 83–109; Sr. Laureen Grady, "Afterword to *A Pistle of Discrecioun of Stirrings,*" *Contemplative Review* 10 (1977): 1–6; David Knowles, "The Excellence of the *Cloud,*" *Downside Review* 52 (1934): 71–92; Robert Englert, "Of Another Mind: Ludic Imagery and Spiritual Doctrine in the *Cloud of Unknowing,*" *Studia Mystica* 8, no. 1 (1985): 3–12.

91. Hodgson, *Deonise Hid Diunite,* pp. 44–45.

92. Ibid., p. 2.

93. E. D. Blodgett, "Chaucerian *Pryvetee* and the Opposition to Time," *Speculum* 51 (1976): 477–93 provides a lengthy word study of *pryvetee* and its oblique forms, emphasizing its spatial connotations. My subsequent discussion of the word will privilege its *audible* (or more properly nonaudible) connotations. Compare Kendrick's treatment in Kendrick, *Chaucerian Play,* of this word; following Lacan, she prefers a sexual meaning to the term: for her "God's privity" in the Miller's Tale refers to God's private parts.

94. Phyllis Hodgson, ed., *The Cloud of Unknowing and The Book of Privy Counselling,* EETS 218 (London: Oxford University Press, 1944), p. 136.

95. Ibid., pp. 143–44.

96. Ibid., pp. 23–24.

97. Ibid., p. 38.

98. For a selective list of explications of Julian, see John Lawler, "A Note on the *Revelations* of Julian of Norwich," *Review of English Studies,* n.s. 2 (1951): 255–58; Sr. Carol Marie Peloquin, "All Will Be Well: A Look at Sin in Juliana's *Revelation,*" *Contemplative Review* 13 (1980): 9–16; Barry A. Windeatt, "Julian of Norwich and Her Audience," *Review of English Studies,* n.s. 28 (1977): 1–17; Muriel Lewis, "After Reflecting on Julian's Reflections of Behovabil Synne," *Studia Mystica* 6, no. 2 (Summer 1983): 41–57; Roland Maisonneuve, "Julian of Norwich and the Prison of Existence," *Studia Mystica* 3, no. 4 (Winter 1980): 26–32; and Grace M. Jantzen, *Julian of Norwich: Mystic and Theologian* (New York: Paulist Press, 1988).

99. For the important treatments of the God-as-Mother theme, see Caroline Walker Bynum, *Jesus as Mother: Studies in the Spirituality of the High Middle Ages* (Berkeley: University of California Press), pp. 110–69; Jennifer P. Heimmel,

"*God Is Our Mother*": *Julian of Norwich and the Medieval Image of Christian Feminine Divinity* (Salzburg: Institut für Anglistik und Amerikanistik, 1982); Ritamary Bradley, "Mysticism in the Motherhood Similitude of Julian of Norwich," *Studia Mystica* 8, no. 2 (1985): 4–14; Valerie M. Lagorio, "Variations on the Theme of God's Motherhood in Medieval English Mystical and Devotional Writings," *Studia Mystica* 8, no. 2 (1985): 15–37; Boenig, "The God-as-Mother Theme"; Ricki Jean Cohn, "God and Motherhood in *The Book of Margery Kempe*," *Studia Mystica* 9, no. 1 (1986): 26–35; and Maria R. Lichtmann, "Julian of Norwich and the Ontology of the Feminine," *Studia Mystica* 13, nos. 2–3 (Summer-Fall 1990): 53–64.

100. Edmund Colledge, O. S. A., and James Walsh, S. J., eds., *A Book of Showings to the Anchoress Julian of Norwich* (Toronto: Pontifical Institute of Medieval Studies, 1978), p. 362.

101. Ibid., p. 364.

102. Ibid., pp. 367–69.

103. For Julian's use of "prevytes" in a different context, see Kendrick, *Chaucerian Play*, p. 10.

# Chapter 2. Experience and Authority

1. For the best book-length study of Kempe, see Clarissa W. Atkinson, *Mystic and Pilgrim: The Book and the World of Margery Kempe* (Ithaca: Cornell University Press, 1983). Watson, *Richard Rolle*, p. 23, briefly mentions the similarity between the two.

2. Sanford Brown Meech, ed., *The Book of Margery Kempe*, EETS 212 (London: Oxford University Press, 1940), p. 203.

3. Ibid., p. 143.

4. See Roger Ellis, ed., *The Liber Celestis of St. Bridget of Sweden*, EETS 291 (London: Oxford University Press, 1987).

5. For some comments about Kempe's connection to previous texts about women, particularly St. Cecelia and St. Catherine of Siena, see David Aers, *Community, Gender, and Individual Identity: English Writing, 1360–1430* (London: Routledge, 1988), pp. 93–95.

6. Meech, *Book*, p. 11.

7. See lines 225–80 of Chaucer's Second Nun's Tale.

8. Meech, *Book*, p. 21.

9. Ibid., p. 23.

10. See ibid., pp. 1–6.

11. For an explication of the astrology behind these lines, see Walter Clyde Curry, *Chaucer and the Mediaeval Sciences* (1942; rpt., New York: Barnes and Noble, 1960), pp. 91–118.

12. Meech, *Book*, p. 145.

13. Ibid., p. 115.

14. Ibid., p. 50.

15. See Caroline Walker Bynum, *Holy Feast and Holy Fast: The Religious Significance of Food to Medieval Women* (Berkeley: University of California Press, 1987); and Rudolph M. Bell, *Holy Anorexia* (Chicago: University of Chicago Press, 1985).

16. See Gen. 1:28, God's command to Adam and Eve to bear children, "Be fruitful and multiply."

17. Meech, *Book,* p. 121.

18. Ibid., p. 160.

19. Ibid., p. 215.

20. Ibid., pp. 152–53.

21. Watson, *Richard Rolle,* p. 40, points out how Rolle himself in the possibly apocryphal story of his removing his secular clothing and fashioning a habit out of two of his sister's dresses may be patterning his life after that of St. Francis, who dramatically threw off his clothes prior to his conversion.

22. A connection between Kempe and the Parson is suggested by Robert N. Swanson, "Chaucer's Parson and Other Priests," *Studies in the Age of Chaucer* 13 (1991): 55: Kempe's parish priest was well read in the mystics, suggesting that Chaucer's Parson was as well.

23. Meech, *Book,* p. 126.

24. Robert Easting, ed., *St. Patrick's Purgatory,* EETS 298 (Oxford: Oxford University Press, 1991), p. 91.

25. For this redirection, see Pearsall, *Canterbury Tales,* pp. 288–89.

26. Meech, *Book,* p. 67.

27. See Thomas Bestul, "Chaucer's Parson's Tale and the Late-Medieval Tradition of Religious Meditation," *Speculum* 64 (1989): 600–619; and John M. Hill, *Chaucerian Belief* (New Haven: Yale University Press, 1991), pp. 2–3.

28. For the best analysis of the Parson's Tale, see Lee W. Patterson, "'The Parson's Tale' and the Quitting of the 'Canterbury Tales,'" *Traditio* 34 (1978): 331–80.

29. See Pearsall, *Canterbury Tales,* pp. 321–25.

30. For a facsimile edition of this work originally printed in 1506 from a late-fourteenth-century or early fifteenth-century manuscript, see Robert Boenig, ed., *Contemplations of the Dread and Love of God (1506)* (Delmar, N.Y.: Scholars' Facsimiles and Reprints, 1990).

31. Robert Boenig,"*Contemplations of the Dread and Love of God,* Richard Rolle, and Aelred of Rievaulx," *Mystics Quarterly* 16 (1990): 27–33.

32. Boenig, *Contemplations,* p. 7.

33. The editor (Wynkyn de Worde) or scribe before him mistakenly writes "thre" here.

34. Boenig, *Contemplations,* p. 9.

35. The preceding three and a half paragraphs are taken from Boenig, Introduction, *Contemplations,* pp. 4–5.

36. For information on the sources of the Parson's Tale, see Wenzel, *Summa Virtutum,* pp. 2–11; and Germaine Dempster, "The Parson's Tale," in W. F. Bryan and Germaine Dempster, eds., *Sources and Analogues of Chaucer's "Canterbury Tales"* (Chicago: University of Chicago Press, 1941), pp. 723–60.

37. See Wenzel, *Summa Virtutum,* p. 9.

38. See H. J. Thomson, ed. and trans., *Prudentius,* vol. 1 (Cambridge: Harvard University Press, 1969), pp. 274–343.

39. For the classic explication of Prudentius's *Psychomachia,* see C. S. Lewis, *The Allegory of Love* (London: Oxford University Press, 1936), pp. 66–73.

40. For introductions to the literature of penance, see Allen J. Frantzen, *The Literature of Penance in Anglo-Saxon England* (New Brunswick, N.J.: Rutgers University Press, 1983), pp. 1–94; and Robert Boenig, *Saint and Hero: Andreas and Medieval Doctrine* (Lewisburg, Pa.: Bucknell University Press, 1991), pp. 30–54.

41. See Audrey Ekdahl Davidson, ed., *Hildegard von Bingen: "Ordo Virtutum"* (Kalamazoo, Mich.: Medieval Institute Publications, 1984).

42. Bestul, "Chaucer's Parson's Tale," pp. 600–619.

43. See W. Meredith Thompson, ed., *Þe Wohunge of Ure Lauerd,* EETS 241 (London: Oxford University Press, 1958).

44. Boenig, *Contemplations,* pp. 5–6.

45. See J. R. R. Tolkien, ed., *Ancrene Wisse: MS Corpus Christi College Cambridge 401,* EETS 249 (London: Oxford University Press, 1962).

46. See John Ayto and Alexandra Barratt, eds., *Aelred of Rievaulx's "De Institutione Inclusarum": Two English Versions,* EETS 287 (London: Oxford University Press, 1984).

47. See Denise Despres, *Ghostly Sights: Visual Meditation in Late-Medieval Literature* (Norman, Okla.: Pilgrim Books, 1989), pp. 19–56; John V. Fleming, *An Introduction to the Franciscan Literature of the Middle Ages* (Chicago: Franciscan Herald Press, 1977); and David L. Jeffrey, *The Early English Lyric and Franciscan Spirituality* (Lincoln: University of Nebraska Press, 1975).

48. See Despres, *Ghostly Sights,* pp. 57–88.

49. For the meditative roots and aspects of seventeenth-century poetry, see Louis Martz, *The Poetry of Meditation,* 2d ed. (New Haven: Yale University Press, 1962); Anthony Low, *Love's Architecture: Devotional Modes in Seventeenth-Century English Poetry* (New York: New York University Press, 1978); and Arthur L. Clements, *Poetry of Contemplation* (Albany: State University of New York Press, 1990).

50. Ayto and Barratt, *Aelred,* p. 39.

51. Ibid., p. 47.

52. Ibid., p. xiv.

53. Ibid., pp. xix–xxvi.

54. See William Harris Stahl, trans., *Microbius: "Commentary on the Dream of Scipio"* (New York: Columbia University Press, 1952), pp. 87–92.

55. Horstman 1:15–16.

56. Ibid., p. 16.

57. Ibid.

58. See Kolve, *Imagery,* pp. 233–48.

59. See John Block Friedman, "A Reading of Chaucer's *Reeve's Tale,*" *Chaucer Review* 2 (1967): 8–19; Rodney Delasanta, "The Horsemen of *The Canterbury Tales,*" *Chaucer Review* 3 (1968): 29–36; Beryl Rowland, *Blind Beasts: Chaucer's Animal World* (Kent, Ohio: Kent State University Press, 1971), p. 130; and Sandy Feinstein, "The *Reeve's Tale*: About That Horse," *Chaucer Review* 26 (1991): 99–106.

60. Horstman 2:421–22.

61. Ibid., p. 413.

## Chapter 3. Comic Tales

1. For interpretations of the religious aspects of the Miller's Tale emphasizing patristic allegory, see Robertson, *Preface,* pp. 382–86; W. F. Bolton, "The 'Miller's Tale': An Interpretation," *Mediaeval Studies* 24 (1962): 83–94; and Paul A. Olson, "Poetic Justice in the *Miller's Tale,*" *Modern Language Quarterly* 24 (1964): 227–36.

2. See, for instance, E. Talbot Donaldson, *Speaking of Chaucer* (New York: Norton, 1970), pp. 26–27; and Benson, *The Riverside Chaucer,* p. 848.

3. See Riehle, *Mystics*, p. 53.

4. Horstman 2:346.

5. For the courtly love associations of *lemman*, see R. E. Kaske, "The *Canticum Canticorum* in the *Miller's Tale*," *Studies in Philology* 59 (1962): 479–500. Kaske goes on to speak of the influence of the Song of Songs on Absolon's vocabulary with such words as *hony-comb* and *cynamome*. See also Pearsall, *Canterbury Tales*, p. 176.

6. Horstman 2:355.

7. Ibid., p. 353.

8. Ibid., p. 363.

9. Horstman 1:328–29.

10. Boenig, *Contemplations*, p. 64.

11. Horstman 1:331.

12. Ibid., p. 333.

13. There is much critical debate over the role of his spiritual directee, Elzbeth Stagel, in writing his "auto"-biography. See Karl Bihlmeyer, "Selbstbiographie in der deutschen Mystik des Mittelalters," *Theologische Quartalschaft* 114 (1933): 504–44; and Julius Schwietering, "Zur Autoschaft von Seuses Vita," in Kurt Ruh, ed., *Altdeutsche und Altniederländische Mystik*, pp. 309–23 (Darmstadt: Wissenschaftliche Buchgesellschaft, 1964).

14. Tobin, *Henry Suso*, p. 169.

15. Hodgson, *Cloud*, p. 105.

16. For an explication of this phrase in the context of I, 3163–66, suggesting a reading emphasizing God's "private parts," see Kendrick, *Chaucerian Play*, p. 5.

17. See Watson, *Richard Rolle*, pp. 54–72.

18. Easting, *St. Patrick's Purgatory*, p. 93.

19. Bernard F. Huppé, *A Reading of "The Canterbury Tales"* (Albany: State University of New York Press, 1964), p. 85.

20. See Lee Patterson, "'No Man His Reson Herde': Peasant Consciousness, Chaucer's Miller, and the Structure of the *Canterbury Tales*," in Lee Patterson, ed., *Literary Practice and Social Change in Britain, 1380–1530*, pp. 113–55 (Berkeley: University of California Press, 1990), p. 137.

21. See C. David Benson, *Chaucer's Drama of Style* (Chapel Hill: University of North Carolina Press, 1986), p. 96.

22. See Donald R. Howard, *The Idea of "The Canterbury Tales"* (Berkeley: University of California Press, 1976), p. 242.

23. See Ruggiers, *Art*, p. 56.

24. Charles Muscatine, *Chaucer and the French Tradition* (Berkeley: University of California Press, 1957), pp. 224–25.

25. Geoffrey Cooper, "'Sely John' in the 'Legende' of the Miller's Tale," *Journal of English and Germanic Philology* 79 (1980): 4, points out that John the carpenter's epithet has a range of meaning (holy, innocent, etc.) congruent with the saint's life, leading to Chaucerian irony; see also Paul Strohm, "Politics and Poetics: Usk and Chaucer in the 1380s," in Patterson, *Literary Practice and Social Change*, p. 110.

26. Helen Cooper, *The Structure of "The Canterbury Tales"* (Athens: University of Georgia Press, 1984), p. 115.

27. C. David Benson, *Drama*, p. 90 ff.

28. Donaldson, *Speaking*, p. 29.

29. Pearsall, *Canterbury Tales*, p. 172.

30. See Patterson, "'No Man His Reson Herde,'" p. 143; and Patterson, *Subject of History*, p. 270.

31. For a persuasive case that the Friar's Tale should be read as a religious tale, see V. A. Kolve, "'Man in the Middle': Art and Religion in Chaucer's *Friar's Tale*," *Studies in the Age of Chaucer* 12 (1990): 5–46.

32. For a different analysis of the two that comes to a similar conclusion, that each "discredit[s] himself at the same time" (p. 53), see Peggy Knapp, *Chaucer and the Social Contest* (London: Routledge, 1990), pp. 53–60.

33. An exception is Janette Richardsen, "Hunter and Prey: Functional Imagery in 'The Friar's Tale,'" in A. C. Cawley, ed., *Chaucer's Mind and Art*, pp. 155–65 (London: Oliver and Boyd, 1969).

34. See, for instance, Traugott Lawler, *The One and the Many in "The Canterbury Tales"* (Hamden, Conn.: Archon Books, 1980) pp. 37–38.

35. See Riehle, *Mystics*, p. 102, who also sees a mystical valency of this word. Compare the entry in the *MED*.

36. Horstman 2:106–23.

37. Ibid., p. 119.

38. Ibid., p. 120.

39. See Huppé, *Reading*, p. 196.

40. For irony in the Friar's Tale, see Earle Birney, *Essays on Chaucerian Irony*, ed. Beryl Rowland (Toronto: University of Toronto Press, 1985), pp. 85–108.

41. I suggest this deconstruction of his own text accounts for the inconsistencies in the Friar's character and voice described by Paul N. Zeitlow, "In Defense of the Summoner," *Chaucer Review* 1 (1966): 15; and H. Marshall Leicester, Jr., "'No Vileyns Word': Social Context and Performance in Chaucer's *Friar's Tale*," *Chaucer Review* 17 (1983): 21–39.

42. Harley, *A Revelation*, p. 60.

43. For an analysis of the term "brother" in this tale, see Strohm, *Social Chaucer*, pp. 98–99.

44. For the influence of Scholastic philosophy on Chaucer, see Roney, *Theories of Scholastic Psychology*.

45. See J. Edwin Whitesell, "Chaucer's Lisping Friar," *Modern Language Notes* 71 (1956): 160–61; Charles A. Owen, Jr., *Pilgrimage and Storytelling in "The Canterbury Tales": The Dialectic of "Earnest" and "Game"* (Norman: University of Oklahoma Press, 1977), p. 165; and Pearsall, *Canterbury Tales*, p. 223.

46. See Ruggiers, *Art*, p. 105.

47. Easting, *St. Patrick's Purgatory*, p. 102.

48. Horstman 2:416.

49. George G. Perry, ed. *Religious Pieces in Prose and Verse*, EETS 26 (rpt., London: Kegan-Paul, Trench, Trübner, 1867, 1914), p. 24.

50. Ibid., p. 12.

51. See Robert P. Miller, *Chaucer: Sources and Backgrounds* (New York: Oxford University Press, 1977), p. 237. For a general discussion of antifraternalism, see Penn R. Szittya, *The Antifraternal Tradition in Medieval Literature* (Princeton: Princeton University Press, 1986). For the origins of the Carmelites see David Knowles, *The Religious Orders in England*, vol 1 (1948; rpt., Cambridge: Cambridge University Press, 1979), pp. 194–99. See also Nicholas Havely, "Chaucer, Boccaccio and the Friars," in Piero Boitani, ed., *Chaucer and the Italian Trecento*, pp. 249–268 (Cambridge: Cambridge University Press, 1983), esp. p. 257.

52. See P. Olson, *Good Society*, p. 217; and Penn R. Szittya, "The Friar as

False Apostle: Anti-Fraternal Exegesis and the *Summoner's Tale,*" *Studies in Philology* 71 (1974): 19–46.

53. See Alfred L. Kellogg, *Chaucer, Langland, Arthur: Essays in Middle English Literature* (New Brunswick, N.J.: Rutgers University Press, 1972), pp. 273–75.

54. See P. Olson, *Good Society,* p. 217.

55. Perry, *Religious Pieces,* p. 117.

56. See Miller, *Sources and Backgrounds,* pp. 237–39.

57. Ibid., pp. 255–58.

## Chapter 4. The Prioress's Tale

1. Easting, *St. Patrick's Purgatory,* p. 115.

2. See Bynum, *Jesus as Mother* and Bynum, *Holy Feast and Holy Fast;* and Bell, *Holy Anorexia;* see also Kieckhefer, *Unquiet Souls.*

3. See particularly the analysis of the New Historicism in medieval studies in Patterson, *Negotiating the Past.*

4. For a comprehensive study of the Saint's Life in terms of both its social role and the theoretical problems facing its authors, see Thomas J. Heffernan, *Sacred Biography: Saints and Their Biographers in the Middle Ages* (New York: Oxford University Press, 1988). The two final chapters, "The Passion of Saints Perpetua and Felicitas and the *Imitatio Christi*" (pp. 185–230) and "Virgin Mothers" (pp. 231–99), are devoted to the particular issues attending the lives of female saints.

5. Meech, *Book,* p. 2.

6. For a description and an analysis of Kempe's marriage, see Atkinson, *Mystic and Pilgrim,* pp. 15–17, 20–27, 80–81, 214–15; and Cohn, "God and Motherhood," 26–35.

7. Meech, *Book,* p. 6.

8. Ibid., p. 7.

9. Ibid., p. 7.

10. Ibid., p. 6.

11. Ibid., pp. 16–17.

12. Ibid., p. 21.

13. For an analysis of the interchange between Kempe and her husband that leads to this decision, see Heffernan, *Sacred Biography,* pp. 186–88.

14. For a treatment of the virginity theme in Hildegard von Bingen, who placed particular theological importance upon it, see Barbara Newman, *Sister of Wisdom: St. Hildegard's Theology of the Feminine* (Berkeley: University of California Press), esp. pp. 218–28.

15. Michael Lapidge and Michael Herren, trans. *Aldhelm: The Prose Works* (Cambridge: D. S. Brewer, 1979), p. 63.

16. See Ayto and Barratt, *De Institutione Inclusarum.* For a facsimile of the Vernon Manuscript, in which this text appears, see A. I. Doyle, ed., *The Vernon Manuscript: A Facsimile of Bodleian Library, Oxford MS Eng. Poet. a. l.* (Cambridge: D. S. Brewer, 1987). See also Heffernan, *Sacred Biography,* p. 233.

17. Ayto and Barratt, *De Institutione Inclusarum,* p. 26.

18. Ibid., p. 27.

19. Tolkien, *Ancrene Wisse,* p. 208. For an analysis of this and similar passages from the *Ancrene Wisse,* see Georgianna, *The Solitary Self:* Individuality in the "Ancrene Wisse" (Cambridge: Harvard University Press, 1981), pp. 72ff.

20. Meech, *Book,* p. 87.

21. Mechthild states, "Er trutet se mit voller maht in dem bette der mine," where the Middle High German verb *truten* is roughly synonymous with Chaucer's Merchant's notorious *thringen* (VI, 2353), "to consumate passion"—a modern euphemism where a four-letter word would do all the better. See Riehle, *Middle English Mystics,* p. 38.

22. Meech, *Book,* p. 90.

23. Ibid., p.. 90.

24. Bella Millet, ed., *Hali Meiðhad,* EETS 284 (London: Oxford University Press, 1984), p. 4. See also Heffernan, *Sacred Biography,* p. 251.

25. As Heffernan, speaking of the Lives of female saints, reminds us, "the goal of these women, whether virgins or wives, is a closer union with Christ . . . which depends on a successful outcome of the struggle not only with their own sexuality but also with that of the men in their lives. The war is with men, not with mankind" (*Sacred Biography,* p. 189).

26. For an account of her exertions to avoid marriage, see Bynum, *Holy Feast and Holy Fast,* pp. 167ff. For accounts of her life and writing, see Joseph Berrigan, "The Tuscan Visionary Saint Catherine of Siena," in Katharina M. Wilson, ed., *Medieval Women Writers* (Athens: University of Georgia Press, 1984); and Suzanne Noffke, *Catherine of Siena: The Dialogue* (New York: Paulist Press, 1986). For the contemporary account of her life, see Suzanne Raymond of Capua; *The Life of St. Catherine of Siena,* George Lamb, trans., (New York: P. J. Kenedy and Sons, 1960).

27. See H. Logeman, ed., *The Rule of S. Benet,* EETS 90 (London: N. Trübner, 1888), p. 21.

28. Ibid., pp. 69–70. The punctuation is modernized.

29. Owen Chadwick, trans., *Western Asceticism* (Philadelphia: Westminster Press, 1958), pp. 316–17.

30. Horstman 1:329.

31. Avril Henry, ed., *The Pilgrimage of the Lyfe of the Manhode,* vol. 1, EETS 288 (London: Oxford University Press, 1985), p. 166.

32. See Susan K. Hagen, *Allegorical Remembrance: A Study of "The Pilgrimage of the Life of Man" as a Medieval Treatise on Seeing and Remembering* (Athens: University of Georgia Press, 1990), pp. 3, 110.

33. Kieckhefer, *Unquiet Souls,* p. vii.

34. Ibid., p. 37.

35. Mary S. Serjeantson, ed., *Legendys of Hooly Wummen by Osbern Bokenham,* EETS 206 (London: Oxford University Press, 1938), p. 68.

36. Carl Horstman, ed., *The Early South-English Legendary,* EETS 87 (London: Oxford University Press, 1887), p. 264.

37. Ibid.

38. Ibid., p. 267.

39. Ibid., p. 269.

40. For a study in part about the possible influence of Bede's *Commentary on the Apocalypse* on Chaucer's *House of Fame,* see Robert Boenig, "Chaucer's *House of Fame,* The Apocalypse, and Bede," *American Benedictine Review* 36 (1985): 263–77.

41. J.-P. Migne, ed., *Venerabilis Bedae Opera Omnia,* vol. 4 in Migne, ed., *Patrologia Latina,* vol. 93 (Paris, 1830), cols. 161–62.

42. Rev. Edward Marshall, trans., *"The Explanation of the Apocalypse,"* by

*Venerable Beda* (Oxford and London: James Parker and Co., 1878), pp. 70–71. The paragraphing has been condensed and the diction freed from archaism.

43. See the facsimile of Florens Deuchler, Jeffrey M. Hoffeld, and Helmut Nickel, eds., *The Cloisters Apocalypse* (New York: Metropolitan Museum of Art, 1971).

44. Carolyn P. Collette, "Sense and Sensibility in the *Prioress's Tale*," *Chaucer Review* 15 (1982), 138–50 suggests that the Prioress's Tale reflects the same late-fourteenth-century tenderness and sensibility that produced the mystics. She appeals to Julian of Norwich's hazelnut and emotional elements in the visual art of the time.

45. Bynum, *Holy Feast and Holy Fast,* p. 4.

46. Ibid., pp. 170–75.

47. Carelton Brown in his section of Bryan/Dempster, "The Prioress's Tale," pp. 448–50 indicates that in most of the earlier versions of this tale, the Jews bury the boy in the earth or inside a house; only "Group C" includes the privy.

48. The physicality, even cannibalism, of the Eucharist in medieval doctrine is a complex and much-studied subject. A theological argument between Ratramnan and Radbert, two ninth-century monks from Corbie, developed into a major theological debate in the eleventh century, which finally led to the condemnation of Berengar of Tours, the strongest proponent of the symbolic nature of the Eucharist, as a heretic. The term *transubstantiation* was first used in the twelfth century by Peter Damian. See Charles E. Sheedy, *The Eucharistic Controversy of the Eleventh Century against the Background of Pre-Scholastic Theology* (Washington, D.C.: Catholic University Press, 1947); A. J. MacDonald, *Berengar and the Reform of Sacramental Doctrine* (London: Longmans, 1930); Gary Macy, *The Theologies of the Eucharist in the Early Scholastic Period: A Study of the Salvific Function of the Sacrament according to the Theologians, c. 1080–c. 1220* (Oxford: Clarendon Press, 1984); and Robert Boenig, "*Andreas,* the Eucharist, and Vercelli," *Journal of English and Germanic Philology* 79 (1980): 313–31.

49. See Bynum, *Holy Food and Holy Fast,* pp. 269–76.

50. Ibid., pp. 133, 271.

51. In medieval medical theory a woman's milk was thought to originate in her blood. See ibid. pp. 270–71.

52. See ibid., pp. 122–23.

53. Ibid., p. 126.

54. Ibid., pp. 125–26.

55. The Prioress depicts her hero as more vulnerable, little, and powerless than those of the sources and analogues; see Brown, "The Prioress's Tale," p. 465; Pearsall, *Canterbury Tales,* pp. 247–48; Margaret H. Statler, "The Analogues of Chaucer's *Prioress's Tale:* The Relationship of Group C to Group A," *PMLA* 65 (1950): 896–910; and Alan T. Gaylord, "The Unconquered Tale of the Prioress," *Papers of the Michigan Academy of Science, Arts, and Letters* 42 (1962): 633–34.

56. The translation is my own.

57. See Nigel Wilkins, *Music in the Age of Chaucer* (Cambridge: D. S. Brewer, 1979), pp. 92–93.

58. See Sumner Ferris, "Chaucer at Lincoln (1387): The *Prioress's Tale* as a Political Poem," *Chaucer Review* 15 (1981): 298.

59. See Robinson, *Works* p. 735.

60. Frese, *Ars Legendi,* p. 20, calls attention to the Pardoner's alimentary imagery.

61. See, for instance, Collette, "Sense and Sensibility."

62. I am suggesting, of course, a feminist reading based on an intertext roughly contemporaneous with Chaucer. For a feminist reading based on more modern critical modes, see Carolyn Dinshaw, *Chaucer's Sexual Poetics* (Madison: University of Wisconsin Press, 1989). For alternative feminist readings of Chaucer, see Hope Phyllis Weissmann, "Antifeminism and Chaucer's Characterization of Women," in George D. Economou, ed., *Geoffrey Chaucer: A Collection of Original Articles* (New York: McGraw-Hill, 1975), pp. 93–110; David Aers, "Chaucer's Representation of Marriage and Sexual Relations," in David Aers, *Chaucer* (Brighton: Havester Press, 1986), pp. 62–75; and Jill Mann, *Feminist Readings: Geoffrey Chaucer* (Atlantic Highlands, N.J.: Humanities Press, 1991).

63. Horstman, *South English Legendary,* p. 96.

64. Ibid., p. 96.

65. For details about Hildegard's life, see Newman, *Sister of Wisdom,* pp. 4–14.

66. For Catherine's relationship with Raymond of Capua, see Noffke, *Dialogue,* p. 27; Bynum, *Holy Feast and Holy Fast,* pp. 166–75; and Paul M. Connor, O.P., "Catherine of Siena and Raymond of Capua—Enduring Friends," *Studia Mystica* 12, no. 1 (Spring 1989), 22–29. See also Hyacinth Cormier, O.P., *Blessed Raymond of Capua* (Boston: Marlier, Callahan, and Co., 1900).

67. See Bynum, *Holy Feast and Holy Fast,* pp. 27, 140–45; see also Paul Lachance, O.F.M., *The Spiritual Journey of the Blessed Angela of Folgino according to the Memorial of Frater A* (Rome: Pontificium Athenaeum Antonianum, 1984).

68. See Bynum, *Holy Feast and Holy Fast,* pp. 397–98.

69. See Greenblatt, *Shakespearean Negotiations.*

70. See Bell, *Holy Anorexia,* p. 60.

71. For the paradigmatic and circular nature of Saints' Lives, see Heffernan, *Sacred Biography,* pp. 3–18.

72. See Brown, "The Prioress's Tale," pp. 447–85.

73. See Carleton Brown, "The Man of Law's Headlink and the Prologue of *The Canterbury Tales,*" *Studies in Philology* 34 (1937): 465; Pearsall, *Canterbury Tales,* pp. 247–48; Statler, "Analogues," 896–910; and Gaylord, "Unconquered Tale," 633–34.

74. See Roger Ellis, *Patterns of Religious Narrative in "The Canterbury Tales"* (Totowa, N.J.: Barnes and Noble, 1986) , p. 73.

75. See Carleton Brown, "Headlink," p. 449; and Ellis, *Patterns,* pp. 80–81.

76. See Brown, "Headlink."

77. See Sr. Nicholas Maltman, O.P., "The Divine Granary, or the End of the Prioress's 'Greyn,'" *Chaucer Review* 17 (1982): 163–70, who argues this as the solution to Chaucer's addition of the grain to his sources, against Albert B. Friedman, "The Mysterious 'Greyn' in the *Prioress's Tale,*" *Chaucer Review* 11 (1977): 328–33.

78. Cooper, *Structure,* p. 166.

79. Ibid., p. 165.

80. See Riehle, *Mystics,* pp. 94–95; Despres, *Ghostly Sights,* pp. 125–26; and Dinshaw, *Chaucer's Sexual Poetics,* p. 8; Stephen Spector, "Empathy and Enmity in the *Prioress's Tale,*" in Robert R. Edwards and Stephen Spector, eds., *The Olde Daunce: Love, Friendship, Sex and Marriage in the Medieval World* (Albany: State University of New York Press, 1991), p. 211; and Hill, *Chaucerian Belief,* p. 103.

81. Hodgson, *Cloud,* p. 47.

82. Harley, *A Revelation of Purgatory*, p. 59.

83. See Barbara E. Wykes, ed., "Edition of Book I of *The Scale of Perfection, by Walter Hilton*," (Ph.D. Diss., University of Michigan, 1958), p. 95.

84. For a comment about Rolle and the Prioress, see Hill, *Chaucerian Belief*, p. 101.

85. See S. J. Ogilvie-Thomson, ed., *Richard Rolle: Prose and Verse*, EETS 293 (London: Oxford University Press, 1988), p. 42.

86. Among the others, Julian of Norwich is particularly fond of this topos. See Colledge and Walsh, *Showings*, pp. 364, 403, 509, and 664.

87. Horstman 1:89–90.

88. Horstman 1:27–28.

89. Horstman 2:359.

90. See Robert B. Burlin, *Chaucerian Fiction* (Princeton: Princeton University Press, 1977), p. 187.

91. Avril Henry, ed., *The Mirour of Mans Saluacioun: A Middle English Translation of Speculum Humanae Salvationis* (Philadelphia: University of Pennsylvania Press, 1987), p. 69.

92. Horstman 2:348.

93. Ibid., p. 361.

94. Ibid., p. 362.

95. Ellis, *Liber Celestis*, p.

# Chapter 5. Good Women

1. See Patterson, *Subject of History*, pp. 283–84.

2. See Benson, *Riverside Chaucer*, Prologue to the *Legend of Good Women*, F, lines 431–41.

3. A dissenting voice from the positive appraisal of Custance is that of Robert B. Dawson, "Custance in Context: Rethinking the Protagonist of the *Man of Law's Tale*," *Chaucer Review* 26 (1992): 293–307.

4. Kolve, *Imagery*, rightly makes much of this controlling image of the tale; see his *Imagery*, pp. 297–358; compare David Raybin, "Custance and History: Woman as Outsider in Chaucer's *Man of Law's Tale*," *Studies in the Age of Chaucer* 12 (1990): 66.

5. See Sheila Delany, "Womanliness in the *Man of Law's Tale*," *Chaucer Review* 9 (1974): 63–72.

6. See Kolve, *Imagery*, pp. 297–358.

7. Raybin, "Custance and History," p. 80, notes Custances's passivity.

8. Ibid., p. 70, Raybin calls attention to the silences attending Custance: the narrator often concentrates on those about her rather than on herself.

9. For a detailed comparison of Chaucer's version to its source, see Edward A. Block, "Originality, Controlling Purpose, and Craftsmanship in Chaucer's *Man of Law's Tale*," *PMLA* 68 (1953): 572–616; and Ellis, *Patterns*, pp. 119–68.

10. For support of this assertion and a full description of the literary relationship between Chaucer and Gower, see John H. Fisher, *John Gower: Moral Philosopher and Friend of Chaucer* (New York: New York University Press, 1964), pp. 204–302; see also Donald R. Howard, *Chaucer: His Life, His Works, His World* (New York: Dutton, 1987), pp. 418–20; Winthrop Wetherbee, "Constance and the World in Chaucer and Gower," in R. F. Yeager, ed., *John Gower: Recent Readings* (Kalamazoo, Mich.: Medieval Institute Publications, 1989), pp. 65–93;

Linda Barney Burke, "Genial Gower: Laughter in the *Confessio Amantis*," in Yeager, *John Gower*, pp. 39–63 esp. p. 39; and Peter Nicholson, "The *Man of Law's Tale*: What Chaucer Really Owed to Gower," *Chaucer Review* 26 (1991): 153–74. For a long-accepted view that Chaucer owed little to Gower, see Block, "Originality, Controlling Purpose, and Craftsmanship."

11. Russell A. Peck, ed., *John Gower: Confessio Amantis* (New York: Holt, Rinehart, and Winston, 1968), p. 124, lines 58–63.

12. See R. E. Lewis, *De Miseria Condicionis Humane*. For a study of the Man of Law's Tale that establishes a tension between the voices of Custance and the narrator and that in part analyzes the Innocentian material, see Ann W. Astell, "Apostrophe, Prayer, and Structure of Satire in *The Man of Law's Tale*," *Studies in the Age of Chaucer* 13 (1991): 81–97. I argue for a stronger contrast between the Boethian and Innocentian material in the tale.

13. For a discussion of Chaucer's probable translation of the work see R. E. Lewis, *De Miseria Condicionis Humane*, pp. 17–30; for an analysis of the role the work plays in the Man of Law's Tale that differs from my own, see Chauncey Wood, *Chaucer and the Country of the Stars* (Princeton: Princeton University Press, 1970) pp. 204ff.

14. Horstman 1:409.

15. R. E. Lewis, *De Miseria Condicionis Humane*, pp. 130–31. This and the following modern English translations are Lewis's.

16. Ibid., pp. 166–69.

17. Ibid., pp. 170–71.

18. Ibid., pp. 128–29.

19. See Huppé, *Reading*, pp. 91–107.

20. See Pearsall, *Canterbury Tales*, p. 265.

21. See Alfred David, *The Strumpet Muse: Art and Morals in Chaucer's Poetry* (Bloomington: Indiana University Press, 1976), p. 129.

22. Ibid., p. 129; compare Pearsall, *Canterbury Tales*, p. 263. That Chaucer elsewhere parodies Boethius has been established by Katherine Heinricks in "'Lovers' Consolations of Philosophy' in Boccaccio, Machaut, and Chaucer," *Studies in the Age of Chaucer* 11 (1989): 93–115.

23. Peck, *Gower*, lines 1226–30.

24. See, for instance, Mikhail Bakhtin, *Problems of Dostoevsky's Poetics* (Minneapolis: University of Minnesota Press, 1984). Compare Strohm, *Social Chaucer*, pp. 169–70.

25. See Bynum, *Holy Feast and Holy Fast*.

26. Kolve, *Imagery*, pp. 297–358.

27. This, of course, is the thesis of Caroline Walker Bynum's *Holy Feast and Holy Fast*.

28. This paragraph is quoted from my article, "Music and Mysticism in Hildegard von Bingen's *O ignis spiritus paracliti*," *Studia Mystica* 9, no. 3 (1986): 60–61. For information about Hildegard, see Peter Dronke, *Women Writers of the Middle Ages* (Cambridge: Cambridge University Press, 1984), pp. 144–201; Kent Kraft, "The German Visionary: Hildegard of Bingen," in Wilson, *Medieval Women Writers*, pp. 109–114; Newman, *Sister of Wisdom*, pp. 1–34; and Barbara Newman, ed. and trans., *Saint Hildegard of Bingen: "Symphonia"* (Ithaca: Cornell University Press, 1988), pp. 1–6.

29. Dronke, *Women Writers*, p. 231, translation, p. 145.

30. Biographical details of Catherine's life may be found in Bynum, *Holy*

*Food and Holy Fast,* pp. 165–80; Noffke, *Catherine of Siena,* pp. 3–7; Bell, *Holy Anorexia,* pp. 22–54; and Kieckhefer, *Unquiet Souls,* pp. 62–64.

31. Phyllis Hodgson and Gabriel M. Liegey, eds., *The Orcherd of Syon,* EETS 258 (London: Oxford University Press, 1966), p. 28.

32. For an argument stressing her connections with the Virgin Mary, see James I. Wimsatt, "The Blessed Virgin and the Two Coronations of Griselda," *Mediaevalia* 6 (1980): 187–207. For an argument from a feminist point of view stressing her silence, see Hansen, *Fictions of Gender,* pp. 188–207.

33. For a discussion of the relationship between the Clerk's Tale and Petrarch's version, see David Wallace, "'Whan She Translated Was': A Chaucerian Critique of the Petrarchan Academy," in Patterson, *Literary Practice and Social Change,* 156–215. For the most comprehensive treatment of the relationship between Chaucer and Boccaccio, see David Wallace, *Chaucer and the Early Writings of Boccaccio* (Cambridge: D. S. Brewer, 1985).

34. See J. Burke Severs, "The Clerk's Tale," in Bryan and Dempster, *Sources and Analogues,* pp. 288–332.

35. See, for instance, J. Burke Severs, *The Literary Relationships of Chaucer's Clerkes Tale,* Yale Studies in English 96 (New Haven: Yale University Press, 1942); Alfred L. Kellogg, "The Evolution of the 'Clerk's Tale': A Study in Connotation," in Kellogg, *Chaucer, Langland, Arthur,* pp. 276–329; and Thomas H. Bestul, "True and False *Cheere* in Chaucer's *Clerk's Tale,*" *Journal of English and Germanic Philology* 82 (1983): 500–514.

36. See Kellogg, *Chaucer, Langland, Arthur,* p. 297.

37. Ibid., 298–99.

38. Ibid., p. 308.

39. See Ralph A. Griffiths, *The Reign of King Henry VI* (Berkeley: University of California Press, 1981), p. 688. For the larger political implications of the Clerk's Tale, see Michaela Paasche Grudin, "Chaucer's *Clerk's Tale* as Political Paradox," *Studies in the Age of Chaucer* 11 (1989): 63–92.

40. See Strohm, *Social Chaucer* , pp. 28–29.

41. Horstman 2:47. See also p. 48.

42. Ibid., p. 356.

43. Ibid., pp. 410–11.

44. See John Speirs, "Chaucer (II): *The Canterbury Tales* (I)," *Scrutiny* 11 (1943): 193; reprinted in Andrew, *Critical Essays,* p. 48.

45. See John H. Fisher, *The Tretyse of Loue,* EETS 223 (London: Oxford University Press, 1951), pp. 17–18.

46. See Severs, "The Clerk's Tale," in Bryan and Dempster, *Sources and Analogues,* pp. 310–11.

47. For the importance of the word *ynough* for the tale, see Jill Mann, "Satisfaction and Payment in Middle English Literature," *Studies in the Age of Chaucer* 5 (1983), 17–48.

48. For a perceptive analysis of *sad* in this tale supporting the meaning of "serious" or "constant," see Derek Brewer, *Chaucer: The Poet as Storyteller* (London: Macmillan, 1984), pp. 41–2. For a comprehensive analysis of the word's semantic range, see C. S. Lewis, *Studies in Words* (Cambridge: Cambridge University Press, 1967), pp. 75–85. Neither Brewer nor Lewis recognizes the devotional aspect of the word. See also S. S. Hussey, *Chaucer: An Introduction* (London: Metheuen, 1971), p. 173; and Priscilla Martin, *Chaucer's Women: Nuns, Wives, Amazons* (Iowa City: University of Iowa Press, 1990), pp. 24–25.

49. See Severs, "The Clerk's Tale," in Bryan and Dempster, *Sources and Analogues*, p. 310.

50. Horstman 2:423.

51. Boenig, *Contemplations*, p. 16.

52. Theresa A. Halligan, ed., *The Booke of Gostlye Grace of Mechtild of Hackeborn* (Toronto: Pontifical Institute of Mediaeval Studies, 1979), p. 330.

53. Boenig, *Contemplations*, pp. 11–12.

54. Horstman 1:329.

55. Ibid., 1:357.

56. Ibid., 1:321.

57. Kathryn L. Lynch, "Despoiling Griselda: Chaucer's Walter and the Problem of Knowledge in *The Clerk's Tale*," *Studies in the Age of Chaucer* 10 (1988): 52 notes Walter's habit of "concealing himself."

58. Griselda's godlike qualities are well explicated by Mann, "Satisfaction and Payment."

59. Kendrick, *Chaucerian Play*, p. 52, suggests that Griselda "'becomes' Walter by conforming her will to his."

60. For an explication of the rhetorical aspects of the Clerk's Tale, see Karl P. Wentersdorf, "Chaucer's Clerk of Oxenford as Rhetorician," *Medieval Studies* 51 (1989): 313–28.

61. See C. David Benson, *Drama*, pp. 136–37.

62. See G. H. Gerould, "The Second Nun's Prologue and Tale," esp. in Bryan and Dempster, *Sources and Analogues*, pp. 664–84, p. 676. Pope Urban there shows up to baptize those converted during the trial. For a source study emphasizing Chaucer's other changes to his source, see Sherry L. Reames, "The Cecelia Legend as Chaucer Inherited It and Retold It: The Disappearance of an Augustinian Ideal," *Speculum* 55 (1980): 38–57.

63. See Paul E. Beichner, "Confrontation, Contempt of Court, and Chaucer's Cecelia," *Chaucer Review* 8 (1973): 204.

64. See Ellis, *Patterns*, p. 90.

65. Compare C. David Benson's statement, "The poet [of this tale] firmly believes in the power of words to change, convert, and save. All of the Christian characters use language well" (*Drama*, p. 137).

66. Hodgson, *Cloud*, p. 95.

67. Horstman 2:47

68. Colledge and Walsh, *Julian*, p. 284.

69. Gerould, "The Second Nun's Prologue and Tale," in Bryan and Dempster, *Sources and Analogues*, p. 674.

## Chapter 6. Other Women

1. Douglas Berger, "Deluding Words in the *Merchant's Tale*," *Chaucer Review* 12 (1978): 103–10.

2. See Bertrand H. Bronson, "Afterthoughts on *The Merchant's Tale*," *Studies in Philology* 58 (1961): 596; Robert M. Jordan, "The Non-Dramatic Disunity of the Merchant's Tale," *PMLA* 78 (1963): 293–99; and T. W. Craik, *The Comic Tales of Chaucer* (London: Methuen, 1964), p. 153.

3. See E. Talbot Donaldson, *Chaucer's Poetry* (1958; rpt., New York: Wiley, 1975), p. 921; and Donaldson, *Speaking*, pp. 30ff. See also J. S. P. Tatlock, "Chaucer's Merchant's Tale," *Modern Philology* 33 (1936): 367–81.

4. See Emerson Brown, Jr., "Chaucer, the Merchant, and their Tale: Getting beyond Old Controversies, Part II," *Chaucer Review* 13 (1979): 247ff.

5. See Jay Schleusner, "The Conduct of the *Merchant's Tale*," *Chaucer Review* 14 (1980): 237ff.

6. See C. David Benson, *Drama*, pp. 116ff.

7. See, for instance, Huppé, *Reading*, p. 152; and Pearsall, *Canterbury Tales*, p. 199.

8. For the artistic effect of this euphemism, see C. David Benson, *Drama*, p. 126.

9. Henry, *Mirour*, p. 53.

10. See Roy J. Pearcy, "Modes of Signification and the Humor of Obscene Diction in the Fabliaux," in Thomas D. Cooke and Benjamin L. Honeycutt, eds., *The Humor of the Fabliaux: A Collection of Critical Essays* (Columbia: University of Missouri Press, 1974), pp. 179–96; and Thomas D. Cooke, *The Old French and Chaucerian Fabliaux: A Study of Their Comic Climax* (Columbia: University of Missouri Press, 1978), pp. 107–8.

11. Hodgson, *Privy Counselling*, p. 153.

12. See, for instance, Donaldson, *Speaking*, pp. 34, 37; and C. David Benson, *Drama*, pp. 118–21.

13. See Mary C. Schroeder, "Fantasy in the 'Merchant's Tale,'" *Criticism* 12 (1970): 169.

14. Ibid., see also Benson, *Drama*, p. 123.

15. See Pearsall, *Canterbury Tales*, p. 199; and Martin, *Chaucer's Women*, p. 58.

16. See Donaldson, *Speaking*, pp. 36–37, for perceptive comments on "softeley."

17. See George Lyman Kittredge, "Chaucer's Discussion of Marriage," *Modern Philology* 9 (1911–12): 435–67.

18. See, for instance, Ruggiers, *Art*, pp. 226–7.; Owen, *Pilgrimage*, p. 203; Cooper, *Structure*, p. 149; P. M. Kean, *Chaucer and the Making of English Poetry*, 2d ed. (London: Routledge and Kegan Paul, 1972), p. 266; Kathryn Jacobs, "The Marriage Contract of the *Franklin's Tale*: The Remaking of Society," *Chaucer Review* 20 (1986): 132–43; and John M. Fyler, "Love and Degree in the *Franklin's Tale*," *Chaucer Review* 21 (1987): 321–39.

19. Joseph Allen Hornsby, *Chaucer and the Law* (Norman, Okla.: Pilgrim Books, 1988), p. 53.

20. See Robertson, *A Preface to Chaucer*, pp. 276, 470–72. See also Howard, *Idea*, p. 269.

21. Huppé *Reading*, p. 168.

22. Alan T. Gaylord, "The Promises in *The Franklin's Tale*," *ELH* 31 (1964): 331–35.

23. See also, for instance, Burlin, *Fictions*, pp. 199–201; David, *Muse*, p. 189; and Pearsall *Canterbury Tales*, pp. 148–51.

24. For the surface morality of the tale's characters, see Russell Peck, "Sovereignty and the Two Worlds of the *Franklin's Tale*," *Chaucer Review* 1 (1966): 253 71.

25. For an analysis of "truth" in the tale, see Strohm, *Social Chaucer*, pp. 105–6.

26. See Huppé, *Reading*, p. 168; and Howard, *Idea*, p. 268.

27. A stronger voice is that of R. A. Shoaf, "The *Franklin's Tale*: Chaucer

and Medusa," *Chaucer Review* 21 (1987): 274–90, who develops the connections between Dorigen and Medusa.

28. See Robertson, *Preface,* p. 274; and Burlin, *Fictions,* pp. 199–201.

29. Burlin, *Fictions,* p. 200.

30. See Anne Thompson Lee, "'A Woman True and Fair': Chaucer's Portrayal of Dorigen in the *Franklin's Tale*," *Chaucer Review* 19 (1985): 169–78.

31. Jacobs, "Marriage Contract," 135.

32. Bynum, *Holy Feast and Holy Fast;* see esp. chap. 7, "Food as Control of Circumstance," pp. 219–44.

33. For an account of her exertions to avoid marriage, see Bynum, *Holy Feast and Holy Fast,* pp. 167ff. For accounts of her life and writing, see Bell, *Holy Anorexia,* pp. 22–53; Kieckhefer, *Unquiet Souls,* pp. 62–64; Berrigan, "The Tuscan Visionary"; and Noffke, *The Dialogue.* For the contemporary account of her life, see Lamb, *Raymond of Capua: The Life of St. Catherine of Siena.* For her relationship to English mystics like Margery Kempe, see David Wallace, "Mystics and Followers in Siena and East Anglia: a Study in Taxonomy, Class and Cultural Mediation," in Marion Glasscoe, ed., *The Medieval Mystical Tradition in England* (Cambridge: D. S. Brewer, 1984), pp. 169–91.

34. See Bynum, *Holy Feast and Holy Fast,* pp. 116, 121, 222. For the medieval account of her life, see Thomas of Cantimpré, *Life of Lutgard of Aywières,* in *Acta sanctorum . . . editio novissima,* eds. J. Bollandus and G. Henschenius), 4:196 ff.

35. See Bynum, *Holy Feast and Holy Fast,* pp. 115, 227. For the medieval account of her life, see Jacques de Vitry, *Life of Mary of Oignies,* in Bollandus and Henschenius, *Acta sanctorum,* 5:568.

36. See Bynum, *Holy Feast and Holy Fast,* pp. 125, 204.

37. See ibid., 131.

38. See ibid., pp. 146–48.

39. Ibid., p. 148.

40. For Christina's life see C. H. Talbot, ed. and trans., *The Life of Christiana of Markyate: A Twelfth-Century Recluse* (Oxford: Clarendon Press, 1959). See also Robert W. Hanning, *The Individual in Twelfth Century Romance* (New Haven: Yale University Press, 1977), pp. 35–50; Bynum, *Holy Feast and Holy Fast,* pp. 27, 222; Henrietta Leyser, *Hermits and the New Monasticism* (New York: St. Martin's Press, 1984), pp. 13–15; and Georgianna, *The Solitary Self,* pp. 37–42.

41. Bynum, *Holy Feast and Holy Fast,* p. 208.

42. See Germaine Dempster and J. S. P. Tatlock, 'The Franklin's Tale," in Bryan and Dempster, *Sources and Analogues,* pp. 377–97, esp. p. 383.

43. See, for instance, Huppé, *Reading,* p. 174, who votes for the clerk.

44. As Theresa Coletti, "The *Mulier Fortis* and Chaucer's *Shipman's Tale,*" *Chaucer Review* 15 (1981): 236–49, points out, one of the ironies of this tale is the implied contrast with the "perfect wife" of Prov. 31:10–31.

45. Most critics who explicate the Shipman's Tale note the obvious connections between sex and money. Among the more detailed and interesting of fairly recent treatments are Paul Stephen Schneider, "'Taillynge Ynogh': The Function of Money in the *Shipman's Tale,*" *Chaucer Review* 11 (1977): 201–09; Robert Adams, "The Concept of Debt in *The Shipman's Tale,*" *Studies in the Age of Chaucer* 6 (1984): 88–102, who adds a penitential to the sexual and mercantile connotations of the word *debt*); and Gerhard Joseph, "Chaucer's Coinage: Foreign Exchange and the Puns of the *Shipman's Tale,*" *Chaucer Review* 17 (1983): 341–57, who establishes a connection between international currency and language ex-

change, noting Derrida's use of the coin metaphor to analyze language in *Of Grammatology* and *Writing and Difference.*

46. Most notably Cooper, *Structure,* pp. 161–64; and C. David Benson, *Drama,* pp. 104–16.

47. C. David Benson, *Drama,* p. 107.

48. For an analysis of the oaths in this tale somewhat different than the one following, see Strohm, *Social Chaucer,* pp. 100–102.

49. Walter W. Seton, ed., *A Fifteenth-Century Courtesy Book and Two Fifteenth-Century Franciscan Rules,* EETS 148 (London: Oxford University Press, 1914), p. 52.

50. See Cooper, *Structure,* p. 164; and C. David Benson, *Drama,* p. 113.

51. See, for instance, C. David Benson, *Drama,* p. 110.

52. See C. David Benson, *Drama,* p. 112; and Pearsall, *Canterbury Tales,* p. 211.

53. See Lee W. Patterson, "'What Man Artow?': Authorial Self-Definition in *The Tale of Sir Thopas* and *The Tale of Melibee,*" *Studies in the Age of Chaucer* 11 (1989): 162; Patterson, *Subject of History,* pp. 363–64; and Martin, *Chaucer's Women,* p. 88.

54. C. David Benson, *Drama,* p. 114.

55. See, for instance, C. David Benson, *Drama,* p. 113; Owen, *Pilgrimage,* p. 116; Howard, *Idea,* pp. 275–76; Schneider, "'Taillynge Ynogh,'"; Claude Jones, "Chaucer's *Taillynge Ynoughe,*" *Modern Language Notes* 52 (1937): 570; Robert A. Caldwell, "Chaucer's *Taillynge Ynough, Canterbury Tales, B2, 1624,*" *Modern Language Notes* 55 (1940): 262–65; Albert H. Silverman, "Sex and Money in Chaucer's *Shipman's Tale,*" *Philological Quarterly* 32 (1953): 329–36; R. M. Lumiansky, *"Of Sundry Folk": The Dramatic Principle in "The Canterbury Tales"* (1955; rpt., Austin: University of Texas Press, 1980), p. 76; Ruggiers, *Art,* p. 86; and Patterson, *Subject of History,* pp. 351, 359. Compare Hornsby, *Law,* p. 99, who calls attention as well to the contractual pun on *wed.* See also pp. 37, 42, and 76.

56. See Murray Copland, *"The Shipman's Tale:* Chaucer and Boccaccio," *Medium Aevum* 35 (1966): 12 n. 5.

57. C. David Benson, *Drama,* p. 104.

58. See Boenig, *"House of Fame,"* p. 269.

59. Ibid., 270–71.

60. James Dean, "Dismantling the Canterbury Book," *PMLA* 100 (1985): 753.

61. Ibid., 753.

62. William Askins, "The Historical Setting of *The Manciple's Tale,*" *Studies in the Age of Chaucer* 7 (1985): 87–106.

63. See, for instance, Howard, *Idea,* p. 303; Cooper, *Structure,* p. 198; R. D. Fulk, "Reinterpreting the *Manciple's Tale,*" *Journal of English and Germanic Philology* 78 (1979): 490; and John J. McGavin, "How Nasty is Phoebus's Crow?", *Chaucer Review* 21 (1987): 456.

64. See, for instance, Howard, *Idea,* p. 303; Dean, "Dismantling," p. 754; and Mark Allen, "Penitential Sermons, the Manciple, and the End of *The Canterbury Tales,*" *Studies in the Age of Chaucer* 9 (1987): 77–96.

65. See, for instance, Allen, "Penitential Sermons"; and Chauncey Wood, "Speech, the Principle of Contraries, and Chaucer's Tales of the Manciple and the Parson," *Mediaevalia* 6 (1980): 209–27.

66. See James A. Work, "The Manciple's Tale," in Bryan and Dempster, *Sources and Analogues,* pp. 699–722.

67. As many have pointed out, the talkative Manciple is, in another sense,

the appropriate teller for a tale about a talkative crow. See, for instance, Earle Birney, "Chaucer's 'Gentil' Manciple and his 'Gentil' Tale," in Birney, *Essays on Chaucerian Irony,* pp. 125–133; J. Burke Severs, "Is the *Manciple's Tale* a Success?" *Journal of English and Germanic Philology* 51 (1952): 1–16; and V. J. Scattergood, "The Manciple's Manner of Speaking," *Essays in Criticism* 24 (1974): 124–46.

68. Critics often call attention to this word. See, for instance, Donaldson, *Speaking,* p. 27; Pearsall, *Canterbury Tales,* p. 241; Allen, "Penitential Sermons," 83; and Strohm, *Social Chaucer,* p. 175.

69. Horstman 2:354.

70. See John H. Fisher, ed., *The Complete Poetry and Prose of Geoffrey Chaucer,* 2d ed. (New York: Holt, Rinehart and Winston, 1989).

71. See, for instance, Howard, *Idea,* pp. 300, 303; and Allen, "Penitential Sermons," 77.

72. See Dean, "Dismantling."

73. For a defense of Chaucerian "intentions" see Koff, *Art of Storytelling,* pp. 3, 76.

## Chapter 7. Chaucer Himself

1. For the various deficiencies of the Squire as a storyteller, see Marie Neville, "The Function of the 'Squire's Tale' in the Canterbury Scheme," *Journal of English and Germanic Philology* 50 (1951): 167–79; Gardner Stillwell, "Chaucer in Tartary," *Review of English Studies* 24 (1948): 177–88; Wood, *Chaucer and the Country of the Stars,* pp. 84–98; J. P. McCall, "The Squire in Wonderland," *Chaucer Review* 1 (1966): 163–69; Grace Hadow, *Chaucer and His Times* (New York: Holt 1914), pp. 81–82; Nevil Coghill, *The Poet Chaucer* (London: Oxford University Press, 1941), p. 167; Derek Pearsall, "The Squire as Story-Teller," *University of Toronto Quarterly* 34 (1964): 82–92; and J. D. North, *Chaucer's Universe* (London: Oxford University Press, 1988), pp. 263–88, esp. p. 284.

2. For a discussion of the inconsistency between this Chaucer and that of the General Prologue, see C. David Benson, *Drama,* p. 29.

3. See Laura H. Loomis, "The Tale of Sir Thopas," in Bryan and Dempster, *Sources and Analogues,* pp. 486–559.

4. Alan T. Gaylord, in "The Moment of *Sir Thopas:* Towards a New Look at Chaucer's Language," *Chaucer Review* 16 (1982), 311–29 suggests that the tale is not so much a parody of literary romances but an invention of a literary language.

5. See, for instance, Pearsall, *Canterbury Tales,* pp. 160–65; Owen, *Pilgrimage,* pp. 120–22; David, *Muse,* pp. 215–19; Cooper, *Structure,* pp. 168–72; and C. David Benson, *Drama,* pp. 29–37.

6. For the Middle English version of this romance, see M. Mills, ed., *Lybeaus Descanus,* EETS 261 (London: Oxford University Press, 1969).

7. Perry, *Religious Pieces,* p. 85.

8. Owen, *Pilgrimage,* p. 124.

9. Ibid., p. 123.

10. See, for instance, Cooper, *Structure,* p. 168; and C. David Benson, *Drama,* p. 215.

11. The chaos is worse in the manuscripts, where the poem is presented horizontally as well as vertically; the long lines are grouped together with the tail

lines columned to the right, joined to the rest with brackets, and then with the bob-lines columned further to the right, again joined by brackets. The poem is thus visually as well as conceptually and prosodically incongruous. See Cooper, *Structure,* p. 170; and Judith Tschann, "The Layout of *Sir Thopas* in the Ellesmere, Hengwrt, Cambridge Dd.4.24, and Cambridge Gg.4.27 Manuscripts," *Chaucer Review* 20 (1985): 1–13.

12. See Loomis, "The Tale of Sir Thopas," in Bryan and Dempster, *Sources and Analogues.*

13. Pearsall, *Canterbury Tales,* p. 165.

14. Cooper, *Structure,* p. 171.

15. Cooper, *Structure,* p. 170; see also Patterson, "'What Man Artow?'" p. 126; and John Burrow, "*Sir Thopas:* An Agony in Three Fits," *Review of English Studies,* n.s. 22 (1971): 54–58.

16. "This litel tretys" was interpreted by Robertson, *Preface,* pp. 367–68 as referring to the whole *Canterbury Tales.* Owen, *Pilgrimage,* pp. 124–25; Glending Olson, "A Reading of the *Thopas-Melibee* Link," *Chaucer Review* 10 (1975–76): 147–53; Pearsall, *Canterbury Tales,* p. 286; and Thomas J. Farrell, "Chaucer's Little Treatise, The Melibee," *Chaucer Review* 20 (1986): 61–67 argue persuasively against him.

17. See J. Burke Severs, "The Tale of Melibeus," pp. 560–614 in Bryan and Dempster, *Sources and Analogues.*

18. Ibid., p. 565.

19. See, for instance, Gardner Stillwell, "The Political Meaning of Chaucer's *Tale of Melibee,*" *Speculum* 19 (1944), 433–44; and Howard, *Idea,* p. 315.

20. See Pearsall, *Canterbury Tales,* pp. 321–25.

21. See Richard Firth Green, *Poets and Princepleasers: Literature and the English Court in the Late Middle Ages* (Toronto: University of Toronto Press, 1980), p. 143.

22. See Severs, "Melibeus," p. 565.

23. See Patterson, "'What Man Artow?'"

24. See, for instance, Ellis, *Patterns,* pp. 108–10; Howard, *Idea,* pp. 309–15; Bertrand H. Bronson, "Chaucer's Art in Relation to His Audience," in his *Five Studies in Literature,* pp. 1–53 (Berkeley: University of California Publications in English 8, no. 1, 1940), esp. p. 42; and Paul Strohm, "The Allegory of the *Tale of Melibee,*" *Chaucer Review* 2 (1967): 32–42.

25. See, for instance, Trevor Whittock, *A Reading of "The Canterbury Tales"* (Cambridge: Cambridge University Press, 1968), p. 214; Dolores Palomo, "What Chaucer Really Did to *Le Livre de Malibee,*" *Philological Quarterly* 53 (1974): 304–20; John Gardner, *The Poetry of Chaucer* (Carbondale, Illinois: Southern Illinois University Press, 1977), pp. 309–10; and Lumiansky, *Sondry Folk,* pp. 94–95.

26. A translation of Catherine of Siena's *Dialogues;* see Hodgson and Liegey, *The Orcherd of Syon.*

27. See John C. Hirsh, ed., *Barlam and Iosaphat,* EETS 290 (London: Oxford University Press, 1986).

28. C. David Benson, *Drama,* pp. 26–43. Ruggiers, *Art,* p. 19 also notes the contrasting style and suggests an author in control and, by implication, a narrator out of control.

29. An earlier version of this section appeared as "Taking Leave: Chaucer's Retraction and the Ways of Affirmation and Negation," *Studia Mystica* 12, nos. 2–3 (Summer-Fall 1989): 21–34.

30. See, for instance, W. W. Lawrence, *Chaucer and "The Canterbury Tales"* (New York: Columbia University Press, 1950), pp. 157–58; Ralph Baldwin, *The Unity of "The Canterbury Tales"* (Copenhagen: Rosenhilde and Beggen, 1955), pp. 105 ff.; and Donaldson, *Chaucer's Poetry*, pp. 949ff. Compare David Lawton, "Chaucer's Two Ways: The Pilgrimage Frame of *The Canterbury Tales*," *Studies in the Age of Chaucer* 9 (1987): 4–5.

31. Fisher, *The Tretyse of Loue*, p. 32.

32. See Hussey, *Introduction*, p. 23.

33. Ruggiers, *Art*, p. 3.

34. Ibid., p. 41.

35. Hodgson, *Cloud*, pp. 1–2.

36. Ibid., p. 2.

37. Ibid.

38. See Fisher, *Importance*, p. 87.

39. Hodgson, *Cloud*, p. 154.

40. Ibid., p. 125.

41. John Cage, *Silence: Lectures and Writing* (Cambridge, Massachusetts: MIT Press, 1961), p. 109.

42. Donaldson, *Speaking*, pp. 1–12; compare James I. Wimsatt, *Chaucer and His French Contemporaries: Natural Music in the Fourteenth Century* (Toronto: University of Toronto Press, 1991), pp. 77–107.

43. As Robert Worth Frank, Jr., puts it in "Inept Chaucer," *Studies in the Age of Chaucer* 11 (1989): 13, "Chaucer can be inept. He is a very human artist and so shares the human birthright of imperfection. And his imperfections should be identified, analyzed, and accepted. That is one of the responsibilities of criticism."

44. John Burrow, "Poems without Endings," *Studies in the Age of Chaucer* 13 (1991), 17–37, argues that modern Chaucerians often prefer to emphasize the artistic satisfactions of unended Chaucerian works like *The Legend of Good Women, The House of Fame,* and *The Squire's Tale* rather than accept them as accidental fragments. He suggests this attitude as the legacy of Romanticism (34–35). I hope I have demonstrated a medieval attitude, based on Pseudo-Dionysian language theory, that earlier than Dorothy Wordsworth valorizes fragmentation.

# Bibliography

Adams, Robert. "The Concept of Debt in *The Shipman's Tale.*" *Studies in the Age of Chaucer* 6 (1984): 85–102.

Aers, David. *Chaucer.* Brighton: Harvester Press, 1986.

———. *Community, Gender, and Individual Identity: English Writing, 1360–1430.* London: Routledge, 1988.

Alford, John A. "Biblical *Imitatio* in the Writings of Richard Rolle." *ELH* 40 (1973): 1–23.

Allen, Hope Emily. *Writings Ascribed to Richard Rolle, Hermit of Hampole, and Materials for His Biography.* New York: Heath, 1927.

Allen, Mark. "Penitential Sermons, the Manciple, and the End of *The Canterbury Tales.*" *Studies in the Age of Chaucer* 9 (1987): 77–96.

Allen, Rosamund. "'Singuler Lufe': Richard Rolle and the Grammar of Spiritual Ascent." In Glasscoe, *Mystical Tradition,* pp. 28–54.

Ampe, Albert. "La théologie mystique de l'ascension de l'âme selon le bienheureux Jean de Ruusbroec." *Revue d'Ascetique et de Mystique* 36 (1960): 188–201, 303–22.

Andres, F. "Die Stufen der Contemplatio in Bonaventuras *Itinerarium mentis ad deum* und in *Benjamin Major* des Richards von St. Viktor." *Franziskanische Studien* 8 (1921): 189–200.

Andrew, Malcolm. *Critical Essays on Chaucer's "Canterbury Tales".* Toronto: University of Toronto Press, 1991.

Askins, William. "The Historical Setting of *The Manciple's Tale.*" *Studies in the Age of Chaucer* 7 (1985): 87–106.

Astell, Ann W. *The Song of Songs in the Middle Ages.* Ithaca: Cornell University Press, 1990.

———. "Apostrophe, Prayer, and the Structure of Satire in *The Man of Law's Tale.*" *Studies in the Age of Chaucer* 13 (1991): 81–97.

Atkinson, Clarissa W. *Mystic and Pilgrim: The Book and World of Margery Kempe.* Ithaca: Cornell University Press, 1983.

Auger, Alfredus. *De Doctrina et Meritis Joannis van Ruysbroeck.* Louvain: J. van Linthout, 1892.

Ayto, John and Alexandra Barratt, eds. *Aelred of Rievaulx's "De Institutione Inclusarum": Two English Versions.* EETS 287. London: Oxford University Press, 1984.

Bakhtin, Mikhail. *Problems of Dostoevsky's Poetics.* Minneapolis: University of Minnesota Press, 1984.

Baldwin, Ralph. *The Unity of "The Canterbury Tales."* Copenhagen: Rosenkilde and Beggen, 1955.

Barlow, Frank. *Thomas Becket*. Berkeley: University of California Press, 1986.

Barthes, Roland. *S/Z*. Paris: Seuil, 1970.

——. *The Pleasure of the Text*. Translated by Richard Miller. New York: Hill and Wang, 1975.

Beichner, Paul E. "Confrontation, Contempt of Court, and Chaucer's Cecelia." *Chaucer Review* 8 (1973): 198–204.

Bell, Rudolph M. *Holy Anorexia*. Chicago: University of Chicago Press, 1985.

Benson, C. David. *Chaucer's Drama of Style*. Chapel Hill: University of North Carolina Press, 1986.

Benson, Larry, ed. *The Riverside Chaucer*. Boston: Houghton, Mifflin, 1987.

Berger, Douglas. "Deluding Words in the *Merchant's Tale*." *Chaucer Review* 12 (1978): 103–10.

Berrigan, Joseph. "The Tuscan Visionary: Saint Catherine of Siena." In Wilson, *Medieval Women Writers*, pp. 252–68.

Berthold, George C. "Did Maximus the Confessor Know Augustine?" *Studia Patristica* 17 (1982): 14–17.

——, trans. *Maximus Confessor: Selected Writings*. New York: Paulist Press, 1985.

Bestul, Thomas H. "True and False *Cheere* in Chaucer's *Clerk's Tale*." *Journal of English and Germanic Philology* 82 (1983): 500–514.

——. "Chaucer's Parson's Tale and the Late-Medieval Tradition of Religious Meditation. *Speculum* 64 (1989): 600–619.

Bihlmeyer, Karl. "Selbstbiographie in der deutschen Mystik des Mittelalters." *Theologische Quartalschrift* 114 (1933): 504–44.

Birney, Earle. *Essays on Chaucerian Irony*. Edited Beryl Rowland. Toronto: University of Toronto Press, 1985.

Block, Edward A. "Originality, Controlling Purpose, and Craftsmanship in Chaucer's *Man of Law's Tale*." *PMLA* 68 (1953): 572–616.

Blodgett, E. D. "Chaucerian *Pryvetee* and the Opposition to Time." *Speculum* 51 (1976): 477–93.

Bloom, Harold. *The Anxiety of Influence: A Theory of Poetry*. New York: Oxford University Press, 1973.

——. *A Map of Misreading*. New York: Oxford University Press, 1975.

——. *Poetry and Repression*. New Haven: Yale University Press, 1976.

Boenig, Robert. "*Andreas,* the Eucharist, and Vercelli." *JEGP* 79 (1980): 313–31.

——. "Chaucer's *House of Fame,* the Apocalypse, and Bede." *American Benedictine Review* 36 (1985): 263–77.

——. "The God-as-Mother Theme in Richard Rolle's Biblical Commentaries." *Mystics Quarterly* 10 (1984): 171–74.

——. "Music and Mysticism in Hildegard von Bingen's *O ignis spiritus paracliti*." *Studia Mystica* 9, no. 3 (1986): 60–70.

——. "Taking Leave: Chaucer's Retraction and the Ways of Affirmation and Negation." *Studia Mystica* 12, nos. 2–3 (Spring-Fall 1989): 21–34.

——. *Contemplations of the Dread and Love of God (1506)*. Delmar, N.Y.: Scholars' Facsimiles and Reprints, 1990.

——. "*Contemplations of the Dread and Love of God,* Richard Rolle, and Aelred of Rievaulx." *Mystics Quarterly* 16 (1990): 27–33.

———. *Saint and Hero: Andreas and Medieval Doctrine.* Lewisburg, Pa.: Bucknell University Press, 1991.

Boitani, Piero, ed. *Chaucer and the Italian Trecento.* Cambridge: Cambridge University Press, 1983.

Bolton, W. F. "The 'Miller's Tale': An Interpretation." *Mediaeval Studies* 24 (1962): 83–94.

Boularand, E. "L'Eucharistie d'après le pseudo-Denys l'Areopagite." *Bulletin de Littérature Ecclesiastique* 58 (1957): 193–217; and 59 (1958): 129–69.

Bové, Paul A. *Deconstructive Poetics: Heidegger and Modern American Poetry.* New York: Columbia University Press, 1980.

Bowden, Betsy. *Chaucer Aloud: The Varieties of Textual Interpretation.* Philadelphia: University of Pennsylvania Press, 1987.

Bradley, Ritamary. "Mysticism in the Motherhood Similitude of Julian of Norwich." *Studia Mystica* 8, no. 2 (1985): 4–14.

Brewer, Derek. *Chaucer: The Poet as Storyteller.* London: Macmillan, 1984.

Bronson, Bertrand H. *Five Studies in Literature.* Berkeley: University of California Publications in English 8, no. 1, 1940.

———. "Afterthoughts on *The Merchant's Tale.*" *Studies in Philology* 58 (1961): 583–96.

Brown, Carleton. "The Man of Law's Headlink and the Prologue of *The Canterbury Tales.*" *Studies in Philology* 34 (1937): 8–35.

Brown, Emerson, Jr. "Chaucer, the Merchant, and their Tale: Getting beyond Old Controversies, Part II." *Chaucer Review* 13 (1979): 247–62.

Bryan, W. F., and Germaine Dempster, eds. *Sources and Analogues of Chaucer's "Canterbury Tales."* Chicago: University of Chicago Press, 1941.

Burke, Linda Barney. "Genial Gower: Laughter in the *Confessio Amantis.*" In Yeager, *John Gower: Recent Readings,* pp. 39–63.

Burlin, Robert B. *Chaucerian Fiction.* Princeton: Princeton University Press, 1977.

Burns, Robert M. "The Divine Simplicity in St. Thomas." *Religious Studies* 25 (1989): 271–93.

Burrell, David B. *Knowing the Unknowable God: Ibn-Sina, Maimonides, Aquinas.* Notre Dame, Ind.: University of Notre Dame Press, 1986.

———. "Naming the Names of God: Muslims, Jews, Christians." *Theology Today* 47 (April 1990): 22–29.

Burrow, John. "*Sir Thopas:* An Agony in Three Fits." *Review of English Studies* n.s. 22 (1971): 54–58.

———. "Fantasy and Language in *The Cloud of Unknowing.*" *Essays in Criticism* 27 (1977): 283–98.

———. "Poems without Endings." *Studies in the Age of Chaucer* 13 (1991): 17–37.

Bynum, Caroline Walker. "The Spirituality of Regular Canons in the Twelfth Century: A New Approach." *Medievalia et Humanistica* 4 (1973): 3–24.

———. *Jesus as Mother: Studies in the Spirituality of the High Middle Ages.* Berkeley: University of California Press, 1982.

———. *Holy Feast and Holy Fast: The Religious Significance of Food to Medieval Women.* Berkeley: University of California Press, 1987.

Cage, John. *Silence: Lectures and Writing.* Cambridge: MIT Press, 1961.

Caldwell, Robert A. "Chaucer's *Taillynge Ynough, Canterbury Tales, B2*, 1624." *Modern Language Notes* 55 (1940): 262–265.

Caputo, John. "The Nothingness of the Intellect in Meister Eckhart's 'Parisian Questions.'" *The Thomist* 39 (1975): 85–115.

———. "Fundamental Themes in Meister Eckhart's Mysticism." *The Thomist* 42 (1978): 197–225.

Cawley, A. C., ed. *Chaucer's Mind and Art.* London: Oliver and Boyd, 1969.

Chadwick, Owen, trans. *Western Asceticism.* Philadelphia: Westminster Press, 1958.

Châtillon, Jean. "Les trois modes de la contemplation selon Richard de Saint-Victor." *Bulletin de Littérature Ecclesiastique* 41 (1940): 3–26.

Clark, J. P. H. "Sources and Theology in *The Cloud of Unknowing.*" *Downside Review* 98 (1980): 83–109.

Clements, Arthur L. *Poetry and Contemplation.* Albany: State University of New York Press, 1990.

Coghill, Nevil. *The Poet Chaucer.* London: Oxford University Press, 1941.

Cohn, Ricki Jean. "God and Motherhood in *The Book of Margery Kempe.*" *Studia Mystica* 9, no. 1 (1986): 26–35.

Coletti, Theresa. The *Mulier Fortis* and Chaucer's *Shipman's Tale.*" *Chaucer Review* 15 (1981): 236–49.

Colledge, Edmund, O.S.A., and Bernard McGinn, trans. *Meister Eckhart: The Essential Sermons, Commentaries, Treatises, and Defense.* New York: Paulist Press, 1981.

Colledge, Edmond, O.S.A., and James Walsh, S.J., eds. *A Book of Showings to the Anchoress Julian of Norwich.* Toronto: Pontifical Institute of Mediaeval Studies, 1978.

Collette, Carolyn P. "Sense and Sensibility in the *Prioress's Tale.*" *Chaucer Review* 15 (1982): 138–50.

Connor, Paul M., O.P. "Catherine of Siena and Raymond of Capua—Enduring Friends." *Studia Mystica* 12, no. 1 (Spring 1989): 22–29.

Cooke, Thomas D. *The Old French and Chaucerian Fabliaux: A Study of Their Comic Climax.* Columbia: University of Missouri Press, 1978.

Cooke, Thomas D., and Benjamin L. Honeycutt, eds. *The Humor of the Fabliaux: A Collection of Critical Essays.* Columbia: University of Missouri Press, 1974.

Cooper, Geoffrey. "'Sely John' in the 'Legende' of the Miller's Tale." *Journal of English and Germanic Philology* 79 (1980): 1–12.

Cooper, Helen. *The Structure of "The Canterbury Tales."* Athens: University of Georgia Press, 1984.

Copeland, Rita. "Richard Rolle and the Rhetorical Theory of the Levels of Style." In Glasscoe, *Mystical Tradition,* pp. 55–80.

Copland, Murray. "*The Shipman's Tale:* Chaucer and Boccaccio." *Medium Aevum* 35 (1966): 11–28.

Cormier, Hyacinth, O.P. *Blessed Raymond of Capua.* Boston: Marlier, Callahan, and Company, 1900.

Cousins, Ewert H. "Mysticism and the Spiritual Journey." *Studies in Formative Spirituality* 5 (February 1984): 11–20.

———, trans. *Bonaventure: "The Soul's Journey into God," "The Tree of Life," "The Life of St. Francis."* New York: Paulist Press, 1978.

Craik, T. W. *The Comic Tales of Chaucer.* London: Methuen, 1964.

Crane, Susan. "Medieval Romance and Feminine Difference in *The Knight's Tale.*" *Studies in the Age of Chaucer* 12 (1990): 47–64.

Culler, Jonathan. *The Pursuit of Signs.* Ithaca: Cornell University Press, 1981.

Curry, Walter Clyde. *Chaucer and the Mediaeval Sciences.* 1942. Reprint. New York: Barnes and Noble, 1960.

Dady, Mary Rachael. *The Theory of Knowledge of St. Bonaventure.* Washington, D.C.: Catholic University of America Press, 1939.

D'Arcy, Fr. M. C., trans. *Selected Writings of St. Thomas Aquinas.* New York: Dutton, 1950.

David, Alfred. *The Strumpet Muse: Art and Morals in Chaucer's Poetry.* Bloomington: Indiana University Press, 1976.

Davidson, Audrey Ekdahl, ed. *Hildegard von Bingen: "Ordo Virtutum."* Kalamazoo, Mich.: Medieval Institute Publications, 1984.

Dawson, Robert B. "Custance in Context: Rethinking the Protagonist of the *Man of Law's Tale.*" *Chaucer Review* 26 (1992): 293–307.

Dean, James. "Dismantling the Canterbury Book." *PMLA* 100 (1985): 746–62.

DeCatanzau, C. J., trans. *Symeon the New Theologian: The Discourses.* New York: Paulist Press, 1980.

Delany, Sheila. "Womanliness in the Man of Law's Tale." *Chaucer Review* 9 (1974): 63–72.

Delasanta, Rodney. "The Horsemen of the *Canterbury Tales.*" *Chaucer Review* 3 (1968): 29–36.

———. "Chaucer and Strode." *Chaucer Review* 26 (1991): 205–18.

de Man, Paul. *Allegories of Reading.* New Haven: Yale University Press, 1979.

Derrida, Jacques. *Of Grammatology.* Translated by Gayatri Chakravorty Spivak. Baltimore: Johns Hopkins University Press, 1976.

———. *Writing and Difference.* Translated by Alan Bass. Chicago: University of Chicago Press, 1978.

———. *Psyché: Inventions de l'autre.* Paris: Galilée, 1987.

Despres, Denise. *Ghostly Sights: Visual Meditation in Late-Medieval Literature.* Norman, Okla.: Pilgrim Books, 1989.

D'Evelyn, Charlotte, ed. *Meditations on the Life and Passion of Christ.* EETS 158. London: Oxford University Press, 1921.

Deuchler, Florens, Jeffrey M. Hoffeld, and Helmut Nickel, eds. *The Cloisters Apocalypse.* New York: Metropolitan Museum of Art, 1971.

Dinshaw, Carolyn. *Chaucer's Sexual Poetics.* Madison: University of Wisconsin Press, 1989.

Donaldson, E. Talbot. *Chaucer's Poetry.* 1958. Reprint. New York: Wiley, 1975.

———. *Speaking of Chaucer.* New York: Norton, 1970.

Doyle, A. I., ed. *The Vernon Manuscript: A Facsimile of Bodleian Library, Oxford MS Eng. Poet. a. 1.* Cambridge: D. S. Brewer, 1987.

Dronke, Peter. *Women Writers of the Middle Ages.* Cambridge: Cambridge University Press, 1984.

Ducklow, Donald. "Hermeneutics and Meister Eckhart." *Philosophy Today* 28 (1984): 36–43.

Dupré, Louis. *The Common Life: The Origins of Trinitarian Mysticism and Its Development by Jan Ruusbroec.* New York: Crossroad, 1984.

Easting, Robert, ed. *St. Patrick's Purgatory.* EETS 298. Oxford: Oxford University Press, 1991.

Economou, George D., ed. *Geoffrey Chaucer: A Collection of Original Articles.* New York: McGraw-Hill, 1975.

Edwards, A. S. G., and Linne R. Mooney. "Is the *Equatorie of the Planets* a Chaucer Holograph?" *Chaucer Review* 26 (1991): 31–42.

Edwards, A. S. G., and Derek Pearsall, eds. *Book Production and Publishing in Britain, 1375–1475.* Cambridge: Cambridge University Press, 1989.

Edwards, Robert R. "Narration and Doctrine in the Merchant's Tale." *Speculum* 66 (1991): 342–67.

Edwards, Robert R., and Stephen Spector, eds. *The Olde Daunce: Love, Friendship, Sex and Marriage in the Medieval World.* Albany: State University of New York Press, 1991.

Eisner, Sigmund. "Chaucer as Technical Writer." *Chaucer Review* 19 (1985): 179–201.

Elders, Leo. *The Philosophical Theology of St. Thomas Aquinas.* Leiden: E. J. Brill, 1990.

Eliot, T. S. "Tradition and the Individual Talent." In T. S. Eliot, *Selected Essays,* pp. 3–11. New York: Harcourt, Brace and World, 1964.

Ellis, Roger. *Patterns of Religious Narrative in "The Canterbury Tales."* Totowa, N.J.: Barnes and Noble, 1986.

———, ed. *The Liber Celestis of St. Bridget of Sweden.* EETS 291. London: Oxford University Press, 1987.

Emery, Kent, Jr. "The Carthusians, Intermediaries for the Teaching of John Ruysbroeck during the Period of Early Reform and the Counter-Reformation." *Analecta Cartusiana* 43 (1979): 100–129.

Englert, Robert. "Of Another Mind: Ludic Imagery and Spiritual Doctrine in the *Cloud of Unknowing.*" *Studia Mystica* 8, no. 1 (Spring 1985): 3–12.

Ewbank, Michael B. "Diverse Orderings of Dionysius's *Triplex Via* by St. Thomas Aquinas." *Mediaeval Studies* 52 (1990): 82–109.

Farrell, Thomas J. "Chaucer's Little Treatise, The Melibee." *Chaucer Review* 20 (1986): 61–67.

Feinstein, Sandy. "The *Reeve's Tale:* About That Horse." *Chaucer Review* 26 (1991): 99–106.

Ferris, Sumner. "Chaucer at Lincoln (1387): The *Prioress's Tale* as a Political Poem." *Chaucer Review* 15 (1981): 295–321.

Ferster, Judith. *Chaucer on Interpretation.* Cambridge: Cambridge University Press, 1985.

Fish, Stanley E. *The Living Temple: George Herbert and Catechizing.* Berkeley: University of California Press, 1978.

———. *Is There a Text in This Class? The Authority of Interpretive Communities.* Cambridge: Harvard University Press, 1980.

Fisher, John H. *John Gower: Moral Philosopher and Friend of Chaucer.* New York: New York University Press, 1964.

———. *The Importance of Chaucer.* Carbondale and Edwardsville: Southern Illinois University Press, 1992.

———, ed. *The Tretyse of Loue.* EETS 223. London: Oxford University Press, 1951.

———, ed. *The Complete Poetry and Prose of Geoffrey Chaucer.* 2d ed. New York: Holt, Rinehart and Winston, 1989.

Fite, Patricia P. "To 'Sytt and Syng of Luf Langyng': The Feminine Dynamic of Richard Rolle's Mysticism." *Studia Mystica* 14, nos. 2–3 (Summer-Fall 1991): 13–29.

Fleming, John V. *An Introduction to the Franciscan Literature of the Middle Ages.* Chicago: Franciscan Herald Press, 1977.

———. *Classical Imitation and Interprtation in Chaucer's "Troilus."* Lincoln: University of Nebraska Press, 1990.

Foucault, Michel. *The Archeology of Knowledge.* Translated by A. M. Sheridan. New York: Harper and Row, 1972.

Frank, Robert Worth, Jr. "Inept Chaucer." *Studies in the Age of Chaucer* 11 (1989): 5–14.

Frantzen, Allen J. *The Literature of Penance in Anglo-Saxon England.* New Brunswick, N.J.: Rutgers University Press, 1983.

Frese, Dolores Warwick: *An Ars Legendi for Chaucer's "Canterbury Tales:" Re-Constructive Reading.* Gainesville: University of Florida Press, 1991.

Friedman, Albert B. "The Mysterious 'Greyn' in the *Prioress's Tale.*" *Chaucer Review* 11 (1977): 328–33.

Friedman, John Block. "A Reading of Chaucer's *Reeve's Tale.*" *Chaucer Review* 2 (1967): 8–19.

Fulk, R. D. "Reinterpreting the *Manciple's Tale.*" *Journal of English and Germanic Philology* 78 (1979): 485–493.

Fyler, John M. "Love and Degree in the *Franklin's Tale.*" *Chaucer Review* 21 (1987): 321–39.

Ganim, John M. *Chaucerian Theatricality.* Princeton: Princeton University Press, 1990.

Gardner, John. *The Poetry of Chaucer.* Carbondale: Southern Illinois University Press, 1977.

Gaylord, Alan T. "The Unconquered Tale of the Prioress." *Papers of the Michigan Academy of Science, Arts, and Letters* 42 (1962): 633–34.

———. "The Promises in *The Franklin's Tale.*" *ELH* 31 (1964): 331–35.

———. "The Moment of *Sir Thopas:* Towards a New Look at Chaucer's Language." *Chaucer Review* 16 (1982): 311–29.

Geanakoplos, D. J. "Some Aspects of the Influence of the Byzantine Maximus the Confessor on the Theology of East and West." *Church History* 38 (1969): 150–63.

Gellrich, Jesse M. *The Idea of the Book in the Middle Ages: Language Theory, Mythology, and Fiction.* Ithaca: Cornell University Press, 1985.

Georgianna, Linda. *The Solitary Self: Individuality in the "Ancrene Wisse."* Cambridge: Harvard University Press, 1981.

———. "Love So Dearly Bought: The Terms of Redemption in *The Canterbury Tales.*" *Studies in the Age of Chaucer* 12 (1990): 85–116.

Gerson, Paula Lieber, ed. *Abbot Suger and Saint-Denis: A Symposium.* New York: Metropolitan Museum of Art, 1986.

Gilson, Etienne. *La Philosophie de Saint Bonaventure.* Paris: J. Vrin, 1953.

Glasscoe, Marion, ed. *The Medieval Mystical Tradition in England.* Cambridge: D. S. Brewer, 1984.

Gnädinger, Louise. "Der minnende Bernhardus, seine Reflexe in den Predigten J. Taulers." *Cîteaux* 31 (1980): 387–409.

Goldberg, Jonathan. "The Politics of Renaissance Literature: A Review Essay." *ELH* 49 (1982): 514–42.

Grady, Sr. Laureen. "Afterword to *A Pistle of Discrecioun of Stirrings.*" *Contemplative Review* 10 (1977): 1–6.

Green, Richard Firth. *Poets and Princepleasers: Literature and the English Court in the Late Middle Ages.* Toronto: University of Toronto Press, 1980.

Greenblatt, Stephen. *Renaissance Self-Fashioning from More to Shakespeare.* Chicago: University of Chicago Press, 1980.

———. *Shakespearean Negotiations: The Circulation of Social Energy in Renaissance England.* Berkeley: University of California Press, 1988.

———. *Marvelous Possessions: The Wonder of the New World.* Chicago: University of Chicago Press, 1991.

———, ed. *The Power of Forms in the English Renaissance.* Norman, Okla.: Pilgrim Books, 1982.

Griffiths, Bede. *Return to the Center.* Springfield, Ill.: Templegate, 1976.

Griffiths, Ralph A. *The Reign of King Henry VI.* Berkeley: University of California Press, 1981.

Grüber, K. *Der Mystiker Heinrich Seuse.* Greiburg: Herder, 1941.

Grudin, Michaela Paasche. "Chaucer's *Clerk's Tale* as Political Paradox." *Studies in the Age of Chaucer* 11 (1989): 63–92.

Hadow, Grace. *Chaucer and His Times.* New York: Holt, 1914.

Hagen, Susan K. *Allegorical Remembrance: A Study of the "Pilgrimage of the Life of Man" as a Medieval Treatise on Seeing and Remembering.* Athens: University of Georgia Press, 1990.

Hallam, Elizabeth, trans. *The Plantagenet Chronicles.* New York: Weidenfeld and Nicholson, 1986.

Halleux, A. de. "Palamisme et tradition." *Irénikon* 4 (1975): 479–93.

Halligan, Theresa A., ed. *The Booke of Gostlye Grace of Mechtild of Hackeborn.* Toronto: Pontifical Institute of Mediaeval Studies, 1979.

Hamburger, Jeffrey F. "The Use of Images in the Pastoral Care of Nuns: The Case of Heinrich Suso and the Dominicans." *Art Bulletin* 71 (1989): 20–46.

———, ed. *The Rothschild Canticles: Art and Mysticism in Flanders and the Rhineland, Circa 1300.* New Haven: Yale University Press, 1990.

Hamel, Mary. "And Now for Something Not So Different: The Relationship between the *Prioress's Tale* and the *Rime of Sir Thopas.*" *Chaucer Review* 14 (1980): 251–59.

Hanning, Robert W. *The Individual in Twelfth Century Romance.* New Haven: Yale University Press, 1977.

Hansen, Elaine Tuttle. *Chaucer and the Fictions of Gender.* Berkeley: University of California Press, 1992.

Harley, Marta Powell. *A Revelation of Purgatory by an Unknown, Fifteenth-Century Woman Visionary.* Lewiston, N.Y.: Edwin Mellen Press, 1985.

Hathaway, Ronald F. *Hierarchy and the Definition of Order in the Letters of Pseudo-Dionysius.* The Hague: Martinus Nijhoff, 1969.

Havely, Nicholas. "Chaucer, Boccaccio and the Friars." In Boitani, *Chaucer and the Italian Trecento,* pp. 249–268.

Heffernan, Thomas J. *Sacred Biography: Saints and Their Biographers in the Middle Ages.* New York: Oxford University Press, 1988.

Heimmel, Jennifer P. *"God Is Our Mother": Julian of Norwich and the Medieval Image of Christian Feminine Divinity.* Salzburg: Institut für Anglistik und Amerikanistik, 1982.

Heinrichs, Katherine. "'Lovers' Consolations of Philosophy' in Boccacio, Machaut, and Chaucer." *Studies in the Age of Chaucer* 11 (1989): 93–115.

Henry, Avril. *"The Mirour of Mans Saluacioun": A Middle English Translation of "Speculum Humanae Salvationis."* Philadelphia: University of Pennsylvania Press, 1987.

———, ed. *The Pilgrimage of the Lyfe of the Manhode.* Vol. 1. EETS 288. London: Oxford University Press, 1985.

Hill, John M. *Chaucerian Belief.* New Haven: Yale University Press, 1991.

Hirsh, John C., ed. *Barlam and Iosaphat.* EETS 290. London: Oxford University Press, 1986.

Hodgson, Phyllis. *"Deonise Hid Diunite" and Other Treatises on Contemplative Prayer.* EETS 231. London: Oxford University Press, 1955.

———, ed. *The Cloud of Unknowing and The Book of Privy Counselling.* EETS 218. London: Oxford University Press, 1944.

Hodgson, Phyllis, and Gabriel M. Liegey, eds. *The Orcherd of Syon.* EETS 258. London: Oxford University Press, 1966.

Hornsby, Joseph Allen. *Chaucer and the Law.* Norman, Okla.: Pilgrim Books, 1988.

Horstman, Carl, ed. *The Early South-English Legendary.* EETS 87. London: Oxford University Press, 1887.

———, ed. *Yorkshire Writers: Richard Rolle of Hampole and His Followers.* 2 vols. London: Swan Sonnenschein, 1895, 1896.

Howard, Donald R. *The Idea of "The Canterbury Tales."* Berkeley: University of California Press, 1976.

———. *Chaucer: His Life, His Works, His World.* New York: Dutton, 1987.

Howard, Jean E. "The New Historicism in Renaissance Studies." *English Literary Renaissance* 16 (1986): 13–43.

Hughes, Christopher. *On a Complex Theory of a Simple God: An Investigation in Aquinas' Philosophical Theology.* Ithaca: Cornell University Press, 1989.

Huppé, Bernard F. *A Reading of "The Canterbury Tales."* Albany: State University of New York Press, 1964.

Hussey, S. S. *Chaucer: An Introduction.* London: Methuen, 1971.

Ingram, John K., ed. *Middle English Translations of "De Imitatione Christi."* EETS, Extra Series 63. London: Oxford University Press, 1893.

Jacobs, Kathryn. "The Marriage Contract of the *Franklin's Tale:* The Remaking of Society." *Chaucer Review* 20 (1986): 132–43.

Jantzen, Grace M. *Julian of Norwich: Mystic and Theologian.* New York: Paulist Press, 1988.

Jeffrey, David L. *The Early English Lyric and Franciscan Spirituality.* Lincoln: University of Nebraska Press, 1975.

Jennings, Margaret. "Richard Rolle and the Three Degrees of Love." *Downside Review* 93 (1975): 193–200.

Joeressen, Uta. *Die Terminologie der Innlichkeit in den Deutschen Werken Heinrich Seuses.* Frankfort am Main: Peter Lang, 1983.

Jones, Alexander, ed. *The Jerusalem Bible.* Garden City, N.Y.: Doubleday, 1966.

Jones, Claude. "Chaucer's *Taillynge Ynoughe.*" *Modern Language Notes* 52 (1937): 570.

Jordan, Robert M. "The Non-Dramatic Disunity of the *Merchant's Tale.*" *PMLA* 78 (1963): 293–99.

————. *Chaucer's Poetics and the Modern Reader.* Berkeley: University of California Press, 1987.

Joseph, Gerhard. "Chaucer's Coinage: Foreign Exchange and the Puns of the *Shipman's Tale.*" *Chaucer Review* 17 (1983): 341–57.

Kaske, R. E. "The *Canticum Canticorum* in the *Miller's Tale.*" *Studies in Philology* 59 (1962): 479–500.

Kean, P. M. *Chaucer and the Making of English Poetry.* 2d ed. London: Routledge and Kegan Paul, 1972.

Kellogg, Alfred L. *Chaucer, Langland, Arthur: Essays in Middle English Literature.* New Brunswick, N.J.: Rutgers University Press, 1972.

Kelly, C. F. *Meister Eckhart on Knowledge.* New Haven: Yale University Press, 1977.

Kendrick, Laura. *Chaucerian Play: Comedy and Control in "The Canterbury Tales."* Berkeley: University of California Press, 1988.

Kertz, Karl G. "Meister Eckhart's Teaching on the Birth of the Divine Word in the Soul." *Traditio* 15 (1959): 327–63.

Kieckhefer, Richard. "Meister Eckhart's Conception of Union with God." *Harvard Theological Review* 71 (1978): 203–25.

————. *Unquiet Souls: Fourteenth-Century Saints and Their Religious Milieu.* Chicago: University of Chicago Press, 1984.

Kittredge, George Lyman. "Chaucer's Discussion of Marriage." *Modern Philology* 9 (1911–12): 435–67.

Knapp, Peggy. "Deconstructing the *Canterbury Tales:* Pro." *Studies in the Age of Chaucer, Proceedings,* no. 2 (1987): 73–81.

————. *Chaucer and the Social Contest.* London: Routledge, 1990.

Knowles, David. "The Excellence of the *Cloud.*" *Downside Review* 52 (1934): 71–92.

————. *The Religious Orders in England.* Vol. 1. 1948. Reprint. Cambridge: Cambridge University Press. 1979.

————. *The English Mystical Tradition.* New York: Harper, 1961.

Koff, Leonard Michael. *Chaucer and the Art of Story-telling.* Berkeley: University of California Press, 1988.

Kolve, V. A. *Chaucer and the Imagery of Narrative.* Stanford, Calif.: Stanford University Press, 1984.

———. "'Man in the Middle': Art and Religion in Chaucer's *Friar's Tale.*" *Studies in the Age of Chaucer* 12 (1990): 5–46.

Koonce, B. G. *Chaucer and the Tradition of Fame: Symbolism in the "House of Fame."* Princeton: Princeton University Press, 1966.

Kovach, F. J., and R. W. Shahan, eds. *Albert the Great: Commemorative Essays.* Norman: University of Oklahoma Press, 1980.

Kraft, Kent. "The German Visionary: Hildegard of Bingen." In Wilson, *Medieval Women Writers, pp. 109–14.*

Kristeva, Julia. *Desire in Language.* Edited by Leon S. Roudiez, translated by Thomas Gora, Alice Jardine, and Leon S. Roudiez. New York: Columbia University Press, 1980.

Krochalis, Jeanne E. "Postscript: The *Equatorie of the Planetis* as a Translator's Manuscript." *Chaucer Review* 26 (1991): 43–47.

Lachance, Paul, O.F.M. *The Spiritual Journey of the Blessed Angela of Foligno according to the Memorial of Frater A.* Rome: Pontificium Athenaeum Antonianum, 1984.

Ladner, Gerhart B. "Medieval and Modern Understanding of Symbolism: A Comparison." *Speculum* 54 (1979): 223–56.

Lagorio, Valerie M. "Variations on the Theme of God's Motherhood in Medieval English Mystical and Devotional Writings." *Studia Mystica* 8, no. 2 (1985): 15–37.

Lamb, George, trans. *Raymond of Capua: The Life of St. Catherine of Siena.* New York: P. J. Kenedy and Sons, 1960.

Lapidge, Michael, and Michael Herren, trans. *Aldhelm: The Prose Works.* Cambridge: D. S. Brewer, 1979.

Lawler, Traugott. *The One and the Many in "The Canterbury Tales."* Hamden, Conn.: Archon Books, 1980.

———. "Deconstructing the *Canterbury Tales:* Con." *Studies in the Age of Chaucer, Proceedings,* no. 2 (1987): 83–91.

Lawlor, John. "A Note on the *Revelations* of Julian of Norwich." *Review of English Studies,* n.s. 2 (1951): 255–58.

Lawrence, W. W. *Chaucer and "The Canterbury Tales."* New York: Columbia University Press, 1950.

Lawton, David. "Chaucer's Two Ways: The Pilgrimage Frame of *The Canterbury Tales.*" *Studies in the Age of Chaucer* 9 (1987): 3–40.

Lee, Anne Thompson. "'A Woman True and Fair': Chaucer's Portrayal of Dorigen in the *Franklin's Tale.*" *Chaucer Review* 19 (1985): 169–78.

Leicester, H. Marshall, Jr. "'No Vileyns Word': Social Context and Performance in Chaucer's *Friar's Tale.*" *Chaucer Review* 17 (1983): 21–39.

———. *The Disenchanted Self: Representing the Subject in "The Canterbury Tales."* Berkeley: University of California Press, 1990.

Leitch, Vincent B. *Deconstructive Criticism: An Advanced Introduction.* New York: Columbia University Press, 1983.

Lewis, C. S. *The Allegory of Love.* London: Oxford University Press, 1936.

———. *Studies in Words.* Cambridge: Cambridge University Press, 1967.

Lewis, Muriel. "After Reflecting on Julian's Reflections of Behovabil Synne." *Studia Mystica* 6, no. 2 (Summer 1983): 41–57.

Lewis, Robert E., ed. *Lotario dei Segni: De Miseria Condicionis Humane.* Athens: University of Georgia Press, 1978.

Leyser, Henrietta. *Hermits and the New Monasticism.* New York: St. Martin's Press, 1984.

Lichtmann, Maria R. "Julian of Norwich and the Ontology of the Feminine." *Studia Mystica* 13, nos. 2–3 (Summer-Fall 1990): 53–64.

Loenertz, Raymond J. "La legénde parisenne de s. Denys l'aréopagite: Son genèse et son premier té moin." *Analecta Bollandiana* 69 (1951): 217–37.

Logeman, H., ed. *The Rule of S. Benet.* EETS 90. London: N. Trübner, 1888.

Low, Anthony. *Love's Architecture: Devotional Modes in Seventeenth-Century English Poetry.* New York: New York University Press, 1978.

Luibheid, Colm, trans. *Pseudo-Dionysius: The Complete Works.* New York: Paulist Press, 1987.

Lumiansky, R. M. *Of Sondry Folk: The Dramatic Principle in "The Canterbury Tales."* 1955. Reprint. Austin: University of Texas Press, 1980.

Lynch, Kathryn L. "Despoiling Griselda: Chaucer's Walter and the Problem of Knowledge in *The Clerk's Tale." Studies in the Age of Chaucer* 10 (1988): 41–70.

MacDonald, A. J. *Berengar and the Reform of Sacramental Doctrine.* London: Longmans, 1930.

Macy, Gary. *The Theologies of the Eucharist in the Early Scholastic Period: A Study of the Salvific Function of the Sacrament according to the Theologians, c. 1080–c. 1220.* Oxford: Clarendon Press, 1984.

Madigan, Mary F. *The Passio Domini Theme in the Works of Richard Rolle: His Personal Contribution in Its Religious, Cultural, and Literary Context.* Salzburg: Institut für Englistik und Amerikanistik, 1978.

Maisonneuve, Roland. "Julian of Norwich and the Prison of Existence." *Studia Mystica* 3, no. 4 (Winter 1980): 26–32.

Maltman, Sr. Nicholas, O.P. "The Divine Granary, or the End of the Prioress's 'Greyn.'" *Chaucer Review* 17 (1982): 163–70.

Manly, John M., and Edith Rickert. *The Text of "The Canterbury Tales."* Vol. 1 of 8. Chicago: University of Chicago Press, 1940.

Mann, Jill. "Satisfaction and Payment in Middle English Literature." *Studies in the Age of Chaucer* 5 (1983): 17–48.

———. *Feminist Readings: Geoffrey Chaucer.* Atlantic Highlands, N.J.: Humanities Press, 1991.

Marshall, Rev. Edward, trans. *"The Explanation of the Apocalypse," by Venerable Beda.* Oxford and London: James Parker, 1878.

Martin, Priscilla. *Chaucer's Women: Nuns, Wives, and Amazons.* Iowa City: University of Iowa Press, 1990.

Martz, Louis. *The Poetry of Meditation.* 2d ed. New Haven: Yale University Press, 1962.

McCabe, Herbert, O.P., ed. and trans. *St. Thomas Aquinas: "Summa Theologiae."* Vol. 3, *Knowing and Naming God.* New York: McGraw-Hill, 1963.

McCall, J. P. "The Squire in Wonderland." *Chaucer Review* 1 (1966): 103–9.

McGann, Jerome J. *A Critique of Modern Textual Criticism.* Chicago: University of Chicago Press, 1983.

McGavin, John J. "How Nasty is Phoebus's Crow?" *Chaucer Review* 21 (1987): 444–58.

McGinn, Bernard. "The God beyond God: Theology and Mysticism in the Thought of Meister Eckhart." *Journal of Religion* 61 (1981): 1–19.

———. ed., with Frank Tobin and Elvira Borgstadt. *Meister Eckhart: Teacher and Preacher.* New York: Paulist Press, 1986.

Meech, Sanford Brown, ed. *The Book of Margery Kempe.* EETS 212. London: Oxford University Press, 1940.

Meyendorff, John. *A Study of Gregory Palamas.* 2d ed. London: Faith Press, 1974.

———. *St. Gregory Palamas and Orthodox Spirituality.* Crestwood, N.Y.: St. Vladimir's Seminary Press, 1974.

Meyendorff, John, and Nicholas Grendle, eds. and trans. *Gregory Palamas: The Triads.* New York: Paulist Press, 1983.

Migne, J.-P., ed. *Venerabilis Bedae Opera Omnia.* Vol. 4 In J.-P. Migne, ed., *Patrologia Latina.* Vol. 93. Paris, 1830.

Miller, Robert P. *Chaucer: Sources and Backgrounds.* New York: Oxford University Press, 1977.

Millet, Bella, ed. *Hali Meiðhad.* EETS 284. London: Oxford University Press, 1984.

Mills, M., ed. *Lybeaus Descanus.* EETS 261. London: Oxford University Press, 1969.

Miquel, P. "*Peira:* Contribution a l'étude du vocabulaire de l'expérience religieuse dans l'oeuvre de s. Maxime le Confesseur." *Studia Patristica* 7 (1966): 355–61.

Mommaers, Paul. *The Land Within: The Process of Possessing and Being Possessed by God according to the Mystic Jan van Ruysbroeck.* Translated by David N. Smith. Chicago: Franciscan Herald Press, 1975.

Montmasson, E. "La Doctrine de l'apatheia d'aprés S. Maxime." *Echos D'Orient* 14 (1911): 36–41.

Muscatine, Charles. *Chaucer and the French Tradition.* Berkeley: University of California Press, 1957.

Nadel, Alan. "Translating the Past: Literary Allusion as Covert Criticism." *Georgia Review* 36 (1982): 639–51.

Neville, Marie. "The Function of the 'Squire's Tale' in the Canterbury Scheme." *Journal of English and Germanic Philology* 50 (1951): 167–79.

Newman, Barbara. *Sister of Wisdom: St. Hildegard's Theology of the Feminine.* Berkeley: University of California Press, 1987.

———, ed. and trans. *Saint Hildegard of Bingen: "Symphonia."* Ithaca: Cornell University Press, 1988.

Nicholson, Peter. "The *Man of Law's Tale:* What Chaucer Really Owed to Gower." *Chaucer Review* 26 (1991): 153–74.

Noffke, Suzanne, O.P., trans. *Catherine of Siena: The Dialogue.* New York: Paulist Press, 1986.

North, J. D. *Chaucer's Universe.* London: Oxford University Press, 1988.

Ogilvie-Thomson, S. J., ed. *Richard Rolle: Prose and Verse*. EETS 293. London: Oxford University Press, 1988.

Olmes, Antonie. "Sprache und Stil der englischen Mystik des Mittelalters, unter besonderer Berücksichtigung des Richard Rolle von Hampole." *Studien zur Englische Philologie* 76 (1933): 1–100.

Olson, Glending. "A Reading of the *Thopas-Melibee* Link." *Chaucer Review* 10 (1975): 147–53.

Olson, Paul A. "Poetic Justice in the *Miller's Tale*." *Modern Language Quarterly* 24 (1964): 227–36.

———. *"The Canterbury Tales" and the Good Society*. Princeton: Princeton University Press, 1986.

Owen, Charles A., Jr. *Pilgrimage and Storytelling in "The Canterbury Tales": the Dialectic of "Earnest" and "Game."* Norman: University of Oklahoma Press, 1977.

Ozment, Steven E. *Homo Spiritualis: A Comparative Study of the Anthropology of Johannes Tauler, Jean Gerson and Martin Luther (1509–16) in the Context of Their Theological Thought*. Leiden: E. J. Brill, 1969.

Palomo, Dolores. "What Chaucer Really Did to *Le Livre de Melibee*." *Philological Quarterly* 53 (1974): 304–20.

Patterson, Lee W. "The 'Parson's Tale' and the Quitting of the 'Canterbury Tales.'" *Traditio* 34 (1978): 331–80.

———. *Negotiating the Past: The Historical Understanding of Medieval Literature*. Madison: Univeristy of Wisconsin Press, 1987.

———. "'What Man Artow?': Authorial Self-Definition in *The Tale of Sir Thopas* and *The Tale of Melibee*." *Studies in the Age of Chaucer* 11 (1989): 117–75.

———. "'No Man His Reson Herde': Peasant Consciousness, Chaucer's Miller, and the Structure of the *Canterbury Tales*." In Patterson, *Literary Practice and Social Change*, pp. 113–55.

———. *Chaucer and the Subject of History*. Madison: University of Wisconsin Press, 1991.

———, ed. *Literary Practice and Social Change in Britain, 1380–1530*. Berkeley: University of California Press, 1990.

Pearsall,Derek. "The Squire as Story-Teller." *University of Toronto Quarterly* 34 (1964): 82–92.

———. *The Canterbury Tales*. London: George Allen and Unwin, 1985.

Pearcy, Roy J. "Modes of Signification and the Humor of Obscene Diction in the Fabliaux." In Cooke and Honeycutt, *The Humor of the Fabliaux*, pp. 179–96.

Peck, Russell A. "Sovereignty and the Two Worlds of the *Franklin's Tale*." *Chaucer Review* 1 (1966): 253–71.

———. "Chaucer and the Nominalist Questions." *Speculum* 53 (1978): 759–60.

———, ed. *John Gower: Confessio Amantis*. New York: Holt, Rinehart, and Winston, 1968.

Pelikan, Jaroslav. Introduction. *Maximus Confessor: Selected Writings*. Translated by George C. Berthold. New York: Paulist Press, 1985.

Peloquin, Sr. Carol Marie. "All Will Be Well: A Look at Sin in Juliana's *Revelations*." *Contemplative Review* 13 (1980): 9–16.

Perry, George G. *Religious Pieces in Prose and Verse*. EETS 26. 1867. Reprint. London: Kegan-Paul, Trench, Trübner, 1914.

Poirier, Richard. *The Performing Self: Composition and Decomposition in the Language of Contemporary Life*. New York: Oxford University Press, 1971.

Poly, Jean-Pierre, and Eric Bournazel. *The Feudal Transformation, 900–1200*. Translated by Caroline Higgitt. New York: Holmes and Meier, 1991.

Pratt, Robert. "Some Latin Sources of the Nonnes Preest on Dreams." *Speculum* 52 (1977): 538–70.

Quint, Joseph. "Die Sprache Meister Eckharts als Ausdruck seiner Mystichen Geisteswelt." *Deutsche Vierteljahresschrift* 6 (1927): 671–701.

Raybin, David. "Custance and History: Woman as Outsider in Chaucer's *Man of Law's Tale*." *Studies in the Age of Chaucer* 12 (1990): 65–84.

Reames, Sherry L. "The Cecelia Legend as Chaucer Inherited It and Retold It: The Disappearance of an Augustinian Ideal." *Speculum* 55 (1980): 38–57.

Richardsen, Janette. "Hunter and Prey: Functional Imagery in 'The Friar's Tale.'" In *Chaucer's Mind and Art,* edited by A. C. Cawley, pp. 155–65. London: Oliver and Boyd, 1969.

Riddel, Joseph N. *The Inverted Bell*. Baton Rouge: Louisiana State University Press, 1974.

Riehle, Wolfgang. *The Middle English Mystics*. Translated by Bernard Standring. London: Routledge and Kegan Paul, 1981.

Robertson, D. W., Jr. *A Preface to Chaucer*. Princeton: Princeton University Press, 1962.

Robertson, D. W., Jr., and Bernard F. Huppé. *Fruyt and Chaf: Studies in Chaucer's Allegories*. Princeton: Princeton University Press, 1963.

Robinson, F. N., ed. *The Works of Geoffrey Chaucer*. 2d ed. Boston: Houghton Mifflin, 1957.

Robinson, Pamela. "Geoffrey Chaucer and the *Equatorie of the Planetis:* The State of the Problem." *Chaucer Review* 26 (1991): 17–30.

Roney, Lois. *Chaucer's Knight's Tale and Theories of Scholastic Psychology*. Tampa: University of South Florida Press, 1990.

Rorem, Paul. *Biblical and Liturgical Symbols within the Pseudo-Dionysian Synthesis*. Toronto: Pontifical Institute of Mediaeval Studies, 1984.

Rowland, Beryl. *Blind Beasts: Chaucer's Animal World*. Kent, Ohio: Kent State University Press, 1971.

Rudolph, Conrad. *Artistic Change at St-Denis: Abbot Suger's Program on the Early Twelfth-Century Controversy over Art*. Princeton: Princeton University Press, 1990.

Ruggiers, Paul G. *The Art of "The Canterbury Tales."* Madison: University of Wisconsin Press, 1965.

Ruh, Kurt. *Altdeutsche und Altniederländische Mystik*. Darmstadt: Wissenschaftliche Buchgesellschaft, 1964.

Scattergood, V. J. "The Manciple's Manner of Speaking." *Essays in Criticism* 24 (1974): 124–46.

Schibanoff, Susan. "The New Reader and Female Textuality in Two Early Commentaries on Chaucer." *Studies in the Age of Chaucer* 10 (1988): 71–108.

Schleusmer, Jay. "The Conduct of the *Merchant's Tale*." *Chaucer Review* 14 (1980): 237–50.

Schneider, Paul Stephen. "'Taillynge Ynogh': The Function of Money in the *Shipman's Tale*." *Chaucer Review* 11 (1977): 201–9.

Schroeder, Mary C. "Fantasy in the 'Merchant's Tale'." *Criticism* 12 (1970): 169–79.

Schürmann, Reiner. *Meister Eckhart: Mystic and Philosopher.* Bloomington: Indiana University Press, 1978.

Schweitering, Julius. "Zur Autorschaft von Seuses Vita." In Ruh, *Altdeutsche und Altniederländische Mystik,* pp. 309–23.

Schwertner, Thomas M. *St. Albert the Great.* New York: Bruce Publishing Company, 1932.

Serjeantson, Mary S., ed. *Legendys of Hooly Wummen by Osbern Bokenham.* EETS 206. London: Oxford University Press, 1938.

Seton, Walter W., ed. *A Fifteenth-Century Courtesy Book and Two Fifteenth-Century Franciscan Rules.* EETS 148. London: Oxford University Press, 1914.

Severs, J. Burke. *The Literary Relationships of Chaucer's Clerkes Tale.* Yale Studies in English 96. New Haven: Yale University Press, 1942.

———. "Is the *Manciple's Tale* a Success?" *Journal of English and Germanic Philology* 51 (1952): 1–16.

Sheedy, Charles E. *The Eucharistic Controversy of the Eleventh Century against the Background of Pre-Scholastic Theology.* Washington, D.C.: Catholic University Press, 1947.

Sherwood, P. "Explanation and Use of Scripture in St. Maximus as Manifested in the 'Questiones ad Thalassium.'" *Orientalia Christiana Periodica* 24 (1958): 202–7.

———. "Survey of Recent Work on Maximus the Confessor." *Traditio* 20 (1964): 428–37.

Shoaf, R. A. "The *Franklin's Tale:* Chaucer and Medusa." *Chaucer Review* 21 (1987): 274–90.

Shrady, Maria, trans. *Johannes Tauler: Sermons.* New York: Paulist Press, 1985.

Silverman, Albert H. "Sex and Money in Chaucer's *Shipman's Tale*." *Philological Quarterly* 32 (1953): 329–36.

Sinkewicz, R. E. "A New Interpretation for the First Episode in the Controversy between Barlaam the Calabrian and Gregory Palamas." *Journal of Theological Studies* 31 (1980): 489–500.

Sklute, Larry. *Virtue of Necessity: Inconclusiveness and Narrative Form in Chaucer's Poetry.* Columbus: Ohio State University Press, 1984.

Spector, Stephen. "Empathy and Enmity in the *Prioress's Tale*." In Edwards and Spector, *The Olde Daunce,* pp. 211–228.

Speirs, John. "Chaucer (II): *The Canterbury Tales* (I)." *Scrutiny* 11 (1943): 189–211.

Squire, A. K. "The Idea of the Soul as Virgin and Mother in Maximus the Confessor." *Studia Patristica* 8 (1966): 456–61.

Stahl, William Harris, trans. *Macrobius: "Commentary on the Dream of Scipio."* New York: Columbia University Press, 1952.

Statler, Margaret H. "The Analogues of Chaucer's *Prioress's Tale:* The Relationship of Group C to Group A." *PMLA* 65 (1950): 896–910.

Steinmetz, David C. "Late Medieval Nominalism and the *Clerk's Tale.*" *Chaucer Review* 12 (1977): 38–54.

Stiglmayr, Josef. "Die Lehre von den Sakramenten und der Kirche nach Ps.-Dionysius." *Zeitschrift für Katolische Theologie* 22 (1898): 246–303.

———. "Eine syrische Liturgie als Vorlage des Pseudo-Areopagiten." *Zeitschrift für Katolische Theologie* 33 (1909): 383–385.

Stillwell, Gardner. "The Political Meaning of Chaucer's *Tale of Melibee.*" *Speculum* 19 (1944): 433–44.

———. "Chaucer in Tartary." *Review of English Studies* 24 (1948): 177–88.

Strohm, Paul. "The Allegory of the *Tale of Melibee.*" *Chaucer Review* 2 (1967): 32–42.

———. *Social Chaucer.* Cambridge: Harvard University Press, 1989.

———. "Politics and Poetics: Usk and Chaucer in the 1380s." In Patterson, *Literary Practice and Social Change,* pp. 83–112.

Swanson, Robert N. "Chaucer's Parson and Other Priests." *Studies in the Age of Chaucer* 13 (1991): 41–80.

Szittya, Penn R. "The Friar as False Apostle: Anti-Fraternal Exegesis and *The Summoner's Tale.*" *Studies in Philology* 71 (1974): 19–46.

———. *The Antifraternal Tradition in Medieval Literature.* Princeton: Princeton University Press, 1986.

Talbot, C. H., ed. and trans. *The Life of Christiana of Markyate: A Twelfth-Century Recluse.* Oxford: Clarendon Press, 1959.

Tatlock, J. S. P. "Chaucer's Merchant's Tale." *Modern Philology* 33 (1936): 367–81.

Taylor, Paul B. "Chaucer's *Cosyn to the Dede.*" *Speculum* 57 (1982): 315–27.

Théry, G. "Documents Concernant Jean Sarrazin." *Archives D'Histoire Doctrinale et Littéraire* 18 (1951): 181–96.

Thompson, W. Meredith, ed. Þe *Wohunge of Ure Lauerd.* EETS 241. London: Oxford University Press, 1958.

Thomson, H. J., ed. and trans. *Prudentius.* Vol. 1. Cambridge: Harvard University Press, 1969.

Tobin, Frank. *Meister Eckhart: Thought and Language.* Philadelphia: University of Pennsylvania Press, 1986.

———, trans. *Henry Suso: The Exemplar with Two German Sermons.* New York: Paulist Press, 1989.

Tolkien, J. R. R., ed. *Ancrene Wisse: MS Corpus Christi College Cambridge 402.* EETS 249. London: Oxford University Press, 1962.

Tschann, Judith. "The Layout of *Sir Thopas* in the Ellesmere, Hengwrt, Cambridge Dd.4.24, and Cambridge Gg.4.27 Manuscripts." *Chaucer Review* 20 (1985): 1–13.

Tugwell, Simon, O.P., ed. and trans. *Albert and Thomas: Selected Writings.* New York: Paulist Press, 1988.

Wallace, David. "Mystics and Followers in Siena and East Anglia: A Study in Taxonomy, Class and Cultural Mediation." In Glasscoe, *The Medieval Mystical Tradition in England,* pp. 169–91.

———. *Chaucer and the Early Writings of Boccaccio.* Cambridge: D. S. Brewer, 1985.

———. "'Whan She Translated Was': A Chaucerian Critique of the Petrarchan Academy." In Patterson, *Literary Practice and Social Change,* pp. 156–215.

Watson, Nicholas. *Richard Rolle and the Invention of Authority.* Cambridge: Cambridge University Press, 1991.

Weisheipl, James A., ed. *Albertus Magnus and the Sciences: Commemorative Essays.* Toronto: Pontifical Institute of Mediaeval Studies, 1980.

Weissmann, Hope Phyllis. "Antifeminism and Chaucer's Characterization of Women." In Economou, *Geoffrey Chaucer,* pp. 93–110.

Wentersdorf, Karl P. "Chaucer's Clerk of Oxenford as Rhetorician." *Mediaeval Studies* 51 (1989): 313–28.

Wenzel, Siegfried, ed. *Summa Virtutum de Remediis Anime.* Athens: University of Georgia Press, 1984.

Wetherbee, Winthrop. "Constance and the World in Chaucer and Gower." In Yeager, *John Gower: Recent Readings,* pp. 65–93.

Whitesell, J. Edwin. "Chaucer's Lisping Friar." *Modern Language Notes* 71 (1956): 160–61.

Whittock, Trevor. *A Reading of "The Canterbury Tales."* Cambridge: Cambridge University Press, 1968.

Wilkins, Nigel. *Music in the Age of Chaucer.* Cambridge: D. S. Brewer, 1979.

Wilson, Katharina M., ed. *Medieval Women Writers.* Athens: University of Georgia Press, 1984.

Wimsatt, James I. "The Blessed Virgin and the Two Coronations of Griselda." *Mediaevalia* 6 (1980): 187–207.

———. *Chaucer and His French Contemporaries: Natural Music in the Fourteenth Century.* Toronto: University of Toronto Press, 1991.

Windeatt, Barry A. "Julian of Norwich and Her Audience." *Review of English Studies,* n.s. 28 (1977): 1–17.

Wiseman, James A., O.S.B., trans. *John Ruusbroec: "The Spiritual Espousals and Other Works."* New York: Paulist Press, 1985.

———. "The Birth of the Son in the Soul in the Mystical Theology of Jan van Ruusbroec." *Studia Mystica* 14, nos. 2–3 (Summer-Fall 1991): 30–44.

Wood, Chauncy. *Chaucer and the Country of the Stars.* Princeton: Princeton University Press, 1970.

———. "Speech, the Principle of Contraries, and Chaucer's Tales of the Manciple and the Parson." *Mediaevalia* 6 (1980): 209–27.

Wykes, Barbara E., ed. "Edition of Book I of *The Scale of Perfection* by Walter Hilton." Ph.D. diss., University of Michigan, 1958.

Yeager, R. F. *John Gower: Recent Readings.* Kalamazoo, Mich.: Medieval Institute Publications, 1989.

Zeitlow, Paul N. "In Defense of the Summoner." *Chaucer Review* 1 (1966): 6–19.

Zinn, Grover A. "Personification Allegory and Visions of Light in Richard of St. Victor's Teaching on Contemplation." *University of Toronto Quarterly* 46 (1977): 190–214.

———. "Suger, Theology, and the Pseudo-Dionysian Tradition." In Gerson, *Abbot Suger*, pp. 33–40.

———, trans. *Richard of St. Victor: "The Twelve Patriarchs," "The Mystical Ark," "Book Three of the Trinity."* New York: Paulist Press, 1971.

# Index